Practical Chinese Magic

By Jason Read

© Jason Read 2022
First Edition

All rights reserved. No part of this work may be reproduced, stored in a retrieval system, or transmitted in any form or by any means, electronic, mechanical, photocopying, recording or otherwise without the prior permission of the publisher.

The methodologies in this book stem from the author's own experiences. The Reader must not regard the information as an alternative to medical advice, which he should obtain from a qualified professional. The Reader who thinks he might be suffering from a medical condition should seek medical advice immediately. The Reader who is already in receipt of medical treatment should not discontinue or delay this treatment or disregard medical advice as a consequence of having read the information in this book. The author and the publishers cannot accept legal responsibility for any problem arising out of experimenting with the methods described.

Practical Chinese Magic

By
Jason Read

Dedicated to my soulmate
and Priestess of Hu Xian, Vicky Yun

Contents

Acknowledgements and Preface 7

Part I Theory 9
1. A Journey In Time 11
2. The Manifestation of the Gods 47
3. Heaven, Man, Earth 53
4. YIN and YANG 57
5. Qi, The Life Force 63
6. The Five Elements 66
7. The Eight Holy Symbols 75
8. The Heavenly Stems
   And The Earthly Branches 84
9. Sacred Time and Sacred Space
   Yinli, The Lunar Calendar 91
10. Sacred Geography
    And The Gods Of The Tao 102
11. The Shen, Gods Of The Dao 107
12. Of The Immortals
    And The Chain Of Lineage 127

Part II Training 129
13. The Training of the Magician 130
14. The Six Healing Breaths 138
15. Secrets Of The Golden Light 144
16. The Eight Great Spells 148
17. The Eight Great Spells Of Esoteric Maoshan 150
18. Joining the chain of transmission 169
19. Empowering Of Spirit Water 174
20. Maoshan Fali Meditation
    The Peach Grove Flowers Of Maoshan Neigong ... 178
21. Protection, Condensing And Projection 181
22. Cultivating Jade Wine 184
23. Washing The Marrow
    And Replenishing The Essence 187

24. Basic Qi Gathering 189
25. An Exercise To Gather Qi
     From The Soul Of The Earth 195
26. Jian Jue
     Activating The Sword Finger 198

Part III Ritual and Spellwork 201
27. Basic Spell Work 1 202
28. Making Your First Basic Talisman Step By Step 235
29. The Talisman Of Protection (Hu Shen Fu) 250
30. The House Protection Bagua Talisman
     Of Defence And Fortune (AN BAGUA FU) 264
31. QINGJING FU
     (The Talisman Of Bringing Peace, Calm And Purity) . 283
32. ZHAOCAI CUI KE WANG DIAN FA
     (Ritual Of Money And Prosperity
     Inviting Prosperity And Customers For A Prosperous Business
     Technique) 286
33. Mysteries Of The Nine Stars 300
34. Of Ghosts And Ghouls 335
35. Tools Of The Taoist Magician 347
36. Hand Seals Used
     In Daoist Magic 355
37. Divining With The Ling Gua 378

APPENDIX 383
Conclusions 386
Glossary 387
Index 401
The Chinese Magick Series 409

Acknowledgements and Preface

The book you now hold in your hands is a training book for a real Taoist School somewhat unknown in the West and misunderstood in Asia.

In the West, academics tend to focus on either philosophical Taoism or its manifestation in a distant historical past. In actuality Taoism has moved with the times and has a new vocabulary of which the academic scholar has no inkling. Yet, all Taoism is rooted in over 5000 years of history. One may read an academic text on Tang Dynasty rituals and terminology and think that is how modern Taoists work, which mostly, just isn't the case. Taoism in Asia has developed and evolved.

This is particularly true in folk Taoism which is as far removed from Taoist orthodoxy as much as say Gnosticism is from the Catholic Church.

After my studies with teachers in China and Malaysia. and having returned to the United Kingdom, I looked for books on the subject in English., I found not many at all. Academic works were highly impractical and focused on the past or the Daoist Canon. Most other works were the usual texts on Qigong, alchemy and very westernised approaches to Taoism. There was very little actual material on real Taoist magic, and those that were published were either mostly guesswork or so unwieldy as to be impractical. In other words there was a deficit of actual workable material for those who want a way in. Thus the idea of this series of books was born.

The main focus of this volume is to introduce the reader to the real training methods, theory and spells used by the Chinese schools of magic. It is not an academic study nor a piece of missionary work from some Buddhistic-Taoist mix, such as Quanzhen or other orthodox Taoist 'churches'.

Here you will meet the methods of the Chinese schools of magic, their Gods, their methods and their way of working. If you are wondering why there is no bibliography, that's because the sources are an oral tradition and currently not in print.

I hope it opens the door for you and takes you beyond what you imagined Taoism to be.

I would like to thank my teacher Dr. Liang, now in his 90s yet seemingly ever young.

To my beautiful partner in crime, Vicky Yun.

To my publishers Mogg Morgan and Diti Morgan for their patience and support.

Jason Read

2022 UK

Part I
Theory

Maoshan Zushi, the Maoshan Patriarch

1. A Journey In Time

This is not a history book. I want to make that clear right from the start. If you want a dry and more academic approach to the history of China there are scores of books you can consult and indeed, you'll be all the better for it.

This is a practical workbook introducing you to a whole new world of the Chinese magical paradigm, one that is populated with tales of Emperor sorcerers, journeys to the stars, of great wars and of ghosts and spirits. And it is from this viewpoint we are going to launch into a magical history of China.

Much of the history I am about to share with you is based on legend and myth which illustrates the collective folk experience of the very landscape and natural forces those ancient peoples sought sustenance in and at times were at odds with. For our purposes, as apprentices to the magical arts, this approach is far more valuable and usable. What we receive is a magico-cosmographic map of the spirit of Chinese magic and mysticism.

China is a huge country with a mind-bogglingly long history that stretches far beyond the written language into the realm of oral legend. That history incorporates thousands of years of human experience…its struggle not only with the often terrible scourge of nature but with the constantly shifting political arena and the struggle for power.

We should also take into account that China is made up of many races each with their own unique beliefs, cultural traditions and languages.

The majority of Chinese culture stems from the Han people who had arisen in the region of the Yellow River Valley and it is the Hanzu that makes up 99% of the world's Chinese population. Interestingly, even the Han people are separated by spoken language. A Han native of Fujian who speaks the Hokkien dialect, for example, may not understand a Han person who speaks Mandarin or Cantonese.

I learned Mandarin and at the same time, because of my teacher, I had picked up a Hunan pronunciation peculiar to one city and was barely understood by the inhabitants of another city barely a hundred miles away!

However the Chinese written language is composed of characters (hanzi) which do not vary and so while the Chinese may not share a universal spoken language, they do share a universal written language.

Now let us mentally take our first steps to the mastery of this ancient magic and close our eyes and throw our minds back … back … far beyond to when the cosmos was but a dream…

Open your eyes and your senses. There is utter blackness. Pure stillness. But it is not really black and nor is it really stillness because even those concepts do not exist. What your mind is conveying to you is the primordial Chaos. We could call it nothingness but that implies something, but at this point, there is, in fact, no duality. Yet paradoxically you can sense the vibrant powers humming within, longing to become, to express. This Chaos contains the potential to become anything and everything. It is One and it is All. It is Nothing and Everything.

There you watch and sense the stirrings and tensions of becoming and desire to be. A period of 18,000 years passes according to scholars of the ancient annals.

In the theoretical primordial Oneness, we call Wuji, there is a congealing of substance, a definite point of manifestation. Unknown awesome and unfamiliar forces swirl to create a centre. Some mysterious Mind is causing something to be. This is the Cosmic Egg. Cosmic because it contains the seed of what will become the universe. Mentally you look within the egg and see ribbons of dark Yin energy and bright

Yang energy twisting in desire. Suddenly a being is born. The embryo becomes defined. A massive and colossal giant breaks through the shell cracking into existence with a voice of thunder. He is massive beyond any human conception. Hugely strong and hirsute You sense his single-minded purpose. 'I must create!!'.

His name is Pangu, and he is the primordial giant. You recall that such giants have a long history in the memory of all races, probably originating in the dream knowledge of man's first shamanic journeys. For example, the Nordic Ymir who similarly emerged from primordial chaos from the dual forces of fire and ice.

You watch as this terrible, almost terrifying colossus swipes at the space around him. Bands of bright Yang begin rising, separating painfully from the dark mass of Yin, like oil from water. Pangu eventually rests the brightness in his palms and with the darkness at his feet … slowly he stretches, lifting the heavens further and further from the shadow stuff of Yin. Duality is created. In his struggle to divide the Heavens from the Earth, four mysterious beasts emerge to help his straining efforts. These are the Four Auspicious Beasts, the Dragon, the Tiger, the Tortoise and the Phoenix or Vermillion Bird. We will have a lot to say about these later as they are a constant in Chinese sorcery. To throw a hint out there they represent the arising of the four directions and elemental qualities from the duality of Yin and Yang.

There he is, that tremendous force of will and desire, straining sinews dividing the primordial duality like some Asian Atlas. You sense his purpose is done. His head lolls and in slow motion, the limbs buckle. You realize he is dying. He is falling, but so titanic in size that his keeling over appears as if he is falling through syrup.

Then the magic happens. Through death comes life. The King is Dead, Long live the King.

You watch as the blood torrents out into streams, rivers and oceans, the eyes become the Sun and Moon, each hair becomes a sapling, the last breath becomes a wind that rushes through your hair. Bones become jagged mountains. Echoes of the voice of Pangu become thunders in the storms above you. Magical. The ancient Earth was born.

Yet it is not peaceful. It is seething, chaotic and terrifying. Demons are at war, those colossal shadows of destructive force battle in Heaven and on the Earth. Fires rage, waters jet in destructive boiling gushes. It appears as a broken world, a veritable hell of contending elements.

There is finally a huge flood that destroys everything in its path. So terrible is the deluge that even the very heavens were torn and the twin pillars of duality broken.

Yet what is that in the distance? A towering finger of purple rock its heights hidden behind mists. This is Mount Kunlun, the polar axis of the earth. As we venture closer we spy two figures. One is a beautiful woman with long black silky hair but her lower body appears to be that of a serpent glistening with dragon scales. The other is a man, intelligent in the face, strong and determined. The annals of the sorcerers fail to tell us where they came from though rumours suggest they are the last survivors of the great deluge. We know they are the beautiful Queen Nuwa and her brother and husband, the Emperor God, Fu Xi.

Somehow they are more human to our senses though powerful beyond imagination, Indeed they are the father and mother of humanity and the great first teachers of what it means to be human.

Nuwa repairs the heavens and earth with magical gems vibrant with the five colours (the five elements), the waters recede and the inferno is extinguished. Order begins. Alone they set about to create the first people. Some say they engaged in a cosmic sex act that produced a mass of flesh from which all the first human beings were cut. Others say Nuwa moulded those early humans from yellow clay.

The first humans were feral and mindless. They ate raw flesh and cast aside the bones. Raped rather than loved. It was existence for existence's sake. Pure Id.

Meanwhile, Fu Xi contemplated. He had the fire of mind and intellect, the impulse to be more. He contemplated the earth around him and its meaning. He gazed up at the stars and tried to fathom their stellar mysteries and their relationship to the earth they enveloped.

Armed with their divine knowledge the couple brought law and order to those early humans. They instituted marriage to counter rape, they taught them how to cook and grow rice rather than living like wild predators. Fu Xi taught them about the Heavens and the divine Gods that lived there. In consequence, the clay minds sparked with the fire of consciousness and humanity was forever changed.

Fu Xi was the first magician and mystic. It was he who discovered the Ba Gua or Eight Diagrams. The records of the magicians state that in searching for the mysteries of the cosmos Fu Xi discovered this cosmic code of 8 sets of broken (Yin) and unbroken (Yang) lines. He saw them on the back of either a tortoise or dragon-horse that emerged from the River Luo.

These Eight Diagrams form the basis of Chinese philosophy and occult thought. In fact, they possess incredible occult power and knowledge of which even most I-Jing readers are unaware of. This is a subject we shall return to.

Our mind now travels aeons forwards. Nature is generally in order, and the land we call China is populated by tribes living in the rich river valleys of that country. Life is tough but there is at least a social order. As we venture through one such village we see a recognizable society. Happily, we see children playing, women spinning cloth, some men are training in the arts of war with their spears, at least another tribe chooses to take their women and food. However, it is unlikely it would happen to this tribe. Their leader is Yu the Great.

Emperor Fu Xi with Bagua and Turtle

Yu is not only a wise leader, he is a magician of great power. In fact, his power is so great that every magician today utilizes what he taught. Yu could change into a bear, perhaps the totem of his tribe. His shamanic journeys to the stars are what interest us. It is a journey we still use today. Yu would perform a special dance that catapulted his astral body to the star palaces in the Seven Stars we call the Big Dipper to obtain occult power and teaching. The pace of Yu or Seven Star Stepping with a dragging step, emulating the limp lame legged Yu , is still used.

Yu is most famous for another discovery. The control of water. To understand this you have to understand the Yellow River (Huang He). It has been called both the 'Blessing of China' And the 'Sorrow of China'.

The ancient Chinese had an absolute dependence on the Yellow River and yet its cyclical flooding cost thousands of lives. The Yellow River is so-called because it carries rich fertile silt that gives the river a strong yellowish hue. When this silt is deposited it gives an incredibly rich and fertile soil that is truly a blessing to the farmer and to the belly. Yet this same silt can build up to change the depth or course of the river that leads to terrible flooding. This fact is indelibly printed in the Chinese psyche. It shaped the collective unconsciousness and experience of the Hanzu.

To control the waters was to achieve power. In legend, Yu the Great was the man to do this. In some mysterious way, he used a magical and occult diagram known as the Yellow River Map or Scroll. (He tu). Using the map he established a system of flood control thus bringing in a new era of peace and tribal unity. The Yellow River Map and its associated Luo Shu Square are also common components in Chinese magic and occultism as we shall see.

Now, I must introduce you to another key character in the drama of oriental occultism. This is Huang Di, the Yellow Emperor.

The Dragon King

The Yellow Emperor is perhaps the single most revered figure in the popular imagination. Even if you don't know Pangu, Nuwa, Fuxi and Yu the Great, you will know the Yellow Emperor. No one can be sure exactly when he was born, but some traditional scholars posit the date of his birth around 2700 BC in Shandong among a tribe by the Ji River. His beautiful mother was walking along that gentle river when suddenly a flash of light pulsing out from the Big Dipper penetrated her womb and impregnated her with the future Emperor.

Huang Di was, like Yu the Great, a born shaman. As a young man, he ventured to the mysterious East Sea to converse with a mysterious magical beast and learned the habits of over a thousand magical and supernatural creatures.

He is also assigned the invention of writing via the Bone Oracle Script. These mysterious bones and tortoise plastrons were known to generations of farmers who had dug them up during their labours. They were called dragon bones and were used in local pharmacies, Luckily a scholar on examining them recognized them for what they were.

The oracle bones contain some of the earliest writings known in China. They were used in a form of divination where the shaman would heat the bone until cracks formed. The patterns and distribution of these cracks were believed to convey the will of Heaven…of the Gods and spirits. The shamans would then write the meaning in Chinese characters we now call the Bone Script or Jiagu Wen. This bone script is believed to be the ancestor of all later Chinese characters.

Aside from inventing writing and introducing the culture of silk, the principles of Chinese medicine and the Calendar, the Yellow Emperor was a powerful magician who sought immortality.

Of great interest to the practical magician is the relationship with the goddess Jiu Tian Xuan Nu, the Mysterious Girl of the Ninth Heaven. This mysterious goddess appears to have originally been depicted with the head of a woman and the body of a bird, indicating her origin in the shamanic tradition.

The legends state that the Emperor was engaged in war with a terrible demon who was the scourge of all life on Earth. This creature had cast a magical mist over the earth and the emperor sought refuge. It was then that the Dark Lady descended upon her red phoenix or vermillion bird dressed in a robe of kingfisher plumes that glinted with nine colours

The Dark Lady became the Yellow Emperor's teacher in magic, alchemy, the arts of war magic and invisibility. She also imparted the arts of Double Cultivation, that is the development of occult energies through sex, along with her sister, Su Nu.

We cannot underestimate the importance of Jiu Tian Xuan Nu as a deity of the magical systems of China. She is a key figure in the Maoshan branch of occultism and many operations of magic are associated with her.

She would even appear in the novel *The Water Margin* aiding the outlaws in their battle against the corrupt government. Among the skills she taught was the conjuring of spirit warriors and spells of concealment and invisibility. Usually, this was done by the agency of the Six Jade Maidens who were her closest companions.

Another important work attributed to the Yellow Emperor is the Huang Di Nei Jing (*The Yellow Emperor's Internal Classic*). I cannot emphasise too much the importance of this work. Essentially it is a medical treatise but it introduces key themes that would go on to be a foundation for many doctrines concerning the nature of man and his relationship to the environment, This includes matters such as the five elements, Qi …or the universal spirit of life that pervades the universe, of Yin and Yang and of the classification of the organs of the inner body by their energetic and essential function. All these topics would go on to be central to the Taoist search for longevity and immortality.

The Wu Shamans

Early China is not the unified political state we know now. In the earliest dynasties, China consisted of a number of tribal societies that were mostly independent of each other. Like most tribal societies the religion was largely shamanic. Shamanism has certain key features.

Firstly there is an animistic view of the world in which we live. Everything has life and purpose. We mean not only the obviously living things like animals and birds but every tree, every stone, the fires we cook on and the water we drink ... every cloud. Looking up, even the Sun, the Moon and the stars are great spirits. We as people are part of this great living family of spirit, we are brothers and sisters in the great web of life.

Secondly, we can communicate with that world of spirit. Typically this is done through a specialist, who has certain traits or abilities to interact with this world. In anthropological terms, we refer to such a person as a shaman. The shaman is a medium between the spirit world and the world of man, the life of the tribe. In times of sickness, in times of hunger or war with a neighbouring tribe, or times when the supernatural seems to clash with the world of the living, it is the shaman who sees the underlying spiritual causes and offers solutions.

When there are uncertain times such as the mysterious transitions of birth, of coming of age, of marriages and deaths, the shaman helps keep at bay possible pathologies that can come calling at these delicate liminal moments.

The shaman communes with the spirits by various methods. These usually involve the techniques of ecstasy. The word ecstasy refers to a particular set of altered states of consciousness which in shamanic language can propel the soul into flights to the spirit world or even to the heavens.

Such techniques can involve drumming, deep meditations, entheogens, dance, staring at bright or dark objects, pain, sexual intercourse and so on. The idea is to reach a meeting point between the waking consciousness and a mysterious unknown something beyond everyday human experience. This is often identified as the dream world or the world of spirits. This world in itself is populated with many spirits and is often divided into an upper celestial realm and a lower world that may be populated with nature spirits. Lower still may be the dead and the demons. Of course, this is a very general picture.

Thirdly, tribal shamanism often has a strong respect and sometimes fear of the dead. The ancestors have a continued existence and remain very much part of the tribal family. However there are serious consequences for not respecting that relationship with your ancestors. Another aspect is that the dead, if greatly honoured, can become greater in power to the point of becoming actual demigods and gods.

It is the author's opinion that there is wisdom in remembering the ancestors and in fact, is one of the necessary factors in successful occultism in the Maoshan and Yinshan traditions.

Having defined shamanism albeit in broad terms we can now see how this manifested in China.

The shaman could be male or female, though their techniques and functions could vary. The female shaman was called upon for the more earthy rites of fertility while the male was more geared towards magical acts involving the heavens ... for example, invoking the rains in times of drought.

Some insight into what exactly these shamans were up to is

provided by both historical records and archaeological evidence. The most important contextual evidence is strangely enough given in a poem, Jiu Ge (The Nine Songs) composed by Qu Yuan around 230 BCE.

The poems are full of dramatic imagery and rituals are undertaken by shamans of the Yellow River Tribe, the Chu. Evidence shows that the shaman would don exotic costumes while the invoker would utter songs and spells to cause the deity to possess him. Ecstasy was achieved by bells, music, drum dances and by the use of wine and marijuana. There are descriptions of flights to wonderful paradises peopled with mysterious beings The spirit descending on the shaman not is only attracted by the scent and experience of food but by erotic desire. The shaman, therefore, dresses in an attractive way to woo the spirit, much as a lover courts the desired one. Obviously given the time period and cultural norms male shamans invoked female spirits and females invoked male spirits. It is a fascinatingly erotic relationship filled with yearning and sexual tension. It is also a technique we should bear in mind. In one of the poems, for example, a female shaman invokes a male spirit in her home and is taken on a fantastic spirit journey. Male shamans tend to visit the homes of the female mountain and river spirits rather than inviting them into their homes.

From this early form of shamanism in China developed many of the fundamental techniques still in use in the Taoist and Miao people magical methods ... the importance of food offerings and incense, the journey into the spirit world, the erotic relationship between man and the spirits, the use of music and incantation, and of course mediumship, It is my opinion that these early beings related in these shamanic poems are the ancestors of some of the deities and spirits still worshipped today. The Mountain Immortal Fairy Girl and the Jade Girls are still familiar in modern Chinese magic.

The Masters Of The Method

As the tribal system gave way to a more settled social dynamic based on cities and kingdoms based on more permanent agricultural methods, the shaman transformed into something quite different.

This new breed of wonder worker was called the Fang Shi which can be loosely translated as Master of the Method. The method being the law and techniques of magic and alchemy.

Fang Shi was a general middle-class literati who travelled throughout China looking for wealthy patrons much like the alchemists and court magicians of Medieval Europe. They often claimed to have visited mysterious mountains or islands in the Bohai Sea such as Penglai. Perhaps this is really a reflection or even a sophistication on the old shamanic journey. They would claim contact with mysterious immortals and spirits...gods even who taught them the secrets of magic.

To the reader versed in western magic, this may seem very familiar, and yes, does seem to reflect a familiar pattern of the human spiritual experience. For example, the tales of magicians and witches 'flying' to or going into some mountain or hidden faerie kingdom to learn the arts of sorcery. From the dialogues of Shiva and Shakti heard on Mount Kailasa to the bewitching visions of Isobel Gowdie learning her craft from the Queen of Faerie, the pattern is clear.

And so our Fang Shi would visit his mysterious Mountain or Cave and come away with a new body of occult knowledge.

The Fang Shi would often entertain their clients much in the same way as modern stage magicians, performing simple tricks like mind reading or guessing hidden objects. Mostly they conjured and exorcised spirits to perform certain tasks or obtain secret knowledge. Some were famed for their skill in alchemy. Alchemy in a Chinese context was very similar to its European cousin in that it sought how to make gold and sought the secret of eternal youth and immortality.

The Fang shi also divined the will of Heaven and the state of the flow of Yin and Yang in the landscape. They might use techniques of astrology in calculating complex charts similar to the horary astrology method in the West. One such art is still used today. I learned it in my intermediate training in the Maoshan School. It is called Qimen Dun Jia or the Secret Gates of Escape. I was introduced to this system of divination a few months into my training and it involves analyzing the state of the qi energy fields as indicated by the Heavens using certain positions of the so-called Flying Stars, the Earth by Bagua and location and the querent by using the date and place of birth.

I will talk about this later in the section on Maoshan training, but in truth, the subject requires a book of its own. It is planned that one shall be published in this series of Maoshan training books.

Another method was observing the wind. The wind, in Chinese thought, is considered to be closely allied to Qi, the universal life force. Changes, sounds, colours and directions of the wind were analysed by the Fang Shi to ascertain the state of the subtle energies in the local geography.

Other techniques were developed such as the use of various kinds of lots, the most famous being the Moon Blocks and the yarrow stalks of the I Jing. The fundamentals of what we now call Traditional Chinese Medicine were developed according to the occult view of the universe.

Some of these Fang Shi wrote down their methods in books. Such books contained instructions, the names of spirits and immortals and how to call them, methods to diagnose disease and occult problems, recipes for herbal remedies and alchemical formulae and so on. In other words, the Chinese had their own grimoire tradition. Some of these books passed into folklore. The most famous example being the Luban.

The Luban could be considered the main manual of the folk magician in China. It has the same reputation as saying the Key of Solomon or the Secrets of Albertus Magnus in Europe.

Lu ban is, in fact, the name of a famous carpenter, builder, engineer and inventor of the Zhou Dynasty (507-444BCE). Lu Ban was deified as the patron god of builders. He is particularly revered among the Kam people of southern China. Interesting since the Kam and Miao people have a deep connection with the more primal and witchcraft aspects of far eastern occultism. No one knows for sure where exactly it originated but the Lu Ban Shu (Lu Ban Book) became the ipso facto book of practical magic. This secret book of magic judging by contextual evidence was the work of an anonymous author who was almost certainly a Fang Shi.

On a side note, there is a connection between building and magic. To build safely required not only how to throw a few bricks together but also to possess an intimate knowledge of the land. The builder would be expected to know how to relate to the Land Gods or genii loci and to understand feng shui and the various taboos and rituals of a building. The Kam people mentioned above have the head carpenter of any building project to actually be possessed by Lu Ban. Up to modern times, certain families of builders possess books of magic. Some of it is about exorcising or propitiating spirits and the like However those books also contain some methods to deal with nasty customers. There is a popular story I heard from Singapore. A rich client hired the services of a builder but on completion, there was a strong disagreement between the two and a serious argument broke out between the two.

Finally, the rich man and his family moved into their new house. Then they began to pay the price. Every night they could hear the dreadful wailing and crying of a woman or girl. So awful was the crying it terrified them to the deepest part of their souls. Finally, an expert Taoist was called in and he soon discovered a hollow space behind a loose brick. Inside was an old dried shell of an orange containing the offending talisman of dark magic. The builder had placed it there in his anger.

The Taoists

I should point out that many of the Fang Shi were Taoists in their belief, but the earliest ones were not. I cannot without conscience write this book on magic without saying something about Taoism and its importance in the history of Chinese magic. As this is a book on the Maoshan and Yinshan schools and to a lesser extent, the Miao tradition of witchcraft, we must have a basic understanding of the Tao or more accurately, the Dao.

In the opinion of most scholars, Taoism coalesced from a number of folk and state practices and beliefs. In fact, it is very difficult to exactly pin down a precise definition of Taoism because of its widely diverse expressions.

Trying to find a single definition of Taoism is rather like trying to find a single pattern in a kaleidoscope. You think you have it and then with a slightly different perspective the patterns and colours morph into something quite different but beautiful and unique.

However, popular tradition does assign the creation of Taoist philosophy to one man, Lao Tzu. Because Lao Tzu is one of the chief deities of the Maoshan system it is worth chatting about him a little here. In a sense, if you have no lineage teacher then Lao Tzu must become what tantrics would call your root (adi) guru. You must establish a link with him in meditations and homage much in the same way as Tantric and Tantric Buddhists do. In this way, as we shall explain later, you join the magical chain of Heavenly Masters and you are protected, empowered and inspired by that hierarchy that passes beyond time and space.

Lao Tzu or Lao Zi is a mysterious figure shrouded in myth and legend. Firstly Lao Zi is not a name but a title meaning Old (Lao) Master (Zi). Scholars think his real name was Li Er. I should point out here that the surname or family name comes first, so Li or Lee was his family name. Generally, Lao Zi was believed to have lived around 400 to 500 BCE and is believed to have been a scholar and librarian working in the archival studios of the Zhou kingdom. In popular legend, Lao Zi was the product of a virgin birth. The tradition is that while his noble mother was walking in the garden a shooting star somehow caused her to become pregnant with the future sage. To illustrate the intense wisdom of Lao Zi the gestation was said to have lasted a period of decades. On the day of his birth, his mother leaned on a plum tree in her labour. Of course, Li means plum in Chinese, and Li is his surname. The spinners of yarns swear that when the holy sage was born he was already a little adult with snowy locks and wispy philosopher's beard! He was married and had a son, the famous warrior Li Zong. At some point, he attracted acclaim as a great philosopher, though he had, as far as we know, no formal academy at which he expounded his philosophy.

According to legend, Lao Zi became weary of the cutthroat world of court life and decided to leave society. So the weary old philosopher riding on the back of a water buffalo began his journey out of the country. The legend goes on to tell us that a guard, Yinxi at the gates of the kingdom suddenly recognised the old sage and demanded that the old master commit to writing the essence of his philosophy to paper before allowing him to leave. Of course, that writing is the Dao de Jing. I shan't discuss the Dao de Jing or The Classic of Power in this text. I will admonish you to read it though as it is the foundation book of Taoism and therefore of Maoshan. You must read it and understand it.

Wonderfully, there are new translations based on newly found archaeological discoveries. A complete ancient copy of the text written on bamboo strips with a few interesting variations was unearthed in Hubei. They are called the Guodian Slips.

Where Lao Zi went is unknown. We know he left China on his ox going west. Some say he had fabulous magical adventures with his first student Yinxi. Others say he went to India. But truly he passed into the immortality that only legend can bestow.

At this stage, Taoism appears to have been mainly a philosophical school. At least as far as we know. It is this philosophical mode of Taoism that is familiar to most readers. In fact, it is so much so that one is tempted to declare there is a westernized Taoism based on this limited vision. It has spawned hundreds of interpretations based on personal, often New Age viewpoints quite alien to Taoism.

When one of my fellow students dubbed this California Taoism I had to giggle to myself. In fact whenever I broach the subject of Chinese sorcery some people look at me with either a surprised or blank expression. Typically they think of the Tao in a tunnel vision of letting go, living with nature, Tai Chi and Qigong. Though those things have their place it is a tiny part of the whole picture.

Remember Taoism is a philosophy deeply embedded in society. Those Taoists were often scholars and fang shi, astrologers and alchemists looking for the secrets of immortality.

Immortality was not just a search for extended life but a search for the means of self-transformation into a divine being. Of this, we shall see more later. In their search for this apotheosis, they practised various Dao yin or yogas, meditations and experimented with concoctions of magical herbs, minerals and animal substances. The most prized of these were mysterious kinds of fungi of a magical nature.

Initially, these Taoist mystics lived alone on the mountains, for mountains were of huge magical import, containing titanically ancient and immense power stretching from earth to the heavens. In the mountains, they could communicate with the spirits and immortals who lived there. We may recall here those forlorn shamans yearning for the spirit maidens of the mountains mentioned in the Nine Songs.

However, this was about to change. As the cosmic clock ticks, the hour strikes and events on earth coalesce into just the right conditions for a new expression of Taoism. The many kingdoms of China are in turmoil. Many of these so-called kingdoms are but strict city-states ruled by petty tyrannical warlords. The skies are dark with dread. The price of geopolitical greed is the stench of slaughter. Iron tastes blood. The widows are young. The people are hungry or cowering in the miasma of uncertainty.

It was in these conditions the soldier, the scholar, the warlord, the widow and the hungrily sought hope, and that hope came in the form of a charismatic spiritual leader and magician named Zheng Dao Ling.

The Path Of The Celestial Masters

Zheng Daoling cuts a mysterious figure. Flourishing in the early years of the Han Dynasty he was a native of Sichuan Province.

Sichuan Province was an area of China where shamanism and magic were still a daily fact of life. Zheng Daoling as a younger man seems to have been a scholar in the down to earth and practical philosophy of Confucius. To quickly explain Confucius was all about social order and knowing your place so society could run smoothly. It praised the value of strict education, the role of family and the state as a greater father-like figure. In many ways, this strict paternalistic philosophy was the polar opposite of Taoism. Studying Confucian philosophy was the main qualification for a life of service within the governmental sphere. The exams were tough and a constant source of stress and strain for young scholars. However, if one could pass these exams one's future was assured and the rewards could be rich, especially if you directly served the court. To this day, this Confucian philosophy is embedded in the psyche of the Chinese people. The insistence on orderly family structure, filial piety, respect for the old, the preservation of traditional ways and the importance of education and exam results are still priorities to Chinese in a way that seems at times extreme and rigid to the western society.

Having lived in China I have witnessed how some children still really do not have a childhood. They will study for long hours and after school attend even more classes. Such is the pressure to attain excellence in education parents have been known to bribe teachers with huge amounts of money and failing students have resorted to leaping from 10th-floor windows to avoid the family shame.

It was this rigid and scholarly background that Zheng Daoling seems to have rejected, even refusing a post as a professor in an ancient equivalent of a university. One day he had picked up a copy of the Dao De Jing that made his dry scholarly books seem so sophisticated. It seems this began when Zheng was working as a local magistrate in Chongqing in Southwest China. Whereas in many parts of China the shaman had all but disappeared, Jiangsu, Sichuan and nearby Yunnan were hotbeds of sorcery and magic ... and to a certain extent still are.

Perhaps influenced and attracted to the magical culture surrounding him he appears to have sought a teacher of magic.

Zheng learned all the traditional methods of the shamanic magical path that would form the basis of the new expression of Taoism. There were ecstatic dances, the knowledge of the spirits within man. The physical exercises and use of herbs and fungi. Communication with the Otherworld and nature spirits and the use of signs of power in talismans.

This culminated in one of the most crucial events in Taoist mystical and magical history.

To set the background we must remember that the folk had a long history of venerating the ancestors and Lao Zi was an important ancestor who was remembered and venerated, but not worshipped in local shrines. This has interesting parallels in say Voudon and Quimbanda where the venerated dead can rise up the ranks so to speak and become powerful and immortal souls in their own right. Some even become actual gods.

Zheng was cultivating on Mount Heming in Sichuan, surrounded by swaying pines and sturdy cypresses and its peaks and ranges give the illusion of a crane dipping its head to drink the white frothy waters bubbling in the valley. Suddenly there is a presence ... so beautiful and powerful, Zheng seems to be filled with warm golden oil oozing from every pore, filled with life and bliss. Like the most unselfish orgasm, one could have. Pure bliss full of unspeakable eternal wisdom. It was Lao Zi himself...but somehow he was godlike in his majesty. The hair-fine white gossamer bound in the traditional topknot, robes fluttering in unknown ethereal breezes of cosmic winds ... a fan in his hand depicted the great seal of the Yinyang Taiji. The face scintillated between virgin and unsullied youth and yet extreme age and wisdom.

This was the deified Lao Zi, known to us as Taishang Laojun ... The Great Lord Upon High.

Taishang Laojun is one of the highest deities of not only orthodox Taoism but also of our Maoshan sect. From Taishang Laojun comes great power and he is the wellspring from which the waters of our magic emerge. He is the Ancient Ancestor from whom the chain of brother and sisterhood in the Maoshan sect begins. Even in the Yinshan tradition which is concerned with the Yin World of the dead, Taishang Laojun appears in his wrathful form, with fangs and horns and glistening blue skin not unlike the wrathful guardians of Buddhism. I digress. More of

Zheng Daoling with his totemic tiger

this later when we arrive at the practical portion of this volume.

Taishang Laojun bestowed on Zheng the title of Celestial Master and warned him that the Underworld had released plagues and demons upon the world and that he must spread the Way of the Celestial Masters among the people to allay suffering and protect the weak. Laojun explained various methods by which this could be achieved and that by efforts a man can transcend to become so much more than he is in his present state.

Zheng created the first magical school of Taoism we now call the Way of the Celestial Masters. It had its centre in Sichuan and even formed its own kingdom of 24 parishes. Entry into this Way cost you five pecks of rice, so some nicknamed it the Order of the Five Pecks of Rice.

Central to the Celestial Masters was the cure for disease and health longevity practices. Talismanic water was the main vehicle of the healing power, and it is still the case today. The Way of the Celestial Masters ultimately fragmented into Northern and Southern factions and today its descendent is the Zhengyi Orthodox School of Taoism.

As for Zheng Daoling, he is said to have transformed into an immortal, leaving only his clothes behind in a heap on the floor. Today you can see his image in many temples throughout Asia, the lofty sage riding on the back of an immense tiger.

Ge Hong And The Path Of Immortality

I now must introduce you to Ge Hong. Ge Hong lived during the Eastern Jin Dynasty. Like Zheng, he rejected the life of a government official in the classic Confucian model and sought the spiritual release and transformation that the Dao offered.

Ge Hong made a study of Taoist practices in alchemy and so forth and wrote one of the most important books in Taoism known as the

Baopuzi or The Book of the Master Who Embraces Simplicity. The Baopuzi is one of the foundational texts of cultivation and magic. The most important chapters discuss how the ordinary man can be transformed into an Immortal or Xian. Of the Xian and the method, I will discuss in a later chapter. Naturally in this book, we can only discuss the rudimentary practices of the path to becoming an Immortal, but hopefully, in the near future, a companion volume will be made discussing this topic in full detail.

The Neipan or Inner Chapters discuss the Inner and Outer Methods of alchemy. Alchemy here is all about the transfiguration of the human being into a new transcendent being.

The Outer Methods or Medicine of the Outer Secret uses various herbs, minerals and magical fungi concocted to heal, balance and change the human body. The Baopuzi explains the use of metals in processes that would be familiar to alchemists in the Arabic and Western worlds. Exorcisms and talismans also play their part in the Outer Alchemy or Weidan. The ultimate goal was the Pill of Immortality ... somewhat like the Philosopher's Stone so yearned for by generations of alchemists in Europe and claimed by a few adepts.

Other practices included various physical exercises such as the practice of the martial arts and various calisthenic routines. One such set of exercises would become for example the often misunderstood and ill practised Tai Ji Quan.

Other practices would seem shocking by today's standards and the 'all light and breath' crowd would have frowns of disapproval for sure. While Tai Ji may be practised in your local church hall or community centre, manipulating the dragon's head (penis) or jade grove (vagina) would not. However such sexual techniques in the secret theosophy of China is still the done thing and we should not reject them as they are a genuine and powerful means of Taoyin, the Chinese term for yoga.

The Inner Chapters tell us about the Inner Medicine (Neidan) which involves meditation, visualization and sound. This part would be the most familiar to western students. I would like to point out here though that what we call Qigong is but a lower and often introductory phase of the real neidan.

Unfortunately, over time the Neidan has been corrupted into a few exercises involving the breath into a mere health routine. Partly this is because most teachers are either reluctant to teach the marrow of real Neidan to western students or because those teachers lost that knowledge and practice some martial or medical-based Qigong system. For example with the advent of Communism in China and the ensuing cultural revolution, the government completely banned all occultic practices or aims. Kung fu became a mere gymnastic ballet and qigong a mere tonic for health.

Happily, the tradition has been preserved in the Chinese underground. Indeed the Maoshan school I joined was banned in China and more than once there was fear that that knock at the door was the police ready to bundle us into a black van. I would have been deported and my teacher and colleagues imprisoned, reeducated or executed.

Ge Hong is the first to mention the famous Nine Hand Seals that became widespread and important in Japanese mystical traditions such as Shingon Buddhism and Mikkyo. You may have, for example, seen anime where warriors of the samurai or ninja class form magical hand signs to focus their minds or cast spells. Most of these originate from Taoist magic, in particular Ge Hong's Inner Chapter on Entering Forests and Mountains.

Lingbao, The Wizards Of The Divine Treasure

Ge Hong's family seems to have had a long family tradition. This is often the case in China, those magical traditions are passed down through the family, what we could call the red thread in western occult circles.

The Lingbao School emerged around 400CE and was founded by Ge Chaofu, a descendant of Ge Hong.

Its central text which survives to this day is a wonderful book called the Classic of the Five Talismans or Wufujing. In this book expounded the crux of Lingbao Taoism and it is even for the Maoshan magician a very useful and practical text in the search of immortality and magical ability. Many of the techniques were absorbed into the corpus of Maoshan training.

Interestingly the work attributes some of its techniques to Yu the Great, that primal shaman we visited earlier in this voyage through time.

The book begins with a complex history of the Great Deluge as understood in China and the eventual mastery of the untamed waters of the Yellow River by the magical diagram as we talked about before. It goes on to expound the Doctrine of the five elements and how it relates to the five directions, colours, the internal organs and the Five Divine Emperors. Further chapters concern the creation of one's immortal and magical body by imbibing the essence of the sun and moon, of empowering one's internal gods who rule over various energetic functions within. Later the text gives recipes for various elixirs based on substances such as pine resin, ginger and a particular kind of fungus. I would almost certainly recommend this work to all aspiring magicians. Of course, the talismans are central to the work too and have various protective functions and aid in the process of self-transformation.

Lingbao no longer exists as a stand-alone school, but most Taoist schools retain elements of their teaching, This is especially true of the

Shanqing School. The Shanqing School is the root of the Maoshan and Yinshan School of Magic to which we must now journey. Readers let us now go forth and fly. In the distance you see a network of glistening rivers and lakes mirroring the azure skies...and there is a mountain..girded in living poles of bamboo, and that mountain is Maoshan....

Shanqing, The Masters Of Mao Mountain

Our tale of the wonderful story of Chinese magic takes us to a moderate but not poor house in the thriving community of an unknown town. Plum trees bend heavy with purple orbs as dragonflies playfully weave like children with gossamer wings. We see a girl, perhaps a mere sixteen years old. She is athletic and sinewy and her hair hangs in a velvet black curtain that swishes when she turns her head from her straw paper book. Her mother is stern with worry. Her daughter is not interested in suitors and reading those books!! This is no way for an unmarried girl to behave! The mother smiles to herself, remembering that soon, a young man of a good family will come to tame her daughter. "Come here, a gentleman is on his way...you must put your hair up to show you are marriageable and show that neck ... quickly now. .. and hide those books!!"'.

The young girl tries to hide her protest and indignation beneath a thin veneer of filial piety. The veneer is too thin, the hair swishes too sharply, the book closes too hard, the anger rouges her cheeks too obviously. She dreaded marriage ... the chores ... the bearing of children, the wasted years of domestic drudgery. Her mind was devoted to Tao. She immersed herself in the seductive words of the philosophers. Her inner world questioned the nature of her very existence. Her world was populated with flitting spirits free in the universal winds, the Immortals descending on regal white cranes. She longed to be there herself as light as the immortals riding in the purple breezes of Heaven. Despite her protests, the marriage happened. She bore two children ... but in her heart, she kept that promise, of that inner vision before her. In time, the children were grown. Now was her time.

That dreaming girl became Wei Huacun. She flourished around 300 CE in the area of Shandong. After her children had grown she became a serious practitioner in the Celestial Master faction. Historians of Taoism relate how in seeking for the Pill of Immortality she could be seen gathering herbs of all kinds on nearly a daily basis. She would hike her way back home and then create concoctions and test them on herself. If it had a good effect and had no side effects she would distribute it to the folk. The annals of Taoism go on to say that over time she had imbibed so many medical potions and powders that her body had begun to transform to the point she did not need to eat. The legends state that she impressed the Immortals around her with her attention and devotion to the ways of inner alchemy. This culminated in a visionary experience of Immortals who dictated to her new practices in alchemy that became the foundational text of Maoshan training, the Yellow Court Classic (Huang Ting Jing). Apparently this Immortal had the name of Xu Wang Bao. Initially, she only taught other disciples in an informal way. Her teachings would attract more and more followers. This led to a new school that synthesized many of the practices of the Celestial Masters and the Lingbao called Shanqing which literally translates as the Highest Clarity School. Even today the Yellow Court Scripture is one of the key texts of the Maoshan Pai. Pai means school or sect in Chinese. For example, in this book, you are learning the occult training and secrets of the Maoshan and Yinshan Pai. I should mention here that though the Maoshan Pai taught here is derived from the Shanqing Sect it is not the same as we shall see.

Miss Wei, like many tales of the Masters, did not die. Having attained immortality her compatriots witnessed her ascent to Heaven.

Today she is 'worshipped' as the Immortal Zi Xu Yuan Jun Nan Yue Wei Furen.

The Shanqing school flourished on Mount Mao in Jiangsu, where a faction of the Lingbao School had flourished some years before it was absorbed into the Shanqing. Shanqing was very much a servant of the people and used its skills to lessen the suffering and misfortune of the people who seek their help. They were famous for their medicines and talismans.

Behind the scenes, the Maoshan were practitioners of specialist meditations aiming at ecstatic union with the deities. Deities were literally internalised within one's own body. In other words, a complete spiritual and occult landscape was constructed in one's magical body and this led to an inner transformation of the very substance of the spiritual body. Ultimately this would even translate into actual changes in the physical too. This is, of course, reminiscent of the spiritual internalization of the Celestial Powers in Lingbao which in turn was itself an adaptation of the ancient shamanic practices. That almost if not actual erotic yearning and courting were still very present.

We must also mention the Three Mao Brothers who you will find honour in every Mao Temple. The San Mao Jen Zhun or Three Perfected Mao Brothers all attained immortality. Mao Ying was the eldest and a known expert in alchemy and the Yi Jing. Such was his attainment that he was summoned by the Queen Mother of the West, Xi Wang Mu herself. The Queen of Immortality gave him certain key scriptures on the Taoist arts. Mao Jing and Mao Zhong were his brothers who achieved immortality sometime after their older brother.

Before we leave the Shanqing Masters I would like to note that though they had Temples they were not about communal living and practice. Rather the development was individualistic. You had to train the arts of internal meditation by yourself. This fact is still one of the key factors in the Maoshan and Yinshan Pai.

The Battle Of The Sorcerers

The Master woke suddenly. Something was afoot, The air was wrong. He knew by his training that his senses were picking up on some kind of weird Qi. He focused his eyes to tease out their yin quality. With yin eyes, he could see what others might vaguely sense. Yes! There it was a bluish-black colour in the energy around him as if the very qi that enveloped him had been bruised. He sighed to himself … how could he have been so stupid … for nights he had been having alien dreams of eldritch horrors, He should have put two and two together and known that occult attacks emerging from the Yin World began through the deepest parts of the mind. He had simply brushed them off as dreams caused by hard nights of study. The air palpably thickened and congealed into a knot of grotesque, sickly indigo in the corner of his room. It stunk of the corpse fluids he had often heard sloshing in the biers carried from the village. He knew it was over. This sorcery was powerful and beyond his skill to counter and there was no time to counter with the Golden Light Mantra and hand seal. He tried to focus his Sword Finger to cannon blast the forming ghoul with Qi. Too late, he was poisoned. He let go … and passed into the Yin realm of the dead.

The Ming Dynasty was a high point in the development of magical technology in China. After all, there is nothing like a war to force one to develop one's abilities to seek more power and advantage to defeat the enemy. The Ming period was full of cunning officials and court gentlemen and ladies who hired sorcerers to weaken or kill their enemies. Even the generals employed magicians and seers to fight their cause. A number of infamous sects and schools mushroomed that sought not only immortality but real magical power. Sorcery.

The Maoshan School

Among the leaders of these schools was Maoshan Pai as we now know it. Maoshan Pai is not taught at any temple. It is a family tradition or passed down from a Master to his disciples in a layman setting. The Maoshan Pai is dedicated to the path of the occult, of immortality and of sorcery. In a sense, it is a return to the shamanic path as we shall see in more detail.

Apart from Maoshan, there are several sects that arose specialising in magic. sorcery and alchemy rather than martial arts and philosophy.

My own school of Maoshan is perhaps the most famous of these and since that is what we are mainly presenting in this book we should start there.

Right off the bat, I want to make it clear that Shanqing Maoshan and Maoshan are not the same at all. As we have seen, Shanqing Maoshan was primarily a mystical school. Maoshan Shengong is a school of magic and alchemy. Scholars generally believe that Maoshan shengong developed from Shanqing among the laypeople. It spread throughout southern China so some call it Southern Maoshan.

These sorcerous Maoshan lineages became the bread and butter of folk magicians who worked for various clients throughout the many villages that are dotted throughout China, particularly in Guangdong, Hunan, Fujian and Sichuan. It particularly flourished among the Hakka people. This is the school which I studied at.

Maoshan Shengong has three legendary Ancestors, perhaps a reflection of the Mao Brothers of Shanqing. They are Zhang Zi Xing, Hu Bao Qing and Zhu Zhi Fei. Legends state they travelled to the Mao

San Mao Zhejun, the Three Mao Brother ancestors of the Maoshan lineage.

Mountain to master their magical skills. On the mountain, they were taught by Guo Xiu Quan, an Immortal.

Their teachings spread far and wide, and being the Chaos Magic of the East so to speak was very results orientated. Consequently, it picked up important magical techniques from the Miao people, the Thais and the Malays. Many of these techniques from South East Asia are distinctly witchcraft and necromantic in nature.

The Lushan Pai

Another important school is the Lushan or Lu Mountain Faction. Lushan was founded in the Fujian region of China. You may here note that the area of southern China has always been the cradle of occultism in China. It is a cliche, but it is true that the Chinese preserve traditions that go back thousands of years, and you may again recall that it was southern China where the native animism and shamanism survived.

Laoshan is a mountain that is said to be in the depths of the Minjiang River and only opens every 1000 years to a person who has cultivated the Tao.

Every Laoshan temple has as its focus the Three Ladies of Milk, Chen Jinggu, Lin Jiuniang and Li Sanmiang. These are three ancient mother goddesses which date back to Fujian's early roots in shamanism and witchcraft.

Laoshan Pai has two distinct classes of priests. The Red Priests are largely devoted to the Three Ladies of Milk and so are called the Three Milk School. They are dealers in worship, births and marriages. The Black Faction or Wolfsbane School specialise in funerals and spirit, both demonic and of the dead. Laoshan also has a special Buddhist subschool known as the Pu-er.

Another common feature of the Laoshan magic is known as the

Five Battalions in which special altars invoke the protection of a group of celestial warriors assigned to the five directions.

The Jinying School

The Jinying school was also created during the Sorcerer Wars of the Ming Dynasty. It has as its focal deity the Great Ancestor Jin Ying who appears as a child god. In the stories related by the Jin Ying School, the founding ancestor was Lin Jin Ying. His birth was surrounded by portents, the most famous being that a massive luminous eagle passed over his house as he was being born. Three days after his birth the young baby saw a Taoist priest and shouted 'Master!' as if in recognition. By the age of eight on the fifth day of the third lunar month, the enlightened child ascended into the skies as an immortal treading a road in the sky made of pure golden light. Thus, to this day every Jin Ying Temple has a young child god statue holding the Sun and Moon. Most of the talismans of this sect are incinerated, the talisman burnt and mixed with water to be drunk.

The Chinese Occult Today

It is curious today that magic in China is not only discouraged but illegal, though there are underground followers as I was to find out. For this reason, most magicians are focused on overseas Chinese communities like Taiwan, Hong Kong, Singapore, Malaysia, Indonesia and Thailand. Of course, some of those sorcerers are nestled in the various Chinatowns all over Europe and the United States. For British readers, there is one of my acquaintances in the Chinese community in London.

What you must remember though is that China is the source from which all this Taoist magic arose ... indeed it is embedded in the Chinese mind and in the very landscape. During Mao's cultural revolution there was wholesale destruction and burning of not only occult knowledge but in art, philosophy, history and even the martial arts.

Magic in China pre-Mao was practised in the Temples where a citizen could go and seek the services of a Master of the Tao, by a village lay magician or by a travelling folk magician. There was a time when every home had its own altar to the ancestors and every village had a family who had a hereditary tradition of magic to which the fellow villagers turned.

Such magical folk were not simple folk magicians but intellectuals with a deep knowledge of Taoism, Buddhism and Chinese history and medicine. The Cultural Revolution was a disaster for Chinese occultism and as brutal as the Witch Hunts of medieval and Early Modern Europe. Temples were stripped and burnt, intellectuals dragged through the streets with straw in their mouths. The straw that was found in the toilets of then China and covered in excrement. At best an occultist in this period could expect a trip to a reeducation camp or at worst beaten to death or executed by the Red Guard.

Even today in a more liberal China, occultism and fortune telling is illegal. Recently Zhou Yongkong, one of China's most powerful politicians was imprisoned and 'disappeared' along with his colleague Li Chuncheng for their involvement with the magician and healer Cao Yongzheng.

This censure of occultism even extends to the movie industry. Films about occult powers or ghosts cannot be made or shown in China.

China can be rightly said to have been a Kingdom of the Occult for most of its history. The Emperor was, in reality, a man who stood as the pole between Heaven and Earth. His every action was highly ritualised to maintain the balance between Heaven and Earth. He was surrounded by countless philosophers and mystics who interpreted the will of Heaven. The very architecture of the Forbidden City was a reflection of the Purple Palace where the Jade Emperor held court.

The government's suspicion of occultism can be sympathised with if you look at the history of China. Several revolutions were led by occultists, such as the Yellow Turbans and the Boxer Rebellion. More recently the Falungong and other qigong based cults have been ruthlessly persecuted.

For this reason, you will tend to find the majority of occult practitioners operating openly in overseas Chinese communities.

However there is a small underground community of practitioners in China who preserve and pursue the occult tradition, especially in Southern China, and it was from one of these masters that I had the privilege to learn from.

2. The Manifestation of the Gods

It was my first time, I stepped gingerly into the room, Thick clouds of sweet incense suspended in the air. In front was a high altar. Simple in appearance, a statue of the Lord Taishang Laojun gazing from a thin wispy beard with benevolent intent. The altar was draped in bright vermillion cloth and fruits were piled in bowls. The master stood in his black imperial scholar's gown with edges ornamented in porcelain patterns of blue and white.

As soon as I walked in I just knew it was truly magical. It is hard to describe. It was like walking into a field charged with static electricity and I felt the hairs on the back of my neck stand up as goosebumps sprung up in domino succession from head to toe. Powerful. Powerful, almost humming and throbbing with unseen forces that my senses could only translate in some crude earthly way.

I had, as a tourist, visited the public temples of Taoism. Yet despite their ostentatious displays of statues and priests strutting around like holy pepperpots, there was never anything like this. This was real. It was, in fact, a bit scary.

Behind the altar was a large red tablet of paper with various names and invocations written on it. I would later learn that this tablet was, in reality, a giant talisman or stele that acted as a focus for an occult lineage of masters and immortal Xian that existed in the hidden realms, in what British Occultist Kenneth Grant would likely call the Mauve Zone. This simple but empowered red tablet was like a nexus or focal point for gathering occult energies of twelve Immortals. It stored, transmitted and received like some kind of sorcerous crystal radio set.

'Are you ready?' said the teacher.

I handed him a yellow card painted with Chinese characters that

Taishang Laojun

included my name, address and Tao name. This was a literal letter to the Gods requesting initiation into the lineage of the Maoshan Masters. He attached it to the front of the altar.

Unlike western initiations where you are initiated by a representative of the Gods and/or masters, in Maoshan you have to be directly initiated without the intercession of a priest. The Gods and Immortals themselves are approached by way of the occult; 'transmission station'.

I had previously been coached on the process. And kneeling and kowtowing I read the invocations of the Immortals. This was no game. I could feel it, at points I was rooted to the spot as some mysterious but beautiful ecstatic force poured through me. I can only describe it as being held by some spiritual traction beam as I was 'programmed ' by some magical download. I hope the reader can forgive my clumsy description of the process, but I am grasping for adjectives here.

Afterwards, I really did feel different. There was no psychodrama here, just pure energy at work.

I was presented with a special book or Mishu (Secret Book) which gave the methods for this level of initiation and some basic modes of lesser magic such as healing and protection.

Among other things I had a year ahead in which to begin to transmute not just my soul and spirit, but even my body, to be able to radiate the numinous magical presence required of me. Then there would be a test.

The process was very exact. Not only meditations and herbal formulae, but also the making of certain talismans that were to be reduced to ashes and drunk in 'Yin and Yang Water'.

Reserved and somewhat suspicious of the 'Lao Wei' (foreigner) before, his demeanour had now completely changed. I was in the 'Door' as they term it here in China, and a true Dizi or student.

Xing Cheng Shen Ling

With a cup of hot green tea in a thoroughly modern plastic cup, the teacher engaged me in conversation. After the usual niceties and conversation warm-ups, he suddenly said 'Xing cheng shen ling'.

The meaning of this is that If The Heart Is True, The Gods Reveal Their Presence/Spirit.

This is the essence of Taoist magic, especially when you are a beginning disciple. As a neophyte, you will have little ability of your own and the Gods and spirits must be nearly wholly relied upon.

That is with a true heart and dedicated cultivation (Lian) a man or woman can reveal the power of the Gods. Lian is an interesting word. Originally it signified the process by which silk was refined. Silk begins life as a knotted mass of organic fibres in a chaotic mess in the cocoon of the silkworm. The silk manufacturer would untangle the fine threads and put them through various processes including washing and drying until they were woven into an organised structure that forms the fine gossamer fabric we all know and love.

Similarly for the spiritual transmutation of man, who, as a neophyte, begins life as a disorganised collection of forces, of twisted unbalanced threads of yin and yang. He must unpick the tangled mass of his potential nature, and reorganise and purify that nature.

The magical Tao is sometimes called SHENDAO the Way of the Gods, a term that became Shinto in Japan.

At the basic root of Shendao is TIAN or Heaven. Tian is the source of all created things and is the ultimate source of meaning and the reason for the 'moral' life lived by, say the Taoist. The 'moral' here means doing or acting in the right way, which does not always match the 'moral' structures of ordinary society. Tian expresses itself via a universal cosmic substance, Qi as we saw in an earlier chapter and by the balance of Yin and Yang.

BAO YING is the balance we create by acting in accordance with the basic principles of the absolute reality and understanding of Tian.

This brings us to the nature of man himself. He has a dual nature. Partly Yang and tending to Heaven and partly Earthly and tending to Yin. Consequently, there is a constant war of attrition in the being of humanity, between doing and acting correctly or giving in to entirely earthly desires regardless of the consequences and so neglecting the cultivation of his true nature. This internal struggle was often symbolised in Chinese art by the war of the Dragon (Yang, Heaven, spiritual tendency) and the Tiger (Yin, passive tendency to follow nature). The tiger was not conquered but tamed. Thus great sages were often shown riding the tiger ... not killing it.

This internal nature of man is shown by the existence of two grades of soul. The HUN is the Yang and Heaven tending spirit, intelligent and conscious, immortal. While the Po is that which tends towards the material desires, the yin nature and is mortal. In theosophic terms, we could describe the Hun as the spiritual and higher mental bodies. While the Po is astral and etheric. These are loose associations of course offered to help you understand the concept of the Hun and Po. Taoists, in fact, posit the existence of three hun and seven po.

If a man cultivates his true nature in life he is capable of transmutation into a perfected Yang state we call Xian or Zuxian, Immortal ancestor. If uncultivated, at death he becomes a mere shade of yin, a ghost, or GUI, Zu GUI, a ghostly ancestor.

Tian, the Absolute Reality has a factor inherent in the very substance of the cosmos called the DE or power. By the De, all beings can have the potential to transcend.

The Gods are an expression of the absolute reality of Tian. We can become aware of them by LING the holy and sacred power of the Absolute Reality. This spiritual presence is crystallised into reality by personal cultivation, devotion, respect and reverence. Personal good deeds (Shashi) and cultivation (Xiu xing) are vital in this process and are as important as the reverence of the Gods. This is a reciprocal relationship with the deities that bring about the presence of the sacred numen, or Ling. Spiritual manifestations can show themselves through healing, significant dreams (tuomeng), and possession through mediumship.

Once the knowledge of the Tao is started and cultivation begins, a new awareness begins in the life of the neophyte, KAI WU. This is a deeper understanding of life and its spiritual meaning and responsibilities. This gives rise to a new sense of spiritual destiny given by the Absolute Reality of the Tian known as MING YUN. Meaningful serendipitous events occur known as YUAN FEN, helping one understand the path of Dao.

This is all very academic the reader must be thinking. However, it is important to understand this basic conceptual framework of how the magic works and why we do any of this at all.

3. Heaven, Man, Earth

As I keep saying, this is not a book on Taoism, but it is essential you have a grasp of the very basics of Taoist metaphysics, especially in their relationship to magic. The first concept we should be aware of is the concept of Heaven ... Tian, Earth ... Di ... And Man ... Ren.

This is a concept that dates back to those shamanic times and is a broad conception of the interrelationship between the man who stands between Heaven and Earth. It's best not to think of this as a categorisation or division but rather a relationship between three broad principles.

In Chinese, it is known as the San Cai or Three Potencies and encompasses all known, unknown, visible and invisible phenomena.

For the magician, the concept is a way to understand his or her relationship to both the invisible and visible worlds, worlds in which we are immersed and yet become unaware of at times.

Heaven at its densest expression can be said to be the sky above us. Indeed the word Tian indicates both in Chinese. The Sun, the Moon and the stars as well as the weather, all of which have a profound effect on human beings and on the Earth in general. All is under Heaven.

Certain of these stars and planets are of particular importance to us. In particular, the stars of the Big Dipper are a source of infinite power quite unsuspected to most occultists, and we shall devote an entire chapter to this subject. Yet Heaven also includes what we would call the spiritual worlds, those worlds that vibrate at frequencies so high they are invisible to ordinary human consciousness. For this reason, they can only be explained in terms of symbolism until they are experienced. Fortunately for us, those symbols also allow us to interface with the various realities in those higher realms. Symbolic representations in the forms of pictures and sounds are useful keys to the inner kingdoms we speak of. The symbolic interface of Taoist magic has its own unique language. The Taoist will also use certain meditations, energy exercises, prayers and training methods to gradually experience those worlds. These abilities include what western occultists call clairvoyance and astral travel.

In the Yi Jing, we can equate Heaven with Qian, consisting of three unbroken lines. Qian means, yes, you guessed it ... Heaven. It is the Yang, male father recalling the ancestral sky Lord of most early shamanism in the Eastern world. This Sky Father seems to have been defined (realised?) on the steppes by the world's earliest sorcerers and was the ancestor of such Gods as Zeus, Jove, Yahweh, Tiwaz and Varuna as well as our own Jade Emperor. Qian also indicates the Creative or Initiating, the Source and Beginning.

Heaven is nearly pure Yang. It is a positive and executive spiritual force striving to evolve and is indeed life in its most pure form. It brings order, geometry and mathematical certainty to chaos. It manifests through the desire to be. Though beyond comprehension it can be approached by understanding how it is expressed in the principles of Earth and Man.

Opposite to Heaven, we have the principle of Earth which in the Yi Jing is Kun, the Receptive or Receiving and nourishing principle. Its essential nature is Yin. It is the Great Mother impregnated by the thunder, winds and rains of Heaven.

From a practical point of view, the Earth is understood as our environment and all its energies. The environment in which we live not only shapes our existence but entire cultures and civilizations. Chinese culture can be said to have sprung from the yellow silts of the Yellow River and the Egyptians from the rich black alluvium of the Nile.

In practical terms, every Chinese magician has an intimate

knowledge of the landscape around him and how the dragon forces of Qi flow through that landscape. Rivers and mountains are of particular importance to the sorcerer as we shall see.

There is even a method of observing the Qi of the Earth through clairvoyance that can be a portent of things to come. This skill was often used by magicians working for generals in times before battle.

Humanity is, of course, you as an individual and man as a whole. It's best not to entirely think of yourself as the body. That's not what we mean by man. Your body is really a part of the Earth principle shaped by cause and effect so you, the true human, can experience the environment and interact with it. Ren is, in fact, a portion of the Spirit experiencing life in the Earth principle in order to evolve into the state of Immortality, Xian. Unfortunately, we tend to forget this fact. The body is merely a vehicle and tool for the spirit to experience and grow in the restrictions of an environment of material cause and effect. The spirit (shen) becomes so enamoured with that environment it forgets its true nature and true purpose and its true relationship to Earth and Heaven.

Man is a conscious life. We stand as a link between Heaven and Earth. We are both Yin and Yang, Heaven and Earth. In an ideal role, we stand as a medium between the truth of Heaven and the realm of matter. However, this is rarely the case. There must be a truly balanced alignment between all three principles for man to be a truly executive power...a transmitter and receiver of Heavenly Power. When we become out of synchronicity with Heaven and Earth there is a great disbalance which causes personal and historical powerlessness and impotency.

When we are first born we are full of Yang. As time goes on we become increasingly Yin in nature. This isn't natural according to the Taoist mages. When we incarnate the attractions of the Earth principle are powerful and blind the soul to its true nature. The result is we have a kind of spiritual amnesia, just like Odysseus with Calypso or Tannhauser in Venusberg. Hence we grow old and lose our innate Heavenly immortality. We become buffeted about in the winds of desires and of cause and effect.

Taoism is one of the traditions, it's not the only one that has a remedy. Chiefly this is through Internal Alchemy and meditation. The magical powers of sorcery are in a sense just the executive function of your renewed relationship with the spiritual. Those powers are developed for various reasons, but mainly in the service of ending suffering for yourself and others. Taoist magic is a path of service. This is an idea shared by our Buddhist friends who have their Bodhisattvas. These figures temporarily renounce Nirvana ... the oblivion of enlightenment to serve life and its evolution to spiritual consciousness. It is the same for the Taoist Masters.

This relationship between Heaven, Man and Earth seems to have been better understood by the ancients. We now know that the Pyramids of Giza are a representation of the belt of the Orion constellation, and that other temples somehow are designed to reflect heaven on earth. The original function of a ruler or king was as a kind of shaman or priest who kept the balance between Heaven and Earth. The Pharaohs of Egypt and the Emperors of China were really a kind of human axis through which Heaven transmitted its powers to the nation in which they ruled.

In practical terms, you will constantly see this symbolism in ritual and practice. For example when we analyse ritual space or categorise the Gods or kinds of life force or Qi.

4. YIN and YANG

The concept of Yin and Yang is perhaps the most well known of the fundamental principles of Chinese metaphysics, but also one of the most misinterpreted even by Chinese.

Yin and Yang are incredibly ancient concepts.

In their study of nature over millennia, the Taoist mystics observed that all phenomena exhibit a duality. This duality is an expression of the archetypal forces that when manifesting into the phenomenal world have to sexualise.

To paraphrase Lao Zi "first there is the One and then the Two".

Literally translated, Yin Yang means Dark-Bright. The Hanyu character of Yin represents the shaded side of a hill and Yang the sunlit side.

To save droning on about a concept well known to most readers, we can summarise the YinYang concept by quoting the Twelve Laws of YinYang. These laws were compiled by generations of sages and are applied to traditional Chinese medicine, feng shui and magic. Note them well and remember them.

1. The universe is infinite and its source is beyond phenomena. When the Power manifests itself into the phenomenal world it does so by two tendencies, Yin and Yang, which are the complementary and yet antagonistic poles which coexist in a state of eternal change.

2. Yin and Yang arise continuously from the ceaseless motion in the Infinite cosmos.

3. Yin is centrifugal and Yang is centripetal. Their interaction gives rise to all phenomena by constant tension and change.

4. Yin attracts Yang and Yang attracts Yin.

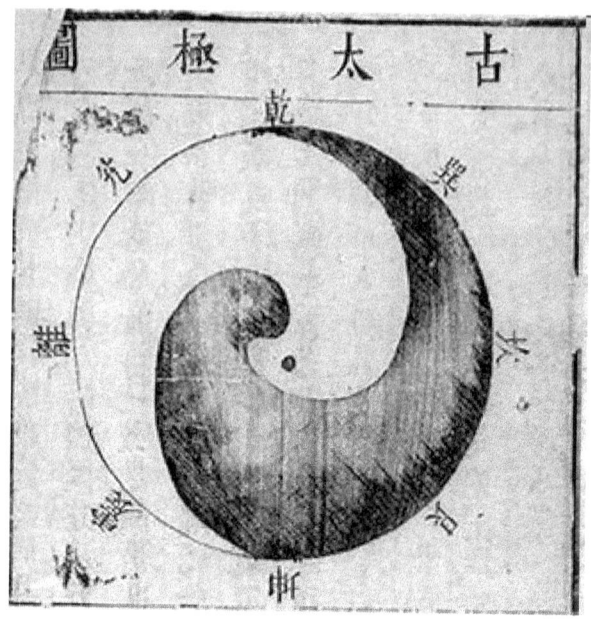
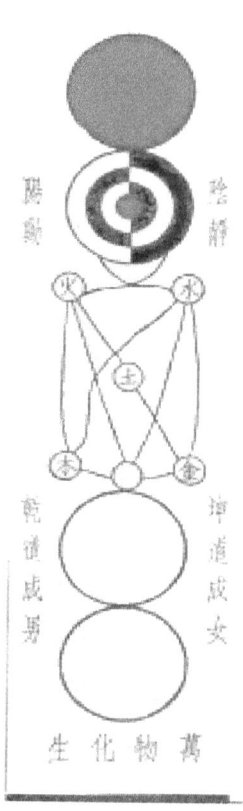

Two forms of Taiji

5. Yin repels Yin and Yang repels Yang.

6. Yin and Yang mix to form an infinite number of combinations in varying proportions giving rise to an infinite variety of created things. The degree to which creations attract or repulse each other represents their similarity or difference.

7. All phenomena exist in a constant state of flux. All creations are constantly shifting towards becoming more Yin or more Yang.

8. Nothing is wholly Yin or wholly Yang. All things are created by both forces.

9. There is no neutrality. All creations have a Yang nature or a Yin nature.

10. Greater Yin attracts Lesser Yin. Greater Yang attracts Lesser Yang.

11. When a phenomenon becomes extremely Yin it changes to Yang, when a phenomenon becomes extremely Yang it becomes Yin. This is one of the Laws of Change. It is the basis of the study of change as for example in the Yi Jing, where Old Yang becomes Young Yin, Old Yin becomes Young Yang and the cycle of change is wrought.

12. Yang focuses on the centre and Yin focuses on the periphery.

These principles should be carefully studied as they are the basis of much in Taoist magic and medicine. I would take time to contemplate each principle so you can apply its wisdom to a study of the universe and yourself.

For example, there is the idea of antipathy and sympathy for things, a principle found in the Neoplatonic and Hermetic systems of magic. For example Heinrich Cornelius Agrippa and Albertus Magnus. Similar to the Hermeticists of old, the Taoist believes in the axiom 'As above, so below'. This means that the very laws which operate in the universe also operate in man. Microcosm and macrocosm. Understand yourself ... understand the universe, understand the universe, understand yourself. In a sense, the apparent division of consciousness and phenomena is an attempt of the universe to express and understand itself.

Yinyang is of course expressed in a number of magical diagrams. The famous Tai Chi or Great Ultimate Diagram is in fact more recent. It shows the circle of the Infinite or Wuji (see next). Within are the 'double fish' one black and one white with a spot of the colour of its opposite to show the potential of change to the opposite.

The Tai Ji shows YinYang at oneness and so is one of the holy symbols of the Tao and you will be required to draw it many times in your Taoist magical career. It is a source of strength when you realize truly what it means and you have mentally charged it so to speak. In fact, its power, when understood, is enough to bring about balance when there is an imbalance.

The second is the older version of the YinYang symbol consisting of concentric circles emerging from the point of the Infinite.

The Wuji And The Tao

Wuji is a more difficult concept to grasp, meaning 'Without Direction' or 'Without a Pole'. The idea is that this is a state beyond matter and three-dimensional space. In modern parlance, it is a state or plane that transcends space and time. Some writers and Taoist scholars translate it as The Limitless. In western terms, we could compare it to the Platonic Archetypal World. A realm where the infinite possibility exists and the origin of all ideas and forms. It could be compared to the Gnostic Pleroma.

In the cosmogenesis diagram of Taijitu Shuo written by Zhou Dunyi in the 11th century CE, the Wuji is represented by a blank circle. We can think of this as zero, but it is not 'nothing' but the root of all. It is at that point where Yin and Yang are so in balance that there is a state of absolute union and non-polarity.

We honestly can not say too much about the Wuji. Any words we try to define it already divide it and present a false picture. It must remain an experiential, gnostic phenomenon.

Though it cannot be verbalised and only pictured with a blank circle, the Wuji can be experienced by contemplation and meditation. A return to the Source. It is a state that is comparable to but not identical to the yogic experience of samadhi. In yogic thought the observer is the cause of the world of phenomena, creating mind waves or Vritti which in a sense disturb the universal equilibrium giving rise to the three Gunas. The three Gunas representing three states of energy, inactive, passive and neutral forms then give rise to observable phenomena and so comes into being the illusory division of the ego and the observed. This is a useful model, and more can be read in the Yoga Sutras of Patanjali. This philosophy is pretty close to the higher Taoist conceptions of the mind and man's relation to the observable universe. The universe is a phenomenon of mind, and we can enjoy it. By cutting ourselves from the universe through ego and division into us and 'it' we have cut ourselves off from the very source of power that ensures our existence and could fill us with life, wisdom and power.

Thus in magical training, the magician seeks this state of Limitless Potential and connects with the Source, a reservoir of immense power. Without this connection, magic is mere theatrics. Man is in a sense a medium or vessel for the expression of this divine superpower. You will find the exercises in the relevant part of this book. Nearly all schools of true magic will develop this, sorry for the cliche, Cosmic Consciousness.

The martial artists among you may even be aware of the Wu Ji posture. This is a standing posture used in connecting with the Wuji in Qigong. However and tragically most teachers will neglect to tell you to connect Wuji at least to the best of your ability before attempting to harness the life force of the universe.

The Tao is also a very ancient concept and is older than what we now call Taoism. Taoism means Way or Path. It is a verb in that the Path is to find one's meaning and purpose in the Universe by a greater understanding of your relationship with Nature and beyond. It is also a noun not only describing the Path but also the mysterious x-factor which is the driving force behind all phenomena. There we must stop. It cannot be known except by experience.

5. Qi, The Life Force

It is a universal belief among the ancients that there is a spiritual life force that interpenetrates and gives life to all things. Often this mysterious force was associated with the wind and or breath. In most languages, the words for spirit, soul and wind are related thus revealing an ancient idea. Neshamah can mean soul and breath in Hebrew and the word Spiritus and Pneuma imply the same in Latin and Greek. The Breath of Life is Qi in Chinese thought.

Qi manifests in many forms. For starters, we can divide Qi according to the San Cai ... Heavenly Qi, Earthly Qi and the Qi of man. By YinYang we can identify Yin Qi and Yang Qi. There's also Qi associated with the Sun, the Moon, the Stars, the Wind and all manifested living things, No one thing is identical in Taoist thought and so Qi manifests in infinite ways.

Qi is a concept that is first recorded in the ancient bone oracles of the Shang Dynasty. Scholars think that the original character for Qi indicates a rising mist between Heaven and Earth. Later the character changed to rice and steam. Steam and mist is the key image here.

Qi is a subtle and usually invisible force that is known by its manifestation. It can be harnessed by people because Qi can follow strong will, visualisation and intention (Yi).

Qi is a medium of thought and spirit and so is the medium of magic as well as alchemy. If you hope for any success in the sorcerous arts you must master Qi.

We are not talking about the kind of qigong (qi skill/work) that you learn from some 10 pound an hour master in the local park or community centre. That kind of qi gong is geared towards health and longevity and there it stops. The training for magical qi gong has more requirements and a greater horizon, though healing of the self is indeed one of them.

A self-repair could be said to be the first stage in fact. Beyond this one has to build up a store of mana or magical power.

Qi is the carrier of thoughts. It is no accident that the words for spirit, aspire, respire, inspire and a spiral is from the same root. Ideas are literally in the air. Qi can and does move in spirals sometimes.

The idea of fascination, better known as the evil eye, has its roots in the idea that an actual force or invisible ray or fluid emanates from the eye carrying the thoughts of hate, avarice or lust to a potential victim. Though a European idea the Chinese magician would recognise this description as projected Qi carrying thought shapes. Healing has long been thought to involve some kind of energy and sudden feats of strength or speed are attributed to the tapping in of this force.

Qi is energy, but it's not just some subtle force you can never see or feel. You can see it everywhere. Matter itself is a Qi that has materialised. The matter is crystallised energy.

There is the concept of the Five Realms in which Qi manifests in minerals, then plants, then animals, then humanity and finally in Spirit.

Within these Five Realms Qi manifests in its own peculiar way, constantly striving upwards to Heaven in its own way.

The Taoists have made an extensive study of Qi in both man and nature. They have come to know its cycles in Nature and in man, which is important for the wizard to understand. The Taoist magician relies on Qi and therefore knows the tides and changes of their interplay.

Shengong or Work\Skill with the spirit is the first stage of any magician's real training. This path has manifold variations but the theme is always the same, cultivate the spirit and build a storehouse of Qi within one's self. Yet we should always remember, especially in the modern 'me me' generation, this energy doesn't come from you and nor does it belong to you. It is from the universe, it is the fire we 'steal' from heaven.

For the magician, there are three main ways to understand and use Qi. There is the Qi of Earth, Di Qi, which we understand through the flow of Qi in the landscape and even in our houses and urban settings. Earth Qi includes the study of minerals and plants which have medical and magical uses.

The Qi of Man, Ren Qi is a study of how Qi flows in man … its cycles and effects. In medicine, we study how Qi flow can be excessive or deficient for example. Then there is the study of Neidan or alchemy which is more or less analogous with the skill and work with the spirit or shengong.

The Qi of Heaven, Tian Qi is the study of the flow of Qi from the Heavens. Initially, we can observe the apparent cycles of the Sun and Moon, the stars, the weather and seasons and so forth. In our training, we ascend higher and higher seeking increasingly finer grades and sources of Qi.

Though we classify all these Qi modes, they are not separate but are interdependent and influencing each other. Remember man stands between Earth and Heaven and in him those two are mingled. If we are to draw a Venn diagram to represent man, draw two intersecting circles. One circle is Heaven and the other, the Earth. Man is their intersection, combining both elements. This explains the curious nature of man, the internal struggle between falling to the centre of Earth and desire, or the rising to Heaven. Like some Push Me-Pull me animal in Doctor Doolittle there is a constant tension between the lower desires and the higher aspirations.

6. The Five Elements

The Five Elements or Wu Xing arise from the most basic combinations of Yin and Yang. These elements, furthermore represent five stages of the life cycle of energy. All energy will exist in one of these states. Essentially it is the same idea as the classical western model of the Four Elements. Also occasionally you may come across another set of Five Elements imported by Buddhists into China.

As Taoists, we should be more reliant on the Wu Xing System. They are in constant use in Taoist magic, medicine, feng shui, the classification of people, music and even cooking.

You should become intimately aware of the Five Elements and their interaction. The Five Elements should be understood as five states in which energy can exist at any given time.

In fact, we can call the Five Elements the Five Motions or Five Phases. Things are not 'stuck' in an element. There are many attributions assigned to the Five Elements and so it can get quite wieldy, try and remember the key points. Let us take a look at how it works from the point of view of a theoretical energy wave.

WOOD (MU):
Energy is born and rises. Try not to think of deadwood such as the desk I am writing on is made of. Think of a living tree in the Spring. It is that sense you get after the last frosts and you feel the life force bursting to grow. The fertile force urging nature to reproduce and expand. The common term for a morning erection is 'morning wood'. It is arousal, fertility, growth, expansion. The planet Jupiter is the Heavenly expression of Wood, hence Jupiter is called Mu Xing, the Wood Star. Similar in thought to western astrology, it is the planet of expansion and growth. In meditation and medicine, the colour is green and its season is quite

naturally Spring. In man, it is associated with the liver (yin) and the gallbladder (yang), the eyes and sight, as well as the index finger. All scaly animals are under it. In magic, its Auspicious animal is the Green or Azure Dragon. The Wood quality emerges as idealism, curiosity and the ability to be spontaneous. Excess wood can be foolish optimism, anger and wearing one's heart on one's sleeve.

FIRE (HUO):
As Wood continues to expand the energy becomes more and more excited it can be visualised as becoming hotter and brighter until finally, it bursts into pure flame. Spring becomes Summer, its natural season. Can you guess the planet? Yes, that's right, it is Mars or Huo Xing, the Fire Star. Its colour is red and it rules all feathered animals. Its magical beast is the Vermillion Bird, which you can think of like a scarlet phoenix. In man, it rules the heart and pericardium(yin) and the small intestine/triple warmer system(yang). It rules the tongue and the sense of taste and middle finger. Fire manifests as passion and intensity but can manifest as violence and hatred when in excess.

EARTH (TU):
The fire cools and what is left are the embers and ashes. The energy has stabilised and is calm yet still fertile, the soil in which things can grow. Stability and discipline are key here. Hence it rules the transitional season of Late Summer when the fruits ripen. Its planet is Saturn (Tu Xing), slow-moving, dependable and serious, which are the very psychological qualities manifesting in a person with strong Earth qualities. It manifests as honesty but also excess anxiety. Of organs, it rules the Spleen and pancreas (Yin) and the stomach(Yang), the mouth, touch and the thumb. It rules the human world. Its colour is yellow in meditation and magic.

METAL (JIN):

The ashes become, over time denser, cooler. It becomes congealed and hardened. It becomes metal. Some like to say gold. Its planet is Venus(Jin Xing). It is mature, logical and rational. Like it's a season, Autumn, it is harvesting and storing in nature. I keep, I retain. Its organs in man are the Lungs (Yin) and the large intestine (Yang), the nose, skin and the ring finger. The smell is its sense. Metal rules all animals with fur and so its magical beast is the White Tiger. The colour in meditation and magic is white. In personality it manifests in reasoning but be warned, it can, in excess, manifest as anxiety, regret and sorrow. This is the element most associated with depression.

WATER (SHUI):

Metal changes, gradually it becomes so dense it must begin to turn into an opposite quality. Think of the heavy metals that become so unstable they throw off particles of radiation and decay. Thus it becomes water. Water is cold and moist. It expresses itself in our solar system as the planet Mercury (Shui Xing). Water is a reflection, physically of the Original Spirit from which life emerges. The ultimate medium that nourishes like some kind of universal amniotic fluid. We can see it expressed in the season of Winter. Things may appear dead but there is secret growth in the darkness, there is conception before erupting into new growth in the return to Wood. All latency is there waiting, hiding in nourishment. In man, it is the kidney (Yin) and the urinary bladder (Yang). I should point out here that the kidney system also includes the sexual function and the Jing, the essence of you and your ancestors. The ears, bones, hearing and little finger are assigned to it. It rules over all shelled animals and hence its magical beast is the Black Tortoise. Its magical and meditational colour is black. In the human personality, it is resourcefulness and wisdom but in excess it is fear.

So these are the five elements or phases. You will see them

constantly in your magical studies so know them well. They appear in things such as calling any group of five spirits, guarding and protecting yourself with the Four Auspicious Beasts, in personal cultivation of the spirit, in sexual cultivation and so on.

In daily life, you can see the phases at work. Let's say I have an idea to write a book. There's the enthusiastic Wood stage of inspiration, passing to manifesting that by action in the Fire stage. Then the initial enthusiasm cools off. It is the earth phase. This is the make or breakpoint. My book is there and it is solidifying into reality. But at this point, you might give up. The metal stage of the project has become real and solid but in the water stage, it is contemplated and edited before final publication ... ie back to Wood.

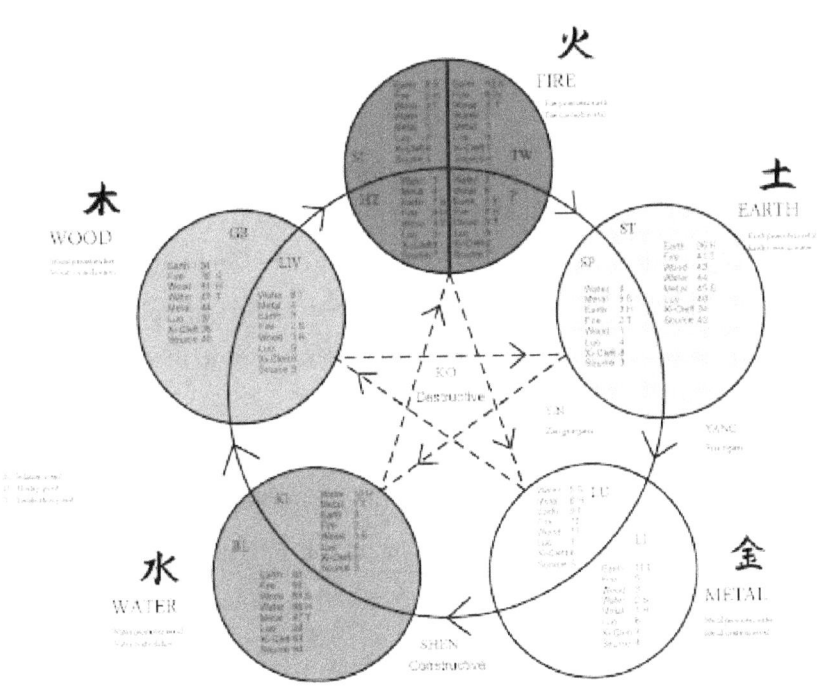

Cycles Of Creation And Destruction

There are two relationships that are very helpful to know in our studies. The Creative and Destructive Cycles are ways to understand transformation in Nature. Most readers will be most familiar with them from their studies in Chinese Medicine. However, their application in magic will also be obvious. Magic, after all, is all about playing with energy. Energy can be understood as the basis of all magic and it too can be understood in terms of Yin and Yang and the Five Phases.

Just as in western traditions of magic one had to master the Four Elements in oneself and in Nature to have any real magical influence (a process symbolised by the Trial of the Elements), so it is so in Taoist magic. Such knowledge of the transformation of things was discovered by generations of alchemists and magicians and transformation has become a key ability in the Chinese occult. It begins by understanding the Elements and understanding the Elements in you and in Nature.

Mystics, philosophers and wizards of all traditions pay a good deal of attention to change. Change is really the natural progression of energy from one state to another state. Simple. There are two processes we must understand. The Cycle of Creation and the Cycle of Destruction. These two processes are essential to not only the calculations of mountain doctors, soothsayers and philosophers but to life and existence itself. The universe is indeed largely illusory if only because the cosmos and everything in it is in a constant state of flux, of coming into being and passing away. Taoists believe as many others do, that this is a temporal reflection in time and space of the Eternal. Time and space are in turn products of having an observer and the observed. All true philosophies, therefore, recognise the Cycles of Creation and Destruction. For example look at your own body, which has both anabolic (creative) and catabolic (destructive) processes. If the anabolic

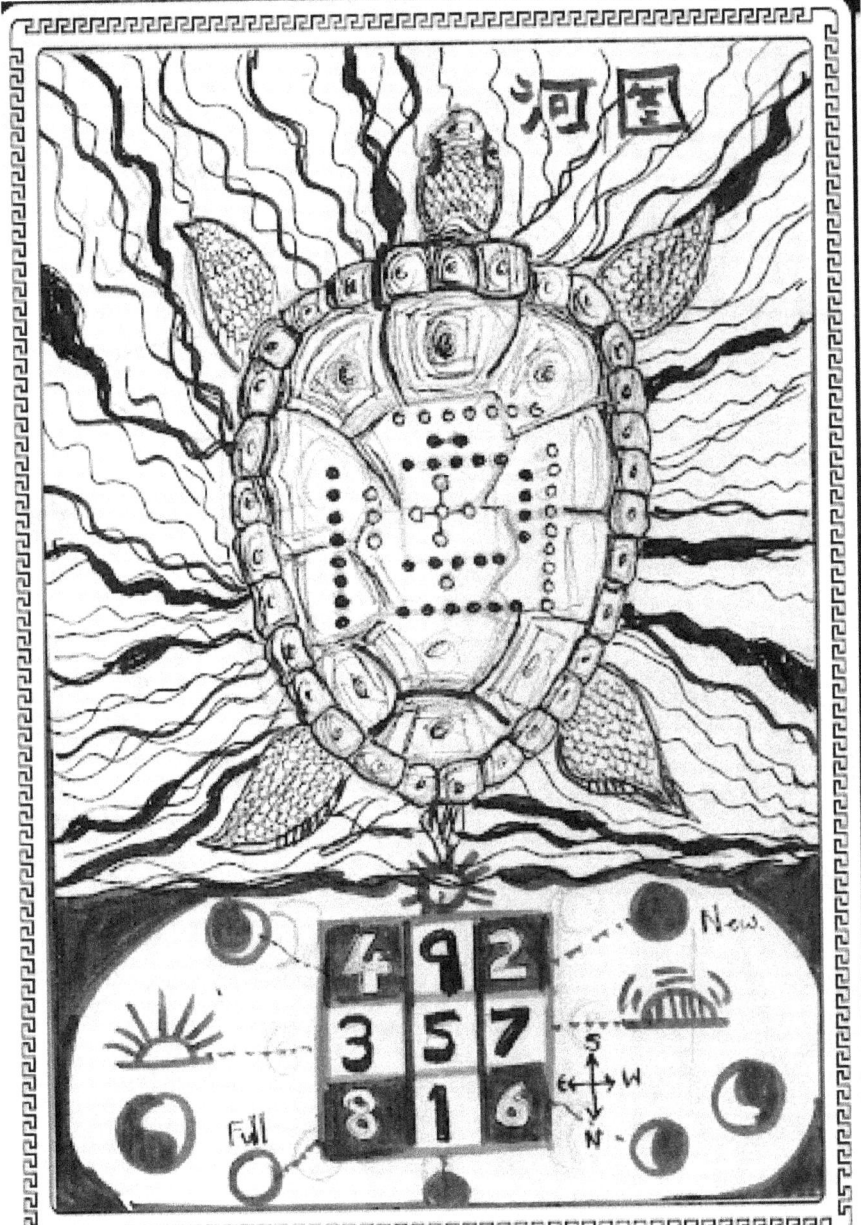

processes were not held in check by the catabolic you would not stop producing bodily tissues and would be a malformed monstrosity until you could no longer be a viable functioning organism. The food that you eat can't be broken down and so on.

Life and death live in tandem and are brother and sister. Eros and Thanatos, I create and I destroy. Sex and death are thus the Great Mysteries of initiation and sources of raw power in Taoism and other schools of the Mysteries. Somehow the modern western consciousness has divorced itself from the reality of the mysteries of Creation and Destruction. Sex is a commodity robbed of its creative power and death is a taboo to be feared. If you are serious about entering the Maoshan door of magic you need a radical shift in attitude.

Now the Cycles of Creation and Destruction are patterns we use to analyse the change in phases of energy in their anabolic and catabolic mode.

The Creative Cycle shows how the five elements or phases support, nourish and derive from each other. It goes like this:

1. WATER nourishes WOOD.

From the conception of the black waters of the womb of water, arises the sapling reaching for the light. I'm growing!! In psychological terms, an idea emerges from the blackness of the subconscious.

2. WOOD feeds FIRE.

Think of the Wood as fuel for the fire. The young idea becomes effort and action.

3. FIRE becomes EARTH.

The fire cools to fertile ash. The idea becomes an actuality.

4. EARTH becomes METAL.

The earth congeals and condenses into metal. The idea is now fixed.

5. METAL becomes WATER.

The metal enhances water. The idea becomes the fertile womb for other ideas.

The diagram shows the Creative Cycle in the traditional pentagonal format going clockwise.

The Destructive Cycle shows how the Five Elements destroy each other and is traditionally shown in the pentagram or five-pointed star. It is kind of like a game of rock, scissors and paper. Let's take a look.

1. WOOD destroys EARTH.

A good mental image is that of the trees and plants sapping the nutrients from the soil. Feeding on the soil until it is bleached of all power.

2. METAL splits WOOD.

The sword cuts the tree. The conservative metal stunts the idealistic wood.

3. FIRE melts METAL.

The solid conservatism of metal is molten in the heat of violent action. Passion melts frigidity.

4. WATER dowses FIRE.

The cold moist waters of the womb mother tame the passions.

5. EARTH fills WATER.

The soil absorbs and fixes water. Time limits timelessness.

Now I hope you can see, even those who are apprentices to this Way, how this can apply to magic, to healing and stages in self-cultivation.

7. The Eight Holy Symbols

The ancient storytellers tell us exactly how the Eight Holy Symbols of Chinese mysticism and magic were discovered. Fu Xi, the primaeval shaman king, had always sought the great mysteries it is told. What he most sought was an essential summary of all philosophy in one glyph or diagram so he could master the occult forces of Earth, Man and Heaven.

However that quintessential knowledge always just seemed out of reach, elusive to grasp.

One day as he walked along the banks of the Yellow River pondering the mysteries of the cosmos his attention was caught by a rippling on the still surface waters of the river. Fu Xi was about to disregard it when to his amazement the waters started furiously foaming and parting as if a door had opened in the very river itself. A burst of supernatural luminescence flashed out from the hollow dip where water should have been. With a furious explosion of movement and limbs there stood before him a dragon-horse, though some of the story weavers tell us it was, in fact, a giant turtle. The white horse was magnificent with dragon-like features enhancing the noblest qualities of the horse. Fu Xi looked closely at the dragon-horse and could see a pattern on the white coat.

That pattern revealed the Eight Diagrams or Ba Gua. Fu Xi had found his key to the mysteries of the universe.

The Western Mysteries have their key in symbol systems such as the qabalah, a system by which the mystic and magician can understand the fundamental cosmic impulses that underlie the very fabric of man, the universe and the environment around him. The Chinese qabalah can be said to begin with Wu Ji, which is very similar to the concept of the Ain Soph, the Limitless Light in Qabalistic thought. The Dao itself can be likened to Kether, the Crown. The first stirrings of creation and the One Source of All. The Supreme Polarity of Yin and Yang emerging from the Dao are the ultimate archetypal expression of the dual forces that Qabalists symbolized by the Twin Pillars of Jachin and Boaz.

The Chinese Qabalah then proceeds with combinations of Yin and Yang, the dual forces, in combinations of three lines to produce the Eight Diagrams. For convenience, we refer to these as trigrams. We saw before how the broken line represents Yin and the unbroken line represents Yang. Combine three of these lines together, for three is the number of manifestations, we have a trigram. By a process of combination, we produce eight such trigrams. Thus we have an analysis of the 8 fundamental forces and qualities which form all possible interpolations of the forces of Yin and Yang as they manifest into reality.

For the Taoist, this is the most Holy of Symbols. Together they are usually arranged in an octagon. This octagon represents the essence of the macrocosm and microcosm. It represents the holy template of the Ultimate Mind, the Logos of Plato. The Reason and means of being. It is cosmic order, the basic geometry and math of the essential laws of creation. Thus, as a symbol, it is not only a source of power and wisdom but a symbol strong enough to break asunder the forces that tend to promote entropy…demons, disease, lost ghosts and the like. The first steps in magic for the practical wizard is, in fact, the magical use of this symbol, the Holy BaGua.

I would like to make a note here at this point. Though I do make analogies with the Chinese system of theosophy to the western systems of the Qabalah I only do so because many of my readers will no doubt be more familiar with those systems. However, we really cannot force the BaGua or the Yi Jing into the Qabalistic framework popularised by Orders such as

The Mystery of the Turtle, The Revelation of the Yellow River and The Golden Dawn. Crowley tried it in Liber 777 and in his works on the Tarot. The attempt was brave but it just does not work, at least in my opinion. To work with the Maoshan and Yinshan systems you just have to empty your cup. You just cannot mix it with other systems comfortably. However, Maoshan Magic can comfortably sit with Tantra and tantric forms of Buddhism.

When I first attempted to find the keys of Chinese magic I did run into some attempts in which the Chinese system was utterly westernised. For example the work of the Choronzon Club or Bertiaux, but I feel a lot is lost. This is why I made the decision to specialize rather than trying to create an eclectic chimaera bonding the western and Maoshan systems. Thus in this book and subsequent volumes, I choose to give you the unaltered system in terms of practice and content. What you do with it however is up to you. With that caveat out the way let's continue.

The Bagua consists of 8 Trigrams. Each has their own images, colours, qualities, powers and attributions, somewhat like the Sephiroth in Western Magic. Let us explore them.

1. QIAN. (Heaven/Sky).
Its image is Sky. The heavens are the source of creation and so some translate it as the Creative. Dating back to the earliest of Shamanic beliefs, we have the Sky Father. He who creates all and who fertilises the Earth principle. It consists of three unbroken lines and so is the ultimate Yang principle. It is the Divine Lingam and Thunderbolt. In a family, it represents the Father, the Emperor. Its animal is the Horse, pure beauty and power. It is strength and persistence. In the microcosm it is the head and brain, the origin of ideas and action to follow. Its traditional colours for meditation are white, grey and silver. The direction can be Northwest or South depending on the arrangement. In magic, it indicates teachers, masters and guides, those who help us, blessing and traveling.

2. XUN (Wind)

Its image is a warm gentle breeze reflecting its quality of gentle penetration and adaptability. The wind is also fecund and carries the sweet energy of creativity from Heaven. It carries the seeds of creation and can be considered to be heavenly Qi, that which impregnates and inspires, fertilises. One recalls that among the ancients the wind was believed to have the power to impregnate. In the family, Xun is the Eldest Daughter, the girl ready to receive the male to her fruitful womb. Hence Xun's season is Summer, the season of fecundity. The trigram has a base of receptive Yin (we read trigrams bottom to top) topped by two yang lines. The direction is Southwest. Its animal is the chicken or bird. Its body parts are the thighs and hips. It has qualities of abundance, prosperity and wealth in magic.

The colours are purple, purple tending blue, purple tending red and brown.

3. KAN (Water)

Its image is dark water. This is not the water you imagine flowing gently but the deep dark waters of the abyss or a deep cave. Dark and primordial, hidden and unknown, it indicates a sense of constant motion. It can be dangerous. It is the Middle Son in the family. Its trigram is Yin at root, Yang in the middle and Yin at top. It indicates the womb and the grave. The waters of life and the waters of death in the West. Its colours are black and dark blue and its body part is the ear. Its animal is the pig or boar and in magic can indicate your career and path in life. This seems a strange attribution but the career and life path are tied to one's karma which is linked to the ancestors in the unknown waters of origin. Its direction is the West. It is linked to the powers of the Moon.

4. GEN. (Mountain)

Its image is the mountain, still, strong, immovable. The Northwest and the Youngest Son. It has a Yang root and is topped by two Yin lines.

The mountain is in Chinese symbolism the abode and access point to the Heavens and the Divine, a fact that becomes increasingly important in our studies. In Maoshan we draw powers from our ancestral mountain or even all five of the Holy Mountains of China. Of course, this belief in the role of mountains as huge sources of spiritual power is universal. In every genuine tradition, there appears some primordial, ancestral mountain of the mysteries. We could list our very own Mao Mountain, Mount Kunlun, Mount Kailash and Meru of the Shiva Tantrics, Mount Fuji of our Japanese brethren, Olympus among the Greeks and even the various mountains in witch lore to which the sorcerers rode to their Sabbats to learn from their Lord. The Mystery of the Primordial Mountain is deep. The direction is the Northwest and its chief quality is stillness. Its colours are blue, black and green. Its body part is the hand. Its animals are the wolf and dog. Knowledge, wisdom and skill are its magical attributes.

5. KUN. (Earth)

Its image is of fallow fields, the earth. Sometimes it's translated as the Receptive or Receiving. It consists of three Yin lines. It is the opposite and complement of Qian. Qian is the Sky Father and so Kun is the Earth Mother. In the family, therefore, it is the Mother. It receives and nurtures energy. It has magical rules over motherhood, love and relationships. Its sacred animal is the cow, the source of milk. Its magical colours are pink, white, beige and red. Pink is the most commonly used. Frankly, whereas Qian is the phallic principle, Kun is the principle of the Yoni. Its direction is in the North.

6. ZHEN. (Thunder)

Is Thunder and the bolt of lightning. Two Yin Lines and atop is the Yang line. The lingam penetrates the yoni. It is the manifested and actual power of Heaven in its most concrete form. It is arousing, exciting and creates change, division and revolution. In family terms, it is the Eldest Son, the young man ready to be a bridegroom, sexually mature and seeking growth and creativity. Of course in every culture Thunder is the medium of the Gods. Thor is a good image of Zhen. The first son of Odin, lusty and a hero battling the Jotun (giants) of primordial Chaos. Yet at times Zhen is not impulsive and acts without wisdom. In Tantric and Taoist symbolism, the Vajra, thunderbolt of phallic action is balanced with the Bell of feminine wisdom. It arises from the East and is associated with Spring. Its colour of magic is green, its body part the feet. Its animal is the Dragon. Its magical attributes include physical health, personal vitality, fertility and virility, the family and growth rooted in things sown in the past.

7. LI (Fire)

The images are flames of scarlet fire. IA Yang root with Yin in the middle and Yang line on top. Li is the Middle Daughter in the family, burning with life and youthful energy. Its quality is clinging as it is dependent on fuel to burn. It is a quick impulsive movement and radiant energy. It is the light of the Sun. It stands opposite to Kan. Fire is the catalyst, beautiful and dangerous if not controlled. In the evolution of man, fire is the catalyst of his development. With fire, he could cook and warm himself. Around the fire, communities emerged. With fire, he could protect himself. The fire became the source of all technology. Fire illuminates the darkness. Yet the fire was also the source of weapons and danger. Fire is a gift from the Gods and many a myth relates that it was 'stolen' and came with a price. Li is associated with the East. Its colours of magic are red, orange and purple. Its body part is the eyes, its animal is the pheasant. Its magical attributes are those of fame, glory and reputation. Success in the material and spiritual worlds.

8. DUI (Lake)

Its image is a calm mirror-like lake that reflects the glory of heaven. She is the Youngest Daughter associated with the Southeast. It has a Yin root with two Yang lines atop. It indicates joy, comfort and satisfaction but it can also indicate stagnation. There is danger in slumbering in bliss like the Eloi in H.G. Wells Time Machine. It can turn from being a Lake to becoming a marsh. Its colours are white, grey and silver…think a metallic mirror. Its organ is the mouth and its animal is the sheep. In magic, it rules over creativity and children.

These then are the Eight Symbols and their main attributes. The aspiring magician should spend some time familiarising himself and meditating on them to feel their energy. They are absolutely essential.

The BaGua is something of a constant in the oriental system of magic. You will see it everywhere and your knowledge must be more than surface-level or intellectual. It must become a part of your being. One way to do this is to simply meditate on the Image and the trigram and contemplate it. Make notes of the sensations and intuitional knowledge that arises.

There are two arrangements of the Bagua, the Pre-Heaven and Post Heaven Sequences.

The Pre-Heaven or Early-Heaven Sequence is used in spiritual matters and interestingly, in feng shui is the pattern used to position tombs of the dead. In the Pre-Heaven BaGua, we are presented with the archetypal pattern of ideal equilibrium between the Heavens and the Earth.

Fu Xi developed the Early Heaven Sequence from another of his discoveries known as the Yellow River Map or He Tu. The Yellow River

Map is a magical diagram which has a numerical basis. In occult legend, the Yellow River Map was used by Fuxi to gain control of natural forces Today the Yellow River Map is still used as a major power source and can be found in Taoist temples, talismans and flags.

So in the Pre-Heaven sequence, all the trigrams are arranged to reflect the primordial perfection of balance.

The Post-Heaven Sequence arranges the BaGua in another way. Sometimes it's called the Manifested or King Wen Sequence.

It is the earthly, material BaGua showing the processes of change and corruption in the manifested world as opposed to the timeless perfection of the Pre-Heaven Sequence. Of course, this is the Bagua we use in practical, earthly matters. For example, in Feng Shui, this is the Bagua used to analyse one's home environment. It is the one used in Chinese medicine, in astrology and the qi men dun Jia divination system.

The Post-Heaven Bagua was said to have been discovered by another Shaman-King we have met earlier, Yu the Great. If you remember, Yu the Great was the sage who learned how to control the flow of the Yellow River whose flooding had caused so much unpredictable misery in early Chinese civilization. Yu discovered another occult diagram called the Luo River Diagram, apparently on the back of a tortoise that emerged from the river Luo. Using Luo Shu he created a new arrangement of the Bagua that we now refer to as the Post-Heaven Sequence.

Western magicians may be interested to know that the Luo Shu is really a magic square, the Square of Saturn and Earth. It may have been a separate discovery or may have even passed to India and Arabian speaking peoples along the Silk Road. It then made its most notable appearance in the works of several Renaissance magicians including The Occult Philosophy of Agrippa. From Agrippa, it went 'viral' appearing in just about every grimoire thereafter, that Saturn is all about control is an interesting parallel.

The Bagua is often used in practical magic for protection of a house. Aside from talismans, you are probably aware of Bagua mirrors which are hung outside a home to reflect bad sha qi. There are also specific hand seals and mantras for each trigram used in meditations to invoke among other things such as different weather conditions and other magical abilities.

The Bagua can be worn not only for protection but as a source of inspiration and power.

Arising from the simple 8 Diagrams are the 64 Hexagrams of the Yi Jing, but that is another matter beyond the scope of this book.

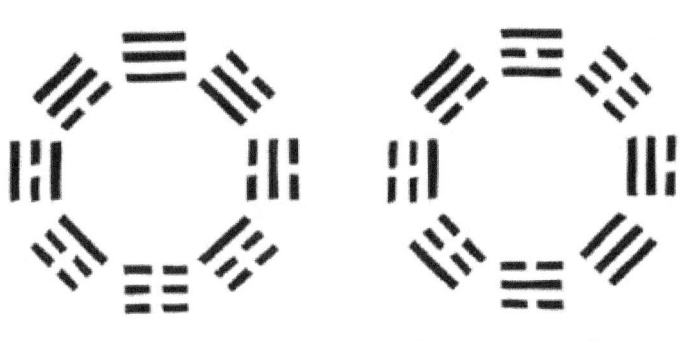

Pre-Heaven Bagua   Post-Heaven Bagua

8. The Heavenly Stems And The Earthly Branches

We are not going to get very far without an understanding of the concept of the Stems and Branches. Again you will notice them constantly appearing in Chinese magic, divination and medicine.

The Stems and Branches are important because they were used by the ancients in the creation of the Chinese calendar. Any magician worth his or her salt knows that the times and seasons are of great import to the workings of their art and this is just as true among the Chinese magical and religious community. This section will thus lead to a discussion concerning the Chinese calendar.

The origins of the Tiangan or Heavenly Stems are lost in history, but we do know they date back to at least the Shang Dynasty and reflected a belief in the powers of the ancestral dead and a belief in Ten Suns, each sun representing a great age or aeon somewhat like the Mayan concept.

These 10 ancient symbols are used as ordinals for counting and are still used today in some circumstances. For us, they are combined with the Earthly Branches which are 12 in number to mark the calendar and indicate its cycles of 60 years and 60 days as we shall see.

Table Of The Heavenly Stems

NAME IN CHINESE	ELEMENT	POLARITY
JIA	WOOD	YANG
YI	WOOD	YIN
BING	FIRE	YANG
DING	FIRE	YIN
WU	SOIL	YANG
JI	SOIL	YIN
GENG	METAL	YANG
XIN	METAL	YIN
REN	WATER	YANG
GUI	WATER	YIN

The Twelve Earthly Branches

The 12 Earthly Branches or Dizhi, will be much more familiar to the western reader as you will know them as the Twelve Animals of the Chinese Zodiac. The Earthly Branches give their name in combination with the Heavenly Stems to hours, days, months and years. Thus we can speak of the year of the Metal Pig. The Heavenly stem gives the Element and the Branch the zodiacal animal quality. This system allows the occultist, diviner or medical practitioner to analyse the general occult forces at play in any given hour, day or year. At its simplest this may be the consultation of a Chinese Almanac, at an advanced level, it requires methods such as Qimen Dun Jia or astrology.

When we say Chinese Zodiac it has a completely different meaning to that of the Western Zodiac. The western zodiac is based on observations of the movement of the Sun along the plane of the ecliptic, i.e. in its apparent orbit around the earth. This takes about a year and this is divided into twelve sections which make up the signs of the zodiac. The ancient Chinese astrologers took as their cosmic base the orbit of Jupiter rather than that of the Sun, which rounded off takes around twelve years. Each year is assigned one of the twelve earthly branches. We combine these with the Heavenly branches to arrive at a calendrical system we call Ganzhi.

Table of the Twelve Branches

Chinese Name	Animal	Time Period	Season	Direction	Element and polarity
Zi	Rat	11pm-1am	Winter	North	Yang Water
Chou	Ox	1am-3am	Winter	Northeast	Yin Water
Yin	Tiger	3am-5am	Spring	Northeast	Yang Wood
Mao	Hare/Rabbit	5am-7am	Spring	East	Yin Wood
Chen	Dragon	7am-9am	Spring	Southeast	Yang Wood
Si	Snake	9am-11am	Summer	Southeast	Yin Fire
Wu	Horse	11am-1pm	Summer	South	Yang Fire
Wei	Sheep	1pm-3pm	Summer	Southwest	Yin Fire
Shen	Monkey	3pm-5pm	Autumn	Southwest	Yang Metal
You	Rooster	5pm-7pm	Autumn	West	Yin Metal
Xu	Dog	7pm-9pm	Autumn	Northwest	Yang Metal
Hai	Boar/Pig	9pm-11pm	Winter	Northwest	Yin Water

Table of the Twelve Branches

Combine the Heavenly Stems and the Earthly Branches and we have a complete calendar that has a cycle of sixty years or 12 multiplied by 5. Thus we can give an energetic value for each year. 2020, the year I am writing this book, for example, is a Yang Year governed by the Metal Rat. This is important knowledge for the occultist and healer.

The Twelve Earthly Branches are also assigned to the hand for use in Taoist magical hand seals as you will see later in the practical magical section of this book.

An interesting concept in Asian culture is that when a person reaches 60 years of age one cycle of the sexagenary cycle has passed, and so 60 is considered the Second Birth is an auspicious year. A special celebration is held and red clothes and vests are worn. The red clothes are the same as those worn by newly born infants. 60 is, therefore, the time of renewal and birth into the higher octave of one's cycle.

Unfortunate ages are said to be 24 and 41 for men and 18 and 32 for women.

The Ten Heavenly Stems

The Twelve Earthly Branches

9. Sacred Time and Sacred Space Yinli, The Lunar Calendar

The Chinese have both lunar and solar elements in the calendar as we shall investigate. The lunar calendar is mostly used in the calculation of religious festivals and holy days so as you can imagine it is crucial for the practising Taoist magician.

One month is the period between a New Moon and the next New Moon, which is around 29.5 days. Naturally, adjustments have been made to fit a standard year. Thus every 3 years there is the 13th month of 30 days or RUNYUE. A Common Year has 12 months and a 13 month year is called a Long Year.

The month can be a Da Yue of 30 days or a Xiao Yue of 29 days.

Each lunar month has a name and an assigned Earthly Branch, an approximate Gregorian date is given for convenience.

Table Of Lunar Months

NAME	CHINESE NAME	BRANCH	APPROX. DATE	MONTH NUMBER
The month of the Square of Pegasus	Zouyue	Yinyue. Tiger Month	21 Jan -20 Feb.	1st.
Apricot Month	Xingyue	Maoyue Rabbit Month	20 Feb -21 March	2nd
Peach Month	Taoyue	Chenyue Dragon Month	21 Mar -20 Apr.	3rd
Plum Flower Month	Meiyue	Siyue Snake Month	20 Apr -21 May	4th
Pomegranate Month	Liuyue	Wuyue Horse Month	21 May -21 June	5th
Lotus Month	Heyue	Weiyue Goat Month	21 Jun -23 July	6th
Orchid Month	Lanyue	Shenyue Monkey Month	23 Jul -23 Aug.	7th
Osmanthus Month	Guiyue	Youyue Rooster Month	23 Aug -23 Sept.	8th
Chrysanthemum Month	Juyue	Xuyue Dog Month	23 Sep -23 Oct.	9th
Month of Dews	Luyue	Haiyue Pig Month	23 Oct -22 Nov.	10th
Month of Reeds	Jiayue	Ziyue Rat Month	22 Nov -22 Dec.	11th
Month of Ice	Bingyue	Chouyue Ox Month	22 Dec -21 Jan	12th

Table Of Lunar Months

The Twenty-Eight Constellations And Lunar Mansions

The 28 Lunar mansions or Ershiba Xiua are 28 points which mark the stations of the Moon in her journey around the Earth. These stations are marked by 28 asterisms or groups of stars that have been recorded as far back as the Zhou Dynasty. The 28 constellations themselves have great importance in the occult arts of the Chinese. You will see them in invocations and talismans for example. They are used in feng shui and other forms of divination and even in certain meditations. In the learning of the talismanic art, for example, the 28 Constellations are assigned talismans all of their own and are connected with one's birth star and fate. Some of these talismans offset the negative effects of certain stars not entirely compatible with ourselves.

The 28 Constellations are in four groups of seven. Each group is headed by one of the Four Auspicious Animals of Chinese occult symbolism. We will discuss these Four Great Beasts later as they are of such importance that they require a separate section of their own.

Constellations Of The Azure Dragon (East)

Name In Chinese	English Name	Main Star	Number	Indications
JUE/JIAO	The Horn	Spica Alpha Vir.	1	Beneficial. Marriage, business, travel, new projects.
KANG	The Neck	Kappa Vir.	2	Tense. Ill in wealth and money.
DI	The Root	Zubenelgenubi. Alpha Lib.	3.	Only good for specific activities depends on the person.
FANG	The House	Pi Sco.	4	Good in love, prayer, burials. Poor for money
XIN	The Heart	Antares Alpha Sco.	5	Ill for finance and legal matters
WEI	The Tail	Xamidimura Mu Sco.	6.	Very favourable for business, construction and marriages.
JI	The Winnowing Basket.	Gamma Sagittarii	7.	Good for collecting money and magic, feng shui and divination.

Constellations Of The Azure Dragon (East)

Constellations Of The Black Turtle Of The North

NAME IN CHINESE	ENGLISH NAME	MAIN STAR	NUMBER	INDICATIONS
DOU	The Southern Dipper	Phi Sagitarii	8.	Favourable except for starting a new business or project. Good for magic and divination.
NIU	The Ox	Beta Cap.	9,	Not good for most things.
NU	The Girl	Albali Epsilon Aquarii	10.	Good for academia and study, writing.
XU	Emptiness	Sadalsuud Beta Aquarii	11.	The star of illness. Not favourable.
WEI	The Roof/Danger	Sadalmelik Alpha Aquarii	12.	Very malefic except for debt collection and the black arts.
SHI	The Encampment	Markab Alpha Pegasi	13.	Good for business, marriage and beginning new projects.
BI	The Wall	Algenib Gamma Pegasi	14.	Good star for business. However ill luck from South. Do not travel South.

Constellations Of The Black Turtle (North)

Constellations Of The White Tiger Of The West

NAME IN CHINESE	NAME IN ENGLISH	MAIN STAR	NUMBER	INDICATIONS
KUI	The Legs	Eta And.	15.	Good for travel and renovations.
LOU	The Bond	Sheratan Beta Arietis	16.	Very beneficial for all things.
WEI	The Stomach	35 Arietis	17.	Good for social activities, feasts, public events, marriages and burials.
MAO	The Hairy Head	Electra 17 Tauri one of the Pleiades.	18.	Unfavourable in most things.
BI	The Net	Epsilon Tauri	19.	Good for land and marriages
ZI	The Turtle's Beak	Meissa Lambda Orionis	20.	Unfavourable. Do not start new projects.
SHEN	The Three Stars	Alnitak Zeta Orionis. One of the stars in Orion's Belt.	21.	Good for most, poor for marriage and burials.

Constellations Of The Vermillion Bird Of The South

NAME IN CHINESE	NAME IN ENGLISH	MAIN STAR	NUMBER	INDICATIONS
JING	The Well	Tejat Mu Gem.	22.	Generally favourable. Good for magic and feng shui.
GUI	The Ghost	Theta Cancri	23.	Only good for burials and yin magic.
LIU	The Willow	Delta Hydrae	24.	Unfavourable, especially for magic and feng shui.
XING	The Star	Alphard Alpha Hydrae	25.	Ill for love and marriage, good for commerce. Bad for burials.
ZHANG	The Cst Net	Upsilon Hydrae	26.	Very beneficial for money and wealth but not good in other spheres.
YI	The Wings	Alkes Alpha Crateris	27.	Bad for all things.
ZHEN	The Chariot	Gienah Gamma Corvi	28.	Good for all things except travelling northwards.

Constellations Of The Vermillion Bird Of The South

Ershisi, The Solar Terms

Having considered the lunar calendar with its months and 28 stations, we must also be aware that there is also a calendar running in tandem with the Lunar Calendar that takes into account the movement of the Sun. The Sun is after all the most powerful and Yang influence on which all life depends. The Sun decides day and night as well as the seasons. Thus we have the so-called 24 Solar Terms or the Ershisi Jieqi. The Solar Terms are 15 degrees apart on the solar ecliptic ...the path that the sun travels around our planet in a year. The main points being the Solstices and the Equinoxes.

NAME	DATE	DEGREE	INDICATIONS
1. LICHUN	Feb. 4th	315	Initiation of Spring
2. YUSHUI	Feb 19th	330	Spring Showers
3. JINGZHE	Mar 6th	345	Insects Awaken
4. CHUNFEN	Mar 21st	0	Spring Equinox
5. QINGMING	Apr 5th	15	Clear and Bright
6. GUYU	Apr 20th	30	Wheat Rains

NAME	DATE	DEGREE	INDICATIONS
7. LIXIA	May 6th	45	Initiation of Summer
8. XIAOMAN	May 21st	60	Animals fruitful
9. MANGZHONG	Jun 6th	75	Wheat on the ear
10. XIAZHI	Jun 21st	90	Summer Solstice
11. XIAOSHU	Jul 7th	105	Lesser Heat
12. DASHU	Jul 23rd	120	Greater Heat

NAME	DATE	DEGREE	INDICATIONS
13. LIQIU	Aug 8th	135	Initiation of Autumn
14. CHUSHU	Aug 23rd	150	Heat withdraws
15. BAILU	Sep 8th	165	White dew
16. QIUFEN	Sep 23rd	180	Autumnal Equinox
17. HANFU	Oct 8th	195	Cold dew
18. SHUANG-JIANG	Oct 23rd	210	Frost

NAME	DATE	DEGREE	INDICATIONS
19. LIDONG	Nov 7th	225	Initiation of Winter
20. XIAOXUE	Nov 22nd	240	Lesser Snows
21. DAXUE	Dec 7th	255	Greater Snows
22. DONGZHI	Dec 22nd	270	Winter Solstice
23. XIAOHAN	Jan 6th	285	Lesser Cold

Summing Up The Calendar

We now have a complete calendar of cycles to work with. We can pinpoint from year to year, month to month, day to day and hour to hour the influences of Yin Yang, the five elements, the 12 Zodiacal animals, the lunar and solar influences. We can pinpoint certain of the stellar influences deemed important by the ancient Taoist Masters, and the Planets as related in the section on the Five Elements are analogous to the Five Elements.

As I write this book, for example, it is April 14th 2020. So the Year branch is Rat (Zi) and the stem is Metal. The month is Metal Dragon. And the day is Fire Pig and it is the 22nd day of the 3rd Lunar Month. This gives me a lot of information. The year of the Rat is excellent for beginning new projects and making new starts but Dragon month is good for action and activity. A Pig day, however, is a good day to focus on the home and family.

To keep a close eye on the calendar, especially before or planning important occasions or transactions….including magical work, one can do no better than consult a Chinese Almanac. Luckily in this internet age, you can find several online resources that will easily give you this information for any day of the week.

Times Of Magic And Times Of Ill: The Maoshan Law Of Days

As a Taoist magician, you have other considerations too. There are certain times when it is auspicious to perform magical acts and times when you should not. In executing acts of magic, for example, drawing talismans, certain hours are favourable and some are taboo.

The forbidden days are:
9th day 3rd Moon.
2nd day 6th Moon.
6th day 9th Moon.
2nd day 12th Moon.

Other days of the destructive pulse and not great for magic are the 17th day of a Greater Month (remember this is any lunar month of 30 days) or the 16th day of a Lesser month (a lunar month of 29 days).

The 5th Moon is a particularly dangerous time for not only magical work but for health. This month is therefore called the Month of Poisons. This esoteric teaching was revealed by Su Nu, the Plain Girl, the sister of Jiu Tian Xuan Nu (the Mysterious Occult Girl of the Ninth Heaven) who revealed it to our friend Huang Di, the Yellow Emperor. Su Nu is one of the goddesses and occult teachers specialising in sexual alchemy and inspired the writings of Su Nu Jing. She taught that on the 16th day of the 5th Moon the Heavens and Earth unite and merge their energies. In practical terms that there means there is a deficiency of Yang Qi making it an unsuitable time for magic, sex...including dual cultivation, and alcohol intake. This is a vulnerable time for health, hence the name of Month of Poisons.

In the 5th Month, there are Nine Poison Days, which are the 5th, 6th, 7th, 15th, 16th, 17th, 25th, 26th and the 27th.

The days before the Equinoxes and Solstices are also 'dead' for magic, though the days themselves are wonderful.

The time of the Dragon Boat Festival is the ideal time to perform greater spells. The hours of Zi, Wu, You and Hai are also excellent.

10. Sacred Geography And The Gods Of The Tao

Taoism has its own sacred geography. In some ways, it is the mythologisation of the land in which the Chinese mystics and magicians lived and the stars upon which they gazed and contemplated, but it is more than that.

This psycho-geography and mapping of the netherworlds can be said to begin with the shamanic journeys made by the ancestors and developed over the course of many generations of sages.

Fundamentally we have a Heaven, a Hell or Underworld and the Earth itself considered in a mystical light. In these schemas, the West and the North have long been considered to be directions or lines of ingress and egress into the mystical worlds. Caves, mountains and rivers are also considered portals into these worlds as we shall see.

In the Heavens those stars we variously call the Big Dipper or the Great Bear are also considered not only a portal but the very point that marks the entry into the sublimity of the Sacred Palace of Purple, the ultimate court of the Gods who hold rulership as Lords of the Earth.

Mount Kunlun

Like most systems of true occult belief, the Taoist system begins with the idea of a sacred pillar, an axis Mundi which passes through all realms and is a point by which the shaman could pass from realm to realm. In shamanic belief, this was the Sacred Pole joining interconnecting realms seen and unseen. The spirit of the shaman, like some Jack on the

Beanstalk, would climb this line or path into the heavens to commune with the high Lords of creation or the Immortal sages and heroes who had passed beyond. We see it constantly in the old ways … the Yggdrasil of the Norse, the heavenly rope or thread of the shamans and the central pole in the Voudon Humfort.

In the Far Eastern mysteries, it manifests as a sacred mountain. In India and in the Tibetan Tantra it is Mount Meru. In Taoism, it is Mount Kunlun.

Both Meru and Kunlun are mountains not to be found literally on the Earth though they are inspired by a real sacred mountain, Kailash.

Kunlun, in essence, is the Western Paradise directly under the Pole Star. In Taoist art, it is shown as an immense pillar with multiple tiers inhabited with wonderful immortals and mysterious flora and fauna. The sages tell us the difficulty of scaling its heights even in its lowest reaches. Deliciously decadent descriptions of Kunlun with rocks of jade and jasper and luminous plants and fungi that can confer supernatural abilities or even immortality has made Kunlun the dream of poets and artists for scores of Dynasties. Strongly associated with Mount Kunlun is Xi Wang Mu, though texts often refer to it as Jade Mountain in association with her. Xi Wang Mu is an incredibly ancient Goddess whose earliest depictions show her with the glistening fangs of a tiger and a swishing leopard's tail. Now she is commonly shown as a beautiful woman with silk clothes riding a phoenix and living in a palace by the Lake of Jewels, surrounded by Immortals who partake of her Sacred Peaches which grant immortality.

Where to find this mountain? Not on earth exactly but on the great spiritual path to immortality.

Wuyue: The Five Sacred Mountains

The Taoists have pinpointed Five Sacred Mountains in China that are of cultural and spiritual significance to us as Taoist magicians. 'Wait 'I hear you say, 'I don't live in China!'. It does not matter. The Lords of the Five Mountains are so powerful that their influence can be invoked no matter where you are geographical. They are the places where the ancestors of the Tao developed and were inspired to create all that you read here. Those mountains are in the sacred internalised geography of every Taoist. In one sense we can consider them as vast psychic energy batteries charged by generations of worshippers and mystics.

The Five Sacred Mountains are as follows:

1. TAISHAN

Is the Great Mountain of the East, and lies in Shandong Province. It has been one of the most significant mountains in Chinese history because of its association with the Emperors, who would solemnly tarry there to make offerings to Heaven at the summit and offerings to the Earth at the base Offerings include food and fine pieces of jade. It has associations with renewal and all the attributes of the wood element.

2. HUASHAN

Is the Great Mountain of the West and can be found in Shaanxi Province. Since early times, Mount Hua was believed to be a portal to the Underworld, and mediums would gather there to connect with the Lords of Hades. Mount Hua was famous for its powerful herbs and was a well-known gathering place for herbs used in the complex processes of the alchemy of immortality. It was the place of the revelations of the Celestial Master School. Today it remains as one of the most dangerous of the hiking trails in China due to its precarious climb on thin boarding.

is the Great Mountain of the South in Hunan Province. In poetry is the mountain where birds flew to escape the harsh winters of Northern China. Naturally, it is associated with the element of Fire.

3. HENGSHAN

The Great Mountain of the South in Hunan Province. In poetry is the mountain where birds flew to escape the harsh winters of Northern China. Naturally, it is associated with the element of Fire.

4. HENGSHAN

(Same name) is the Great Mountain of the North in Shanxi Province. It is not a typo by the way. The Heng here is the same pronunciation as Hunan's Mount Heng. For this reason, we sometimes call them Nan Heng (southern Heng) and Bei Heng (northern Heng).

5. SONGSHAN

is the Great Central Mountain in Henan Province. It is home to one of the earliest of Taoist Temples. Though a major Taoist centre, the general public may know it today for its famous Shaolin Temple.

Penglai

Penglai, Abode Of The Immortals

Penglai is said to be a fabulous mountain on a mysterious island in the Bohai Sea with four other islands around it. Fangzhang, Yingzhou, Daiyu and Yuanjiao.

Famously Emperor Qin attempted to find the physical Penglai in his quest for immortality but was doomed to failure. Penglai is in fact, as the Taoist Canon makes clear, a realm of the accomplished adepts, similar to Devachan or the Blessed Land of the West. The Abode of the Immortals or Mount Penglai is in description like those early folk descriptions of Cockaigne, the land of plenty in English medieval legend, of the Candy Mountain of American folk ballads. A land of virtually no suffering. There are fruits and foods in abundance, gold and jewels are scattered everywhere. The buildings are made of gold and platinum and the trees hang heavy with ripened jewels In legend only the Immortals can reach the blessed island mountain of Penglai

For us, as mere mortals, it must remain as a source of inspiration and another reality that can be accessed by meditation, visualisation and soul flight. Many invocations addressed to the Gods are also asking them to come from Penglai.

11. The Shen, Gods Of The Dao

Shen is a word that can mean spirit and God or even 'spirit power'. The word is not well represented by the word God in the sense that we use it in English. Perhaps the ancient Egyptian term Neter comes closer. Spiritual power.

It is a surprise to some first-timers to the realm of Chinese magic that some of these Gods were once real, historical people who lived on earth. In Chinese belief, one does not stop cultivating even after death. So yes a remarkable hero, sage or scholar can become a god going up the ranks so to speak of being an ancestor, then a saint until they achieve divine status. This is all helped along by a reciprocal relationship between man and the ancestors and the Gods as we shall investigate more deeply in the section entitled Shendao.

The vast array of gods and spirits in China is dizzying. You could write several encyclopedia sized volumes on that subject alone. Even at a local level, the village or even a single house may have its own God of the Place. Such Gods are rather like genii loci in the European tradition.

However, we can here introduce to you the Gods you are most likely to meet in practising the occult mysteries of the Maoshan and its close cousins, the Lushan branches.

The Gods are said to live in the Heavens. The Heavens are said to be structured like a court. It has its own Emperors, ministers, messengers, specialists in various matters from personal destiny right down to how well you do in your examinations or how your business is flourishing.

The most ancient Gods are easy to spot despite their mandarin court official appearances that tidied up their originally more wild and primaeval appearances.

As we have previously noted, for example, the makers of the bone oracles far back in the Shang Dynasty were addressing a God who was shamanic in nature. His name was Shangdi, the High Emperor. Shangdi, like other shamanic gods, was an abstract sky-father, who was represented simply as a pillar or tablet ... the Cosmic Axis.

Shangdi became an epithet of the Jade Emperor, Yu Di as we shall see in a few moments.

However, first, we must teach you about the three most abstract and spiritual Gods known in Dao.

1. The San Qing, The Three Pure Ones

The highest and most abstract of the deities are the Three Pure Ones. Nearly every system of Chinese magic will have them as the Supreme Deities from which all power flows. On many talismans, for example, you will see three ticks, which represent these three august powers. The San Qing are said to be responsible for the creation, organization and running of the 10,000 created things, a poetic term for the entire scope of the universe. They are the highest Gods of Taoism and the purest manifestation of the Tao.

In Taoist theology, the first of this trinity to arise was YUANSHI TIANZUN, who arose from the primordial chaos. He has no beginning and no end and is representative of pure being His name literally translates as the Original or Primordial One of Heaven. In art, he is shown clothed in the primary colour of blue and holding a pearl of ultimate wisdom.

Yuanshi Tianzun emanated LINGBAO TIANZUN, the Lord of the Spiritual Treasures. Lingbao was the one who organized creation, separating Yin and Yang, dividing the heavens and earth, creating time and so forth to manifest the universe as we know it. His primary colour

Yuanshi Tianzun

Lingbao Tianzun

Laoshun Tianzun (DaoDe)

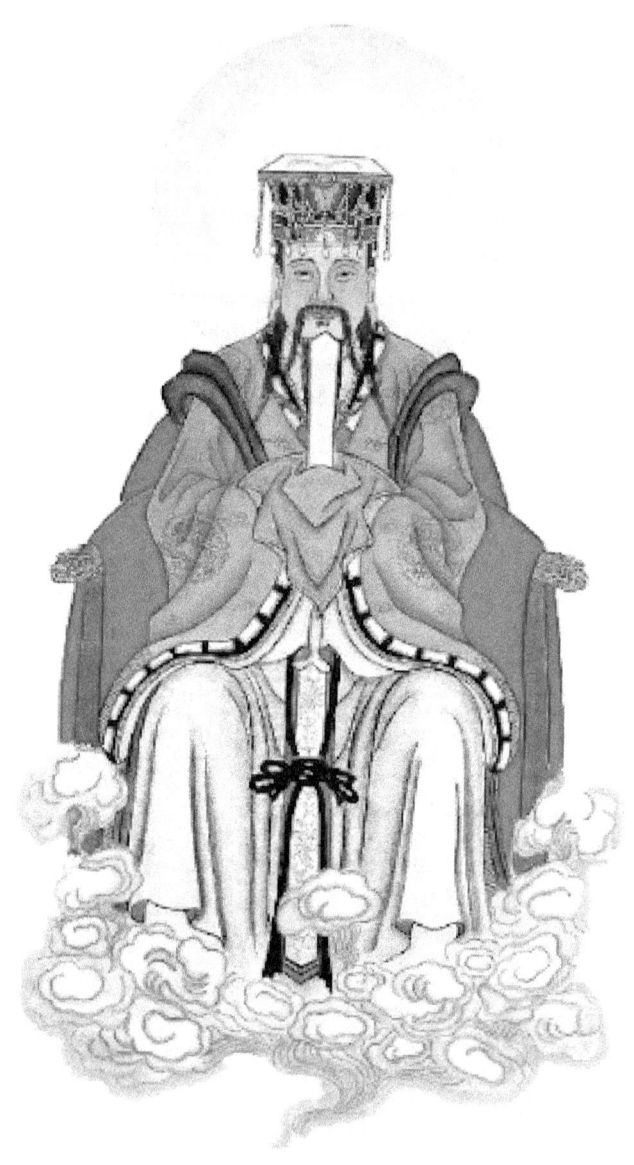

The Jade Emperor

is red. In Taoist art he holds the Ruyi, the measuring stick.

Finally, there is LAOSHUN TAIZUN, the great teacher who has the responsibility of giving the Law and the means of spiritual evolution and advancement to all living beings. Laoshan Taizun has had various incarnations in our world, most notably Fuxi and Lao Zi. His incarnation Laozi is the most significant to Taoists and he is the most 'human' of the San Qing. He is the supreme ancestral master of nearly all lineages. If no other God is on the Altar, Laoshun Taizun will be. His robes are in yellow and are often shown holding a fly whisk or the Yin and Yang Fan.

2. Yu Di, The Jade Emperor

The Jade Emperor is one of the most beloved of all the Gods. The common folk refer to him as the heavenly grandfather. He is the great ruler of the Court of Heaven from where he rules the universe, dispensing order and wisdom as well as punishment. He is usually shown as a powerful middle-aged Emperor in imperial robes and sat upon his throne. His robes are embroidered with the royal dragons. He wears the Imperial Cap with its flat mortarboard like a top from which hang 13 red tassels strung with pearls. It is to the Jade Emperor that many petitions are addressed in Temples throughout China, especially those seeking justice for wrongs done to them but corruption prevents any real earthly justice. In very ancient times he was simply called SHANGDI or Highest Emperor. As a point of reference, we can compare the Jade Emperor to those fatherly sky gods well known in western mythology such as Zeus and Jupiter. At the head of his court, he is the supreme governor of the Earth and the Heavens, overlooking all the affairs of mankind. He shows great kindness and yet is a great warrior capable of dispensing wise and fair advice. The Jade Emperor himself is said to be a reflection of Yuanshi Tianzun. His special day is on the 9th day of the First Moon.

The place of his residence is of course, high in the heavens and is envisioned as a massive purple palace. From here the Jade Emperor runs a court that administers to the universe. There is literally an official for every conceivable phenomenon in the universe and in the affairs of humanity.

3. The Great Queen Mother Of The West

Xi Wang Mu is one of the most mysterious and ancient of the deities of China. Her origins are most certainly lost in the early rituals of the Wu shamans and she is mentioned in the oracle bones of Shang. In her earliest appearances, she is a wet and wild goddess with tiger teeth and leopard tail who ruled in the west and punished those who ignored her with plagues and disease.

In the Taoist scriptures, Xi Wang Mu is the deity presiding over the powers of immortality and she exists on Kunlun Mountain in the West. There she holds court in her paradisiacal realm surrounded by her beautiful courtesans who are goddesses in their own right. She also guards over the Peaches of Immortality, the Pantao.

Interestingly this seems to be reflected in worldwide mythology. The golden apples of Greek and Norse legend A mysterious western island, mountain or garden associated with immortality seems a basic belief throughout the world. Our own British Avalon is said to mean Isle of Apples and appears to be a literary reinterpretation of such a belief.

In Chinese art, a popular image is of the Eight Immortals of Taoism venturing to the annual Feast of the Peaches in their boat. Sun Wu Kung, the monkey king so beloved in Asia and to watchers of the 1980s

Xi Wang Mu. Queen Mother of the West

Japanese extravaganza, Monkey, will know that he feasted on those same peaches to achieve his immortal status.

Xi Wang Mu is in a sense a far more magical Goddess than the Jade Emperor. The Jade Emperor is in a way more concerned with order, while Xi Wang Mu is a shamanic goddess associated with sorcerous power and the arts of internal alchemy and cultivation. She is indeed a worthy goddess for the Taoist magician.

Lao Zi, the grand patriarch of Taoism was said to have received teachings from her. She is the natural Mistress of all-female adepts.

4. Jiu Tian Xuan Nu

Of all the Gods, Jiu Tian Xuan Nu is one of the most revered in the school of Maoshan to which I belong. She is certainly the most mysterious and occult of all the deities and literally that is what her name means. Jiu Tian Xuan Nu translates as the Mysterious/Dark/Occult Girl of the Ninth Heaven

Her most ancient depictions, again break open her shamanic origins. With her female head springing from the body of a bird. Of course, the bird being a creature that is strongly linked as a messenger between Heaven and Earth.

Her most early tales are associated with the Yellow Emperor, Huang Di. In the infancy of mankind, say the legends, there was a time when the very existence of mankind teetered on the brink of annihilation There was an almighty King, said to be demonic in nature named Chiyou. At this point I would like to mention that Chiyou was the leader of the Nine Tribes and is considered holy and sage-like among the Hmong People...so there is a certain perspective we should be aware of. The battle between Huangdi and Chiyou had so far lasted over a terrible and blood-soaked decade. Chiyou finally resorted to his immense powers of

Jiu Tian Xuan Nu. The Mysterious Girl of the Ninth Heaven.

magic and breathed a dark fog over the land of China. Soon the thick dark fog had blocked even the light of the Sun. At a loss, Huangdi called upon the Heavens themselves.

Then the magic happened. A burst of light eased itself into the mortal world, and soon the battle-weary Emperor saw a wondrous sight. A red phoenix as bright as holy cinnabar, and on its back was the most beautiful woman he had ever seen, dressed in garments made from a thousand feathers scintillating with the hues of nine iridescent colours of the kingfisher. Even the very reins by which she mastered the phoenix were composed of cloudy phosphorescent vapours. This was indeed the most powerful maiden goddess.

Jiu Tian Xuan Nu taught the Emperor the secrets of the occult, including the occult arts of war. Her sister, the so-called Plain or Dark Girl, Su Nu, taught her the secrets of sexual magic. These secrets were subsequently revealed in the Su Nu Jing.

Among the gifts the Mysterious Girl gave to the Emperor were the knowledge of the Six Jia and Six Ding, magic still taught in Maoshan to this day.

In appearance you may see her with her hair bound in the nine-dragon and flying phoenix fashion, wearing a silk red gown and elegant body and snow-white skin. Sometimes she is white-robed, the robes dazzling with the 'light of Venus'. She is sometimes seen in golden armour and holding the Jian, the Chinese straight sword.

5. Guan Yin

It may seem strange here to see a Buddhist deity in the Taoist pantheon, but the influence of Guanyin cannot be overstated. So beloved is Guanyin that she is one of the few purely Buddhist deities to be fully incorporated into Maoshan Taoism.

Guanyin, the Great Goddess of Mercy and Love

Jade Girl and Gold Boy. Associated with wealth and prosperity, magic and fertility. They were often seen at the feet of Guanyin

Legends state that in life Guanyin was a princess named Miao Shan, a devoted Buddhist who through her diligence had earned the right to pass into the eternal bliss of nirvana. Just as she was about to do so, she heard a cry of suffering and renounced her entry into paradise until all suffering in the realms of existence had been vanquished. Such compassion was revealed in stories from her life. In one case a fisherman had caught a carp and put it in the market for sale. In fact, the carp was an incarnation of a Dragon King. Recognizing the fact she rescued the fish and set it free.

Guanyin began life as Avalokitesvara, a Bodhisattva who looks down upon the suffering of all beings. In other words, Guanyin is the Buddha of pure compassion who hears and responds to the tears and cries of the suffering. Guanyin, in Indian art, began life as a male deity, but the modern image is that of a compassionate mother or maiden dressed in white robes and strikingly similar to depictions of the Virgin Mary. There is, in fact, a scriptural basis for this form as given in the Lotus Sutra.

This beautiful white-robed Guanyin is the most common form and indeed it is a suitable image of her ability to relieve suffering, offer kindness and grant children to the motherless. In her hand, she often holds a jar of nectar-like water that ends suffering and a willow branch. She has two children playing at her feet, Longnu (the girl) and Shancai (the boy) who are her disciples. The white parrot or cockatoo is also her symbol. Her mantra is perhaps the most well known of all mantras...OM MANI PADME HUM. Indeed it is of great power and has a very secret meaning.

6. The Thunder Gods

When lightning cracks and thunder rolls across the sky the ancients were in awe. To the sages, it was a magnificent demonstration of the immense power of Heaven. Pure elemental power.

Thunder was associated with the God Lord Lei Gong. Of all the Gods his appearance is the most striking. Humanoid with immense strength, his human face had the hooked beak of an eagle and his feet were eagle-like talons. His large hammer caused the lightning to spring up and the thunder reverberated from his drum. One is tempted to question whether this is the image of the ancient shaman with an eagle mask and drum? Very possibly.

Lei Gong is one of many thunder gods. The Taoists in their usual careful classification envisioned a whole hierarchical 'Thunder Bureau' with different gods compartmentalised to control winds, the rains and the very thunder and lightning itself.

The thunder gods become important in Taoist magic because there is a whole branch dedicated to this called Lei Fa, the thunder method or law. The idea of thunder magic is not the control of thunder as a weather phenomenon, but the channelling of raw heavenly yang qi into acts such as healing and exorcism. This process was a mixture of special internal alchemy and ritual magic. Whole schools of thunder magic evolved and often concerned themselves in applying their skills on behalf of various warlords. Today thunder magic has become one of the fundamental training methods of most schools including Maoshan.

7. The Five Emperors

The Five Emperors or Wufang Wudi are also very important figures in Taoist magic. Yes, you will have noticed the constant recurrence of

Gods in groups of five. Five is the basic number associated with the five directions and the five elements. The Five Emperors, therefore, are rulers of the directions and the elements and other cognate symbols such as the Five Mountains. They are again of extremely ancient heritage and are found in some of the oldest books on Taoist practice such as Lingbao School's 'Book of Five Talismans'.

In this text, the Emperors are envisioned as associated with their respective colours and with the organs of the body. This internalisation of the deities is a practice that passed from Lingbao into Maoshan, especially by way of The Yellow Court Classic the foundational text of basic training in the Maoshan lineage.

A wonderful expression of the Five Emperors is through the Five Dragon Kings, Wu Long Wang. Instead of five Imperially dressed monarchs, the Five Emperors assume the form of the Five Dragons in

The Five Emperors

their respective elemental colours. In this form, you will meet them later in the practical part of this book.

The Wufang Wudi literally means Five Directional Five Emperors, they are as follows:

1. DONGFANG QINGDI. is the Blue or Green Emperor of the east and the element of wood.

2. NANFANG CHIDI is the Red Emperor residing in the south and represents the element of fire.

3. ZHONGYANG HUANGDI is the Yellow Emperor of the central position and represents the element of soil.

4. XIFANG BAIDI is the White Emperor of the West and is the ambassador of the element of metal.

5. BEIFANG HEIDI is the Black Emperor of the North and rules over the element of water.

8. Miscellaneous Gods

Yan Luo. Is the Lord of the Underworld. He is important in many of the rituals of practical magic that deal with the soul after death or even in aspects of magic such as wealth. It is interesting the correlation of wealth with the Underworld as other civilisations as far away as Greece and Rome held a similar view. Yan Luo is the judge of the dead and is said to possess a mirror that, in true Dorian Grey style reflects the true nature of the soul.

Zaojun, The Kitchen God. In reality a God of the Hearth and home. In Daoist lore he reports to the Heavens the goings on in a household, good and bad to the Emperor in Heaven. Thus each year, his image is smeared with honey at the New Year and his image replaced.

Yan Luo. Is the Lord of the Underworld.

Zaojun, The Kitchen God.

12. Of The Immortals And The Chain Of Lineage

These are the main deities of Chinese occultism. We could list many more but it seems pointless at this juncture. Some of the more occult deities are more specialist and we will introduce them at the right moment as you progress through this book, Sanshan Jiu Hou, is very unique to the Maoshan method for example and must be understood within context. The Three Mothers are also very specific. Hehe, are the twin Gods of harmony used specifically for creating harmony in relationships.

As well as the Gods themselves, there are the Immortals or Xian. Sometimes we can view them as ascended Masters who have attained the pinnacle of spiritual and occult attainment, others are specific in function rather like patron saints. The classic example is the Snow Mountain Immortal who is called to create coldness or bring cool environmental ambience. For example to cool a fevered patient. Another is the Peach Blossom Immortal who is evoked purely for love spells. The list is seemingly endless.

There are Immortals who teach you the skills of magic (shengong), immortals that protect, immortals that aid in longevity, in healing, and just about every other sphere of life.

Many of these Immortals were once human. Having cultivated on earth as living beings they attained through dedication and internal alchemy the freedom of immortality, and so liberated they have the power and compassion to aid humanity.

There is an implication here in the Tao that there is a system of evolution, a promise of elevation into true being. From man to higher or true man (Zhen ren) to Immortal (Xian) and finally to a God (Shen).

The schools of magical Taoism (Fulu pai) in fact do posit a chain of hierarchy that passes beyond the Earth. A magical school is not confined to its earthly members but extends into the unseen realms. On joining the student or Dishi is connected to, and empowered and protected by this chain of initiates. The idea is, of course, universal, and it probably hearkens back to the ancestral devotions of the shamans. The Secret Chiefs of western Hermeticism, the Root Gurus of the tantras of the Kashmiri and Tibetans, the Mahatmas of the Theosophical Society, the ancestral chain of Vodou and Quimbanda all point to the same universal concept.

In the Brazilian tradition of Quimbanda for example, many of the spirits or Exus(male) and Pomba Giras (female) were once mortal, but by personal gnosis and by devotion by disciples on Earth have attained a kind of immortality and spiritual power, and prove their presence by working their power through magical manifestation.

In the processes of Daoist magic and alchemy, this goal of personal transformation to Immortal should be the primary consideration.

Part II
Training

13. The Training of the Magician

The Cursed Girl And The Poison Of Gu

The Maoshan school is in many ways quite different from western esoteric schools. Though the actual practices are fairly secretive it has a public face, the master dealing with clients on a regular basis. In this sense, it reflects the Cunning Man model of early and pre-Industrial Europe or the Spirit Doctors of Hoodoo and Dutch Hex Masters in the United States. The magician of Maoshan is a beloved if sometimes feared member of the community with a service to offer. This can range from finding appropriate dates to say open a business or set a marriage, finding a good location for burial, finding a thief or lost item, helping a failing business and so on. Though there is a high magic component behind the scenes, the Maoshan magician does employ magic on a day to day basis. Most of this lesser magic is pretty mundane, but occasionally I witnessed something entirely extraordinary. One that sticks in my mind is the cursed girl, let's call her Miss Wang.

Miss Wang was a local girl, a successful entrepreneur in the light industry popular in Shenzhen, dealing with electronic parts. She was no country farm girl with a penchant for superstition. She had even studied abroad in one of our very own Universities in the UK and held an MBA. She had been involved with an older gentleman in China, who did have an interest in occultism and was also a successful businessman. They had split up on bad terms and money and property was involved. About two months after the breakup Miss Wang had felt peculiarly sick and nauseous and had woken up with the feeling that someone else was in the room. Then the bad dreams began to occur.

At first, like most of us would, she put it down to the stress and uncertainty of the relationship break up. A few weeks later she had begun to notice strange and uncharacteristic acne on her torso. Seeking medical help the doctor had given her medicine to help what he diagnosed as a fungal infection. The medicine helped not one bit. Soon it was a wine coloured streak across her torso and a good inch across in places. She then knew it was no fungal infection or some psychosomatic reaction to stress.

The Master took one glance at the girl and knew she had been cursed or infected with a spiritual poison known as Gu in Taoist circles. As the girl, she could have only been nineteen, explained the situation he nodded amiably but with visible concern corrugating his forehead. He motioned me to watch. He observed her face to telltale signs such as a darkening of certain areas of the face and certain blood vessel formations in the eyes.

It was definitely Gu. Gu is a general term for a spiritual poison. It can be an actual physical substance or the spirit of a poison sent by magical means. Often this can be in the form of sending the yin spirits of insects, serpents and scorpions to infect the po of the individual.

The Master told her to come back on a specific date and to bring a dressing gown, the reasons for which became obvious at a later date.

On that day the girl came in. She lay on a couch and opened her dressing gown under which she only had her underwear. She was actually a very beautiful girl with pristine skin, so the streak of claret coloured marking across her torso was striking. I noticed there were boil like protuberances dotted within the streak too, It looked as if someone had made a diagonal cut from just above her pubic line to just below her breast. I was shocked.

The teacher lit two white candles and had arranged bowls of colourful fruits on the altar.

Incense was burning in the pot and the sweet jasmine immediately seemed to relax the girl.

After the usual invocations to empower the ink and brush he began to my surprise to draw on the girl. As he did so he was mumbling, making the appropriate invocations. I had never seen a talisman being drawn directly on the skin in this manner before. I was used to paper, cotton cloth and even clothes talismans, but not this. The brush did its work and I could see her muscles twitch slightly at the touch of the cold ink. In ten minutes, he had finished. Across her back and winding round to her front were two centipedes whose mouths seemed to 'eat' at either end of the red slash like a mark that tried to shame her beauty. He explained, ' This fellow has used poison to mark this girl. These spiritual centipedes work for us. The greater poison shall eat the lesser poison.'.

Later he had me write down this very spell in my Mishu or 'secret book'.

He repeated the process a number of times, and sure enough, the mark diminished.

I have to admit that at this stage I was trying to rationalise this whole process. Desperately seeking some kind of intellectual answer ... I went through the usual explanations, the psychosomatic theory ... you know the one, if you believe in voodoo it can kill you! No, it did not gel. I had to admit there was something very real going on here.

The Dark Gate

Training sessions occurred in a typical Chinese apartment block. From a distance, it looked all rather ramshackle like badly shuffled vintage playing cards stacked precariously. The apartments were a kind of dirty brown colour, the result of decades of Shenzhen's heavy traffic. I walked towards this unlikely haven of Taoist knowledge. On the sides of the streets, hawkers displayed a kaleidoscope of exotic fruits and vegetables. I felt their eyes on me, the 'Lao Wei'. Not many foreigners were seen in this part of the city and I anticipated these curious looks and these days were quite used to them.

I buzzed myself in at the bottom entrance, the guard or bao-an giving me a smile as if to say, 'What the hell is this guy doing here?'

Like many of these blocks, there was no elevator. So up I went. I reached the characteristically security-conscious metal door of the Master's house. I noticed the red lucky paper pasted on the outside as he had indicated in his text message.

I entered nervously. I cannot quite explain the feeling but in these situations, you always feel like the outsider 'invading' Chinese space, a plunderer and an appropriator of Chinese culture. However, that feeling quickly dissolved. There were a couple of younger men in their late twenties and four men in their late forties to early fifties. There were a couple of women too. One in her thirties and another about forty. It is hard to tell the age of many far eastern women, who seem ageless at times. This was my first formal lecture 'in the club' so to speak.

We were all armed with hot green tea, everyone sat relaxed on the couches and chairs provided. Only the Master sat apart in a single, very worn and comfortable looking leather chair.

Everyone introduced themselves, and when it was my turn, no one looked surprised as I thought they might have. Later I discovered that I wasn't the first foreign student, a few years ago there had been a German guy.

Today was more or less a history lecture with some definitions, purely introductory stuff to put the tradition in context.

The Master spoke.

"Maoshan has a long history. You could say it has been around longer than the name Maoshan itself.

You see, the most ancient masters had no schools and no name to call themselves. They were wild men, free and living in the holy mountains and in the forests. Only later did distinct schools arise. Even then these were not big formal institutions like you see now. Usually, it would be like a small family, a Master with a few apprentices. It was understood that such apprentices would leave when the time was right. People might call upon such wild masters to solve village problems or for healing.

This all changed with the influence of the Celestial Master Society in Sichuan. By the vision of their master, many gathered together to form a small kingdom that lived according to Taoist principles. However, their downfall was politics. They got too powerful in the worldly and political arena, there instigated rebellions and that sealed their fate. They lost the spirit of the Tao…"

The Master continued relating the various risings and fallings of the manifold Taoist societies. He explained that much of the modern structure of Taoist monasteries and societies were in fact not Taoist at all but adoption from Buddhism, a later interloper into the Chinese religious and philosophical scene. He felt that monasticism is a shoe that really doesn't fit the Taoist foot. Such things as monasteries, monks, nuns and scripture standardising was a mere reaction to rivalry with the growing influence of Buddhism in medieval China.

Finally, he arrived at a more interesting part.

"From the Celestial Masters arose the mysterious Lingbao. Lingbao has set the standard for many of our practices. For example the practice of inhaling the Five coloured Qi from the different directions, the practice of personal transformation by invoking or awakening the very Gods within yourself and how this all relates to the calendrical cycles of the Ten Heavenly Stems and Twelve Earthly Branches. In turn, these practices passed to Shanqing on that blessed mountain we call Mao.

Eventually, certain disciples were either banished from Maoshan or took up wandering. They began to focus on mainly the purely magical aspect of the Maoshan tradition ... yes they even improved it and specialised in it. Thus the Folk Maoshan was born. This is not the same as orthodox Shanqing which is also, somewhat confusingly, also called Maoshan.

Maoshan as we practice here was passed among a few families originally. They continued developing its techniques. Some were adapted from practices they had learned in their own native hometowns or through places they passed in their journeys. Many of these new practices and witchcraft would never have been approved of by their ancestral Shanqing masters. Some of these Masters would find new homes in other countries. They set up home in Thailand and Malaysia for example.

Some of these Masters, particularly in Malaysia, became very famous. For some reason, Maoshan flourished in Malaysia, perhaps because it was there that new methods were learned that breathed a new life into the Maoshan method, specifically the Bawang shamans and other indigenous magical methodologies."

I should explain that though the Master was living in Shenzhen he was, in fact, a Malaysian born Chinese, so he may be a bit biased on the insistence that the Malay brand of Chinese magic is superior to others.

"Now let's talk about your first steps" The room visibly stirred as from a trance typical of such lectures in the hope of doing something more practical. I had taken along a notebook and was furiously scribbling notes.

"The first practices are somewhat lengthy. When a man first enters the path he is broken and blind. He cannot act and he cannot speak, eat, breathe or even think properly. He cannot even fuck." The room giggled nervously together as if it were some funny moment at a movie in the cinema.

"Before you can do anything you have to repair yourselves and crystallise your being. You might think you are a being in your own right but you are not. Your sense of being real is largely an illusion constructed from chaotic elements that you've strung together and called 'self'. There is a true self but it is only a potential that you must actualise through hard work. That true self once crystallised is capable of acting and having a true real existence. It is no longer a victim of every passing influence but can truly act as according to the Tao."

This was really interesting. It reminded me somewhat of Gnosticism and also of the teachings of the Georgian mystic G. I. Gurdjieff. In fact, I recalled that Gurdjieff had learned some aspects of his Fourth Way in Tibet and China.

"To fix yourself is to heal yourself. Before you can gather and store mana or magical power (shen li) you need to fix. If you do not fix yourself it will be like pouring wine into an old leaky bottle. You may get some small results and smell of wine, but you will still be, in reality, empty". I smiled to myself as I remembered the Christian parable of putting new wine into old bottles.

While the teacher lectured we were encouraged not to interrupt though I had a thousand questions ricocheting like a bullet in a ribcage.

I had this picture now, that the average man or woman is a vague pencil sketch, a mere grey and colourless and confused scribble of what he should really be. A mere collection of reactions to the environment, including education, parental and peer pressure and so on. By the processes of the Taoist yoga of magic, every line is redrawn and consolidated, till something special emerges, defined and actually emerges, Art.

The first practice was one I was well aware of. I could have predicted it by contemplating it. Every occult tradition in the world insists on balance before training magic. In the Western Mysteries, this was often symbolised by The Trial of the Elements. In ancient medicine, every man was considered to have four humours or fluids related to the Four Elements. Health, both physical and mental, was defined as having these four humours in balance. Furthermore, we were all born with a tendency to emphasize one of these elements. The apprentice to the Mysteries had as his first task to redress this imbalance.

Maoshan was no different. The terminology was more or less the same though the concepts wore different, exotic clothes.

The Wuxing or five elements in man in Chinese metaphysics are Wood, Fire, Soil, Metal and Water. My dominating element was metal. Each of these xing had a seat in the human body, rather like the humour theory in classical European medicine. However, this was more energetic (etheric?) thing rather than a physical thing. Chinese occult anatomy tends to look at the energetic function rather than the form. The seats of these elemental energies are associated with five of the so-called hollow or Yin organs.

Wood is associated with the liver, Fire is associated with the heart, Soil is associated with the spleen, Metal with the lungs and Water with the kidneys.

He proceeded to explain the Exercise of the Six Healing Breaths. I had heard of this as it was a pretty well-known exercise with the Tai Chi and Qigong crowd, but in this instance, it put the exercise in its magical context.

14. The Six Healing Breaths

The student stands or sits in his posture. This posture can be a full lotus if he or she has the capability of a half lotus, tailor position or even sitting in a chair. The posture is less important than the inner work, but there are still important factors. It should be relaxed, but not so relaxed that it is loose and sloppy. The spine is straight. Think of each vertebra stacked neatly as a pile of coins to form a straight column. Some variations require certain movements of the arms, but these are not included here, as we are going for the purely meditational variation.

Relax. Completely relax. When settled you can begin NATURAL BREATHING. The natural breath is how we should be breathing, though through ill health and bad habits this is rarely the case. We need to get rid of the habit of breathing high up in the chest. From now on the breathing process must be sunk to the lower abdomen, This point is called the LOWER CINNABAR FIELD or Dan Tian. You will be using this point a lot. Specifically, the Dan Tian is around 1 to 1.5 inches below the navel. It is in the centre of the torso and NOT a surface point. It can be imagined as a golf ball-sized sphere with the spine passing through its axis. It is similar in idea to the Kanda, a Nadi or psychic nerve in a bulb or egg shape said to be roughly where the Dan Tian is, in tantric yoga. Do not at this stage attempt to imagine or visualise it but just be aware of its presence. The tongue tip should be on the roof of the mouth, behind the teeth but touching the palate.

With natural breathing, your abdomen pushes out as you inhale slowly. This should all be very relaxed without tension. Relaxed and unforced. The inhalation should last around 6 to 7 seconds and be as relaxed and as noiseless as possible. The abdomen wall slowly pushes outwards in unison with the breath. On exhaling the abdomen slowly

Practical Chinese Magic ∞ 139

falls inwards, naturally, again for around 6 to 7 seconds. Set up the rhythm consciously until you no longer have to think about it.

Now adopt a gentle smile. This is the Taoist Laugh. It may sound strange to western occultists of the stern type but this is an age-old practice. It is not a big beaming grin but a slight smile of the type you may have seen on statues or pictures of the Buddha for example.

The smile has a wonderful way of relaxing the body, perhaps due to the hormonal response to that facial expression. Now, let this smile seem to have an energetic form and quality that passes down the front of your body like hot, melted golden butter. The energy of the smile relaxes each body part while simultaneously sweeping up all worries, tensions, negativities, untying knotted muscles and so on. At the level of the shoulders, it passes down your arms and out through your fingers while also passing down the front and interior of the body and out through the feet. The same smile oozes over the back of your head and passes down the back, doing the same wonderful job, and out through the heels.

Relaxed, you are now ready to practice the healing of the elements via the Six Sounds.

Certain sounds can cleanse and purify the organs. Now, these are not mantric sounds vocalised in the usual method of mantra. Rather they are variations of the sound of breath. The breath is 'shaped' so to speak, rather like variations in the sound of wind passing through different objects such as trees, gaps in rocks and so forth. Let us begin.

Note that in this method we are going to tie together sound, colour, organs and their energetic functions and the five fingers, which correspond to the Wuxing.

1. THE WOOD PRACTICE

Inhaling with natural breathing visualising the breath as green as grass. It helps to imagine this blue-green breath as coming from the East and entering every pore of your skin but gathering at the LIVER. Yes, try to

Amitabho, The Great Buddha of the West. He is one of the Buddhas adopted by some Daoist sects including Maoshan and Lushan Pai

visualise the actual place of the liver. You can consult an anatomy chart to fully become aware of the positions of this and the other organs before engaging in this practice. Now breathe out through the mouth, but change the shape of the mouth so you make a windy SSSSSSHHHHHHHHHUUUUU sound. This is the Hsu sound. Repeat 6 to 7 times. Now put the left thumb in the right fist and twist it, gently but vigorously enough to warm it up Finally gently tug the thumb. Repeat on the opposite side.

2. THE FIRE PRACTICE

This time inhale bright scarlet fiery red from the South through the pores in the skin and let it gather to the heart. Exhale with HHHHHHUUUUUHHHHH. Repeat the finger massage process but with the middle fingers instead of the thumb.

3. THE SOIL PRACTICE

Inhaling yellow Qi from the centre (below your feet) through the pores of your skin and into the spleen and stomach. Then exhale with a WHOOOOOOOOOOOOO sound. This time massage the ring fingers.

4. THE METAL PRACTICE

Inhaling white Qi from the West through the pores and into the lungs. On exhalation the sound is SSSSSSSSSSSSSSSSS. The index fingers are massaged.

5. THE WATER PRACTICE

Inhale black energy from the North and into the kidneys. Exhale with a CHWWWWWWWAAAAYYY sound. The little finger is massaged.

The final practice is related to the TRIPLE WARMER. This is the energetic function of body temperature and circulation. Inhale red energy from the South and gather it in a 5-inch belt around the waist. Exhale the sound SSSSSSHHHHHHHHHH from a gap between teeth and tongue. There is no finger massage in this case.

This completes the practice of the Six Breaths. It should be practised consistently for 49 days before attempting to gather Qi or mana.

It is also a wonderful introduction to several practices such as visualisation, breath control and such, linking you to the cosmological universe of Taoism. There are several health benefits that will emerge from this practice ... improved digestion, better circulation, improved eyesight and so on as the elements become empowered and vitalised.

15. Secrets Of The Golden Light

He felt nervous on his journey in the dark. The darkness clung like oil to everything so that the darkness dripped from the skeletal branches of the trees. There was no moon to light the path and no wind to break the silence. Foolishly he had decided to shorten his journey home from work by crossing through the old graveyard. It was unwise. The thoughts of his beautiful wife, the aroma of the hotpot stewing on the stove with the chilli peppers dancing on the playful bubbles of the boiling broth had enticed him to take this stupid risk.

He felt it then. A Yin presence. Dark, lonely and desperate. The chill of its presence stung him like ice on the skin of the back of his neck. He could feel the fear snaking up in panicked jolts of adrenaline. He knew that his fear would give form to the ghostly presence coalescing behind him, but he could not control himself. Suddenly he remembered what his master had taught. He interlaced his fingers and envisioned the seal of the Golden Light, suddenly there was a warmth, an almost visible radiance of golden light. Turning around, emboldened by the ancient powers he wielded, he saw the gape-mouthed thing dissolving in what appeared to be a series of orbs. Turning around and keeping the Golden Light 'switched on' he continued confidently through the graveyard. Unknown to him yin eyes scrutinised him, backed away in dark corners …"… cannot touch … cannot touch …" they whispered.

The Master spoke and I listened carefully. "Magical power is not just some abstract mental element, it is a real and tangible substance that can be accumulated and stored and even transmitted. That power is all around us and in all of the ten thousand created things. It can feel like a kind of heat.".

The Master picked up a Chinese bottle gourd he had already

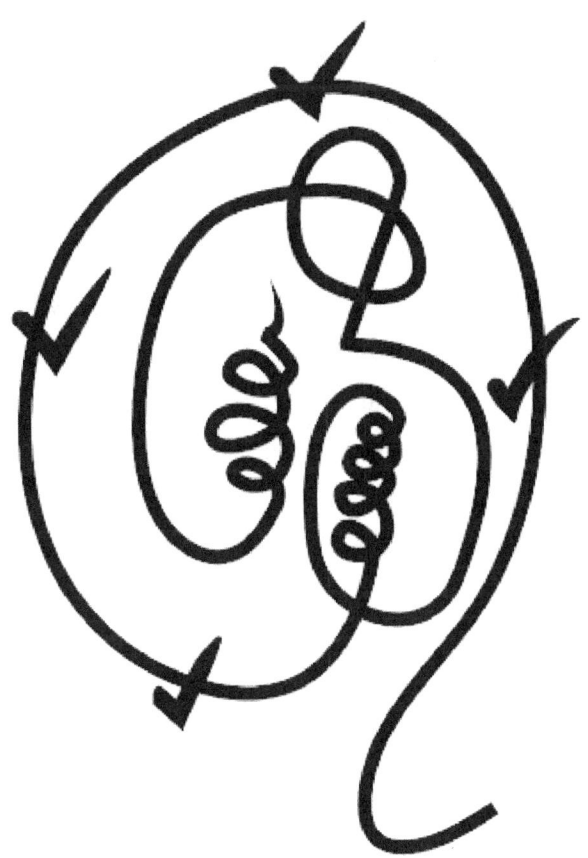

Golden Light Seal

prepared to illustrate his analogy. The human body is like this gourd, it can be viewed as hollow with openings. The Taoist dizhi (disciple) must gather and store the wonderful power of magic, fa li, But it must also be sealed lest it leaks that power."

Someone raised their hand. And asked "How do such leakages occur?"

He appeared to ponder for a moment playing with a single long hair that grew from his chin. Such leaks occur in many ways. The obvious ones are well known to you, such as sex. As you know the human body is a wonderful alchemical apparatus, an alembic of intricate processes. The jing or sexual life essence can either pass out through sexual intercourse to create pleasure, a moment of ecstasy and possibly a child in her womb. Or conversely, we reverse the flow of the jing river inwards and transform it into pure creative magical energy or the Elixir of Immortality. Of course, it's about excess. Making love is a natural expression of the Yin and Yang, but too much may leave you dissipated and old before your time. Balance. There are also ways of lovemaking that fortify the magical energies and the Elixir, but that is another lesson. Too much excess in anything can deplete the energies, including too much listening, too much seeing and too much tasting. Breaking vows to the Gods can thwart your attempts as can boasting and breaking your oaths of secrecy".

He laughed and continued, "Now you must be wondering how to gather this wonderful power and I expect most of you think it is through internal alchemy. Yes and no I say to you. Internal alchemy is a specific practice designed to create the Immortal body and indeed it is vital to your practice. This practice, however, will take decades of hard inner work. Yet the ancient Masters have taught us another and passed from generation to generation a secret chant and meditation that helps us to immediately gather and condense a storehouse of energy. I must point out to you that this power, though we can store it in the body and that we can transmit it, does not in any way belong to you. Magical power must be drawn from the reservoir of the Heavens and Earth. If you were to rely only on your own energies, you would be a dried old withered plum in no time. This practice is called the Chant of the Golden Light and to it, there is a special magical Talisman or Seal that was said to have been transmitted to us by Taishang Laojun himself. This seal encodes all the powers of the Four Auspicious Animals ... the Dragon, the Vermillion Bird, the White Tiger and the Dark Warrior. These cosmic architects are the source of stupendous power, powers that were said to aid Pan Gu himself in the very building of the universe.

There are two ways to do this practice. The first involves the holding of the Seal of Golden Light Mudra, and the second is a special palm magic practice. The mudra method must be mastered first, however."

He went on to explain that the practice should be repeated over a thousand times before it even comes close to its actual potential, but results will appear fairly quickly. The spell can be used in a variety of ways. Like the hero in our little story, it can dissipate Yin beings such as ghosts, it can be used in healing and self-protection, as a precursor to charging talismans and objects and so forth. You will find the method of the Golden Light below in the section on the Eight Great Spells of Esoteric Maoshan.

16. The Eight Great Spells

You Cannot Speak!!

The next session was interesting. We gathered at the Master's apartment. His wife had rustled up some rather delicious baozi. This is a kind of pale steamed bread filled with pork and or cabbage. This time I was offered a cup of coffee, which I was really grateful for. Many Chinese don't really drink coffee as tea is the favoured beverage. I knew that they had specially bought a jar of Maxwell House just for my benefit. This was typically Chinese. Small acts of kindness and regard without the use of speech. I thanked them for the kindness.

I had been practising the Six Healing Breaths and the Spell of the Golden Light for a few weeks. The Golden Light was wonderful and I almost felt the energy on my first attempt.

I was ready for the next lecture. There was some small talk among us students. Some asked about life in England and other typical questions such as if I am married yet, how much money I make and so on. This may sound rude but actually it is normal conversation etiquette in China.

The Master cleared his throat. "You cannot speak!!" At first, I thought he was giving us a rollicking or telling us to shut up. He continued.

"Your words have no power or no meaning, you cannot speak and you cannot be heard. You cannot act or do. You cannot do anything until you are self purified and empowered."

Ah, now I understand. I recalled *The Book of Coming Forth by Day*. This is an ancient Egyptian text that includes such matters as the Ceremony of Opening the Mouth. Without this ceremony, the recently deceased cannot speak. Similarly in Maoshan, you engage in special practices so that the speech function is magically activated. Until then all the spells uttered are of minimum power if any at all. The mouth must be activated or rather its corresponding magical power.

The Master went on to expound the principles of the Eight Great Spells. The Eight Spells are the fundamental work of the apprentice Maoshan warlock. They are really a kind of purification, activation and initiation into the mysteries of the Tao. Whether you are orthodox or unorthodox, Tao the Eight Spells are your first practice, even before meditations and alchemy.

Yes, you have just learned one. The Golden Light Spell is one of the Eight Spells. It has both the Energy version as shown above as well as the chanted version.

Let's look at these spells and how to actually practice them.

You cannot think and you cannot feel. The mind is a knotted mass of snakes of irrelevant thoughts and connections that block the flow of thought. Even when the surface appears calm, there beneath are twisting leviathans influencing and colouring the mind-stuff. The voices of the Gods cannot be heard or when they are heard you hear a twisted version of that voice. Or when you wish to truly see, the mirror of the mind has been so warped and bent by negative programming and personal complexes that, like a fairground mirror, the true vision is bent into grotesque shapes.

Certain nuclei of thought are so powerful they gather a whole seething mass of associated thoughts around themselves to build a complex. Such complexes can even take a life of their own quite independent of the thinker's mind.

In the first spell, we work towards clearing and purifying the mind and ridding of complexes that block the free flow of the mental energies.

17. The Eight Great Spells Of Esoteric Maoshan

Jing Xin Shen Zhou
The Spell Of Purifying The Heart

Purifying the heart really means purifying the mind. The Chinese word Xin, can indicate heart, feeling and mind. Of course the main tool of inner work is the mind. With mind there comes perception. But perception can be coloured and even tainted by wrong belief and feeling. The idea of this exercise is thus to cleanse the mind and prepare it for correct perception uncoloured by prejudice and belief, and as an active executive tool in the path of Tao.

The Purify Heart Seal is envisioned like a red neon light, as red as the sunset says the oral tradition in the centre of the chest on the axis of a line that is drawn from crown acupoint baihui to the perineum point. In other words, in the centre of the body. It is a red and fiery light, illuminating the entire chest cavity, dazzling in its flaming glory.

For the mudra, the left thumb presses the top joint of the middle finger, the right in the Sword Finger.

O Taishang of the Eternal Stars, Moving without end and flowing with eternal change.

Banish all evil demons and bind them with your magical powers!
Protecting my body, the guardian of life,
His wisdom is pure and all is illuminated in its beauteous light,
Bringing spiritual calmness to the Mind,
Forever internalising the Three Pure Spirits,
And so defeating the Earthly Soul and causing it to flee!

Quickly by the Law (of Heaven)!!

Tai Shang Tai xing,
Ying bian wu ting,
Zhi hui ming jing,
Xing shen an ning,
San hun Yong jiu
Po wu sang qing
Ji Ji Ru Lu Ling.

2. Jing Kou Shen Zhou
The Spell Of Purifying The Mouth/Voice

In this spell, we purify and activate the power of the magical speech. The mouth, saliva, teeth and throat are all consecrated to the true expression of the heart/mind.

Purifying the mouth is an important concept in Daoist magic, so your words really represent command and truth. You can compare this concept to the idea in Hermeticism of the Logos or WORD. The word is an emanation of the Mind. This act is thus more than purifying but magically activating the mouth and magical speech. Perhaps the Ceremony of Opening the Mouth in The Book of Coming Forth By Day originally had this purpose.

Now to the inner work.

After saying the Spell you are to visualise strongly the Magical Seal of Purifying the Mouth. It should be envisioned as about the size of the upper knuckle of the thumb and blazing with a white neon luminosity on the middle of your tongue. The inner body meanwhile is seen as a dark hollow space. The Magical Seal should light up the whole oral cavity and inner throat to the point that the teeth and tongue disappear in the sheer dazzling luminosity of the Seal.

The Hand Seal is that the left thumb presses the middle knuckle of the ring finger and the right hand is in the Sword Mudra.

> Cinnabar Elixir, Spirit of the mouth,
> Banish the unclean and purge the gross vapours,
> O Zhen Lun (Right Order), Spirit of the tongue,
> Enhance life and nourish the spirit,
> O Luo Qian (One thousand assembled), Spirit of the teeth,
> You guard the True, banishing demonic forms,
> Hu Bi (Bright Tiger), Spirit of the throat,

gathering qi and spirit from the saliva.
Dan Yuan, (Original Elixir), Spirit of the Heart,
Commanding my comprehension of truth,
Lian Ye (Refining the Secretions), the Spirit of the Mind,
Eternally following the Tao of the Breath.
Quickly by Law!
Dan zhu Kou shen,
Tu hui chu fen,
She shen zheng lun,
Tong ming Yang shen,
Luo Qian chi shen,
Que Xie Wei Zhen,
Hou shen hu bi,
Qi shen yin jin,
Xin shen lian ye,
Tao qi chang cun,
Ji Ji Ru Lu Ling!!

3. Jing Shen Shen Zhou
Spell Of Purifying The Body

Maoshan does not ignore and revile the body, even as many other traditions do. The body is indeed a temporary vessel or container for the spiritual elements of man, but it is also a valuable tool for experiencing not only the sensory world but also the supersensory. Through exercises such as yoga (daoyin), breath control (qigong), herbal formulae and special foods and medicines (weidan) and the martial arts (wushu) the body is kept flexible and strong even in old age.

In the inner work of the Purifying the Body Spell we visualise the Magical Seal of Purifying the Body at the position we would call the third eye. However the Seal is in the centre of the brain, not merely on the surface of the skin. If you drew a line beginning at the fontanelle centre or Bai Hui that passed down to the perineum, this Seal would be on that axis and on the plane of a line drawn from the third eye to the back of the head. The ancient instructions and oral traditions state that the Seal should be envisioned like a bright lamp that casts dazzling white rays outwards and fills the entire hollow interior of the body, filling it with so much light that even the bones cannot be distinguished. The body becomes as bright as an illuminated crystal.

The thumb presses the upper joint of the ring finger and the right is again in the sword mudra.

> Spiritual treasures of the Heavenly treasury,
> Calm and strengthen the body,
> And its companions are the Hun and Po,
> Dark and Mysterious are the Five Organs,
> The Green Dragon and the White Tiger engage in battle.
> The Vermillion Bird and the Mysterious Warrior

guard my True Nature,
Quickly by Law !!!

Ling bao tian zun,
An Wei shen xing,
Di Zi Hun Po,
Wu Zang Xuan ming,
Qing Long Bai Hu
Dui Zhang fen Yun
Zhu Que Xuan Wu,
Shi Wei wo Zhen
Ji Ji Ru Lu Ling.

4. An Tu Di Shen Zhou
Spell To Purify The Spirit Of The Earth

We now pacify the Earth and the local earth spirits and locate Gods such as Tudi and recruit them towards our work in the Tao. In western terms the Genii Loci and the elementals become a help rather than a hindrance.

The body, mind and spirit must live in its environment. In this spell, we create a healthy environment free from undesirable influences. Literally creating peaceful and sacred space while connecting with the Earth God. This one can be used by itself to promote a healing environment or an environment where you wish good fortune to flow … for example a place of business.

The Magician visualises the Magic Seal of the Earth in space before him as golden as the scorching disk of the Sun. When this is clearly visualised, the magician envisions it as spinning in space before him anticlockwise. With each turn it gets bigger and bigger until, in his visualisation it fills the space between Heaven and Earth.

There is no special hand seal in this practice.

> O the Ancient One calms and protects,
> Commanding a vastness of Immortal Spirits,
> And by you, O August Ministers, Yue and Du,
> Let us pay respect to the Earth God,
> Earth God on the left and the God of Grain to the right,
> I have no delusions or fears.
> I have returned to the True Path,
> Clear and pure, within me, without me,
> All is in order and in its place,
> The Temple is prepared and guarded,

I hold the Mandate of Taishang!!
All unclean influences seized and imprisoned,
Protect the Law of the Spirit Kings!!
Protect the recitation of the Scriptures!
Seeking comfort in the Great Tao.
Origin, Endurance, Fortune and Strength!!
Quickly by Law!!

Yuan shi an Zhen,
Pu gao wan ling
Yue du Zhen guan
Tu di Zhi ling
Bu de wang jing
Hui Xiang Zhong tao
Nei wai cheng jing
Ge an fang Wei
Bei shou tan ting
Tai Shang you ming
Sou bu Xie Jing
Hu fa shen wang
Bao Wei song jing
Gui Yi da tao
Yuan, heng, li, Zhen
Ji Ji Ru Lu Ling!!!!

5. Jing Tian Di Shen Zhou
Spell To Purify The Heavens And The Earth

In this spell we call the powers of Heaven and Earth to unite within us and aid us in our work. The highest powers of Heaven and Earth are now invoked to purify and empower the individual and the immediate environment.

The Magical Seal of Purifying Heaven and Earth is envisioned in a bright, sky blue light. It is envisioned as floating in space in a position about a foot above your baihui or crown centre, throwing off thousands of rays of blue light and illuminating the room that you are in.

The Hand Seal is on the left hand, the thumb is on the lower section of the middle finger. On the right hand the thumb is on the upper section of the middle finger. Lightly touch the tip of the right middle finger to the tip of the left middle finger. Keep the index, ring and little finger straight and place the mudra at your heart.

> Heaven and Earth, expressions of Being,
> They banish all the unclean energies,
> Within the cave of the Mysterious Void,
> The Ultimate Origin of All scintillates in a wonderful light,
> Heroic Spirits from eight directions,
> Cause the being-ness of Nature to be,
> The Talismanic Order of the Spiritual Treasury,
> Qian Luo Ta Na
> In the Pole Star Cave of the Great Dark Mystery,
> He executes evil beings and binds demons.
> Passing over tens of millions of people,
> Chanting to the beings of the Central Mountain
> The Jade Writings of the Primordial Cause,

It is held and recited once,
To defend from disease and cause longevity.
Over the Five Mountains, he soars,
And he is heard over the Eight Seas,
O the hands of the Demon King are bound,
And he guards my journey and is present with me,
Eliminating and neutralising all evil detritus,
The Qi of the Tao will merge and exist in eternity,
Quickly by Order of the Law!!!!

Tian Di zi ran,
Hui qi fen san,
Dong Zhong Xuan xu,
Huang Tang Tai yuan,
Ba Tang Wei shen,
Shi wo zi ran,
Ling bao fu ming,
Qian Luo ta na,
Dong gang Tai Xuan,
Zhan ren wan qian,
Zhong shan shen zhou,
Yuan shi yu wen,
Chi song Yi bian,
Que bing yan nian,
An xing wu yue,
Ba hai Zhi wen
Mo wang shu shou,
Shi Wei wo Xuan.
Xiong hui xiao san,
Tao qichang cun,
Ji Ji Ru Lu Ling!!!!!

6. Jin Guang Shen Zhou
Spell Of The Golden Light
(See below where the energetic form is given)

7. Zhu Xiang Shen Zhou
Spell Of The Offering Of Incense

Incense is one of the most important elements of the rituals of Taoism, so incense is offered, usually in odd-numbered incense sticks. See later exactly how incense is properly offered.

In the inner work of the Incense Practice you visualise the seal in the smoke of the incense, luminous like a moon behind the clouds. As the incense passes through the Seal envision the smoke as becoming empowered and passing into the Heavenly dimension.

There is no standard hand seal for this practice.

The Tao is learned in the heart,
And the incense is the vehicle of the heart,
The incense, O how it warms the Jade Urn,
O the heart comes before the Emperor,
The True Immortal looks down from above,
The banner of the Immortal signals the arrival
of the heavenly chariot,
And so the reports of mankind are closed,
We directly communicate with the Nine Heavens.
Quickly by the Law!!!

Tao you xin Xue,
Xin Jia Xiang Zhuan,
Xiang ruo yu lu,
Xin cun Di Qian,
Zhen Ling Xia Pan,
Xian Pei lin Xuan,
Ling Chen guan gao,

Jing du Jiu Tian,
Ji Ji Ru Lu LIng !!!

The powers, spirits, Gods and Immortals descend (Jiang). Commune with the Ancient Ones.

8. Xuan Wen Zhou
Spell Of The Mysterious Gathering

There is no Seal or mudra. This is a direct calling of the Gods and Immortals.

> The Cloud Seal of the Mysterious Void,
> Has been since the beginning of the Great Kalpa,
> Suddenly it is near and suddenly it is far,
> Sometimes sinking and sometimes floating,
> Moving to and fro in the Five Directions,
> Of the assembly of numerous Masters,
> The True Emperor of Heaven,
> He takes up his brush to write in the Book,
> To reveal the Seal of the Cave,
> And the Book of Talismans,
> The Primal Cause descends,
> With courage teaching the true words,
> Illuminating when being,
> Obscuring when not,
> Serious ills are self-healed,
> The strength of those suffering in work
> and in the dust of the Earth,
> Assisting those who are imprisoned in desire,
> Bringing the gift of ascension into the Realm of the Immortals.
> Quickly by the Law!!!!

Yuan Zhuang Tai xu,
Hao Jie Zhi chu,
Zha Xia Zha er,

Huo Chen Huo fu,
Wu fang pai Huai,
Yi Zhang Zhi yu,
Tian Zhen Huang ren,
An bi nai shu,
Yi yan dong zheng,
Ci shu ling fu,
Yuan shi Xia Jiang,
Zhen wen dan fu,
Zhan Zhao qi you
Ming ming qi wu,
Chen Ke Neng zi Quan,
Chen Lao ni ke fu.
You ming Jiang you,
You shi sheng xian,
Ji Ji Ru Lu Ling!!!!

The Golden Light Spell

1. Let the Dizhi sit in his chosen position or stand in his chosen stance. Adopt natural breath.

2. Interlace all the fingers. Let the little fingers stand erect and touch at the tips. Do the same with the index fingers. Then let the thumb tips touch but they point down. The ring and middle fingers remain interlaced to form a 'platform'. (see diagram}.

3. Raise the hands so the tips of the thumbs are at the level of the niwan (third eye).

4. Chant the spell as follows. Note I have given the spell both in English and Pinyin Mandarin Chinese. You can use either, though purists may prefer the Chinese version. Since this is a spell, the sounds themselves aren't magical but the word-image formation is. Only actual mantric sounds will remain untranslated.

5. As you read the spell you must visualise the Seal of the Golden Light above your head. It is a fairly complex structure so I would suggest drawing it out a few times to understand the structure, and for the first few practices. Have it drawn on a card. The seal must be in bright golden light and pulsing with humming and oscillating waves of golden vibrancy. Bright, luminous, powerful.

6. O Heaven, the profound One origin of All,
   We cultivate, spiralling through countless Kalpas.
   To attain transcendence.
   Inside and outside the three realms.
   The Tao is the honoured One,
   O the Seal of Golden Light,
   Covers and protects my body,
   It cannot be seen,
   It cannot be heard,

Encompassing the entire Universe,
Nurturing all beings.
By One Enchantment,
My body radiates the Light,
Protected in the Three Realms,
The Five Emperors welcome me!
Homage is paid by a thousand Gods,
The Thunder is invoked!!
Ghosts are terrified, the evil ones tremble,
The disintegration of monstrous shapes,
Power is produced from within.
Overseen by the Mighty Lords of Thunder,
Wisdom and magical skill blend.
The Five Forms of Qi shine with life.
The Golden Light instantly erupts into being,
By the Logos of the Jade Emperor,
Quickly by the command of the Law !!!!

Tian di Xuan zong,
Wan qi ben gen,
Guang xiu wan Jie,
Zheng wu shen tong,
San Jie nei wai,
Wei Dao du zun,
Fu you jin guan,
Zhao hu wu shen,
Shi Zhi bu Jian,
Ting Zhi bu wen,
Boa Luo tian di,
Yang yu qun sheng,

Shou chi gi hian,
Shen you Guang ming,
San Jie Shi Wei,
Wu-di si ying,
Wan shen Chao li,
Yi Shi Lei ting,
Gui yan sang dan jing,
Guai wang xing'
Nei you pi li,
Lei Shen yin ming,
Tong hui jiao che,
Wu qi teng teng,
Jin Guang su xian,
Fu fu Zhen ren.
JI Ji Ru Luling!!!

Once the spell is recited you can chant the secret mantra of the Golden Light while intensifying the visualisation of the golden light, those tiny flakes of spiritual solar light entering through every pore of your skin, building up to an intense pressure and surrounding you in a wonderfully dazzling auric egg of gold.

OM KOU LI NIU, OM KOU LI NIU, KOU LI NIU OM.
OM KOU LI OM OM, NIU KOU LI NIU.

7. Now still at brow level, let the hands separate. The hands sweep slowly down in arcs to the sides of the body. As you do this, envision a trail of golden light that forms an auric egg of golden light that is seen to cover your whole body like a forcefield.

It is a kind of energy field that can be envisioned as a golden egg that dark entities fizzle out upon if they come into contact with it, rather like one of those UV insect killer lamps you sometimes see in restaurants.

Later when you are confident, you can begin internally storing the golden light in the dantian and even practice channelling it through the hands for healing purposes. Using the Sword Mudra (which see later) you can literally shoot negative entities as if you possess some kind of psychic laser blaster.

Practice consistently at least three to four times a week.

18. Joining the chain of transmission

The student of Chinese magic like in all other systems of magic must have training in order to make his spells and petitions effective. There is a certain training that must be undertaken that takes him from a normal person who is essentially passive to the material world to one who can act within it. Some call this to gain 'Immortal Bones'.

Like in the western and say the yogic traditions of India and Tibet one needs a Master (Sifu). In Taoist magic theory there is a chain of masters that goes beyond time and space and so the student's very first task is to become a link in this 'magical chain'. To become such a link means that he not only draws on his own powers but is plugged into the total pool of ancestral power in his own work.

The student's first task is then to join this chain.

What follows now is the first spell to connect with, astrally so to speak with the Maoshan Master. It must be done with complete sincerity. This can have a number of effects. The Teacher can manifest in dreams, by meaningful coincidences and by an actual living human teacher appearing in your life. It is a simple ritual and there lies the danger. It is so simple it can be hard to stay consistent. However it should be done daily without fail.

Suddenly one day you get the connection and you are one of the chains.

The aspirant should have an altar in a quiet room in the North. North is the direction from which the numerous powers of the celestials pour into our material plane according to the chinese magicians. The altar can be a simple affair. A small table will do and upon it a bowl of

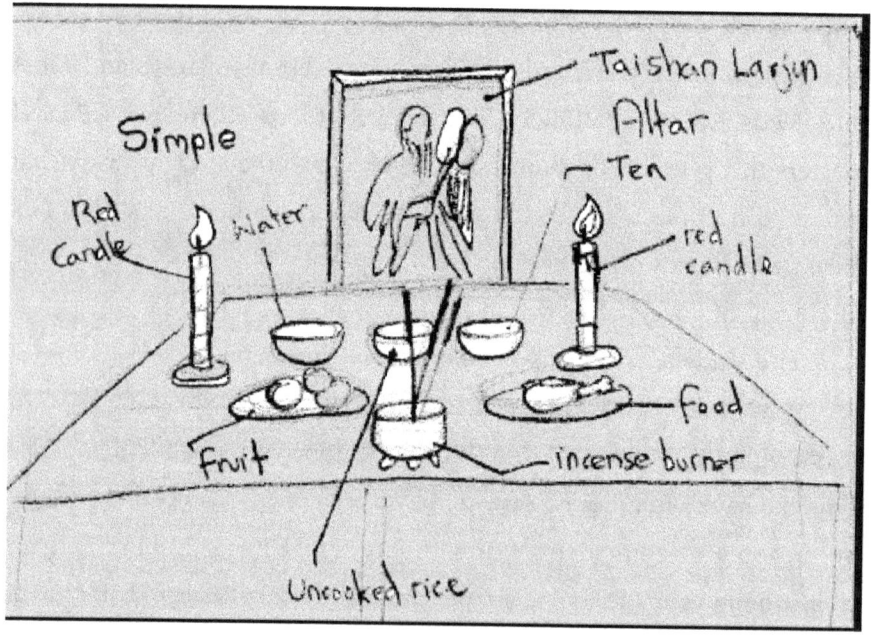

Two red candles on either side represent the Great Lights, the Sun and Moon. At the head of the Altar (tan) is the image of Taishang Laojun. Before Taishang are three bowls. The left one has pure water to represent Yang, the far right one has dark tea to represent Yin, and in the middle is a bowl of uncooked rice to represent the union of Yin and Yang. In front of these three bowls are up to five plates of food even though two will do. One should be fruit and the other(s) should be other foods such as cooked grains and meats. In front of this you have your incense burner. This is a ceramic or metal vessel filled with rice and salt. Arrange three chinese holed coins on the top in a triangle. The incense is inserted through the holes. Do not throw the ash away!! Let the burner build its own power as the consecrated ash mixes with the salt and rice.

Sigil Of The Maoshan Master

water and a bowl filled with a mixture of dried rice and rock salt. Into the rice you can insert one or three incense sticks in a triangular formation.

Adopt the teacher mudra. Fill your heart with longing as if a lover imploring the beloved. Sincerity and passion, lovesick for truth. Read the spell with meaning and sincere desire. It's not a grocery list but a love letter to the Masters. Be humble and passive and non demanding. Be an open cup to receive the nectar of truth.

Tap the teeth together three times.

Three times. The Spell of SHI Tong Zhen.

O my eyes look upwards, the Master in the Blue Heaven is by my side. My eyes gaze to the Heaven's, and the Master is present. The Disciple calls a thousand times and there are ten thousand responses, ten thousand calls, ten thousand spirits. I cannot call my own spirit.

Right hand Sword mudra, Left Ancestor Mudra

JI JI ru lu Ling!

Qi yan guan Qing tian, Shifu zaishen Guang qi yan Wang Qing tian shi fu zai. Yanqian dizi Qian ying wàn jiao Luân Ling dizi bu jiao ziging bu jiao Zi Ling.

JI JI ru lulling!!

Change hands to left ancestral patriarch mudra and right sword mudra. (see chapter 36)

Draw the ancient symbol of the Master over the water with a sword hand and then sip.

Endure till contact is made.

The Teacher Mudra

19. Empowering Of Spirit Water

After requesting the Master the next step is to learn how to empower water. Again the western magician and the tantric will be familiar with this idea in practical magic and religion.

As in the western mysteries, water in Chinese magic is considered a kind of universal solvent, a neutral medium that can be charged by thought, feeling and will in conjunction with the higher powers of Nature. Water has a very receptive and magnetic yin quality that is perfect for capturing and storing spiritual and psychic information.

Water has manifold uses in Chinese occultism and always has a central focus on the altar in one form or another. In some practices water becomes an actual medium or meeting point between the worlds of physical manifestation and the worlds of the spirit. It is not unusual for example for water to be used as a kind of magical mirror to passively skry with 'yin and yang eyes' or to actively engage with the spirit world. In one practice, Maoshan magicians place their ear close to the water's surface to listen to the voices of spirits who communicate via the water.

In this practice called Zhou Shui Tong Ling Fa, literally, 'Water Opens Spirit Method', the water is used to capture the essence of spiritual energy to 'transform' the water into an elixir of powerful transformation which is then drunk. The numinous power is thus incorporated into the being of the trainee magician and subtle changes occur. In the language of Chinese magic, the practitioner is building a store of ling li, spiritual-magical power that some translate by the word mana.

At the heart of this procedure is a character that the magician who chooses to use the psycho-cosmology of Chinese symbolism is the Secret Character of the Purple Palace or Zi Wei Ling.

This character is sacred to Ziwei, and represents the entire essence of the Court of Heaven known as the Central Purple Palace. As an interesting side note, the famous Forbidden Palace in Beijing was supposed to be modelled on it, and to be an earthly representative of the Great Purple Palace. Purple is a sacred colour that represents the perfect balance of the Yin of blue and the red of yang. Thus the Taoist Immortals and Gods often appeared in a diaphanous form of purple mist. To this day you can see its unique purple bricks. The Purple Palace itself represents the sacred axis of the heavens and commands all the movements of the stars, planets and galaxies in our cosmos. Its influence penetrates all things, and by power of its ruler, the Ziwei Emperor, even to the deepest recesses of the Underworld.

The Seal is under the power of Ziwei Da Diwei, the Great Emperor

of the North Star. The character itself is a compound of several characters, most recognisably the character of rain at the top. However as a compound character there is no specific meaning as such, its true power is numerical, for when properly written it consists of twenty-eight strokes. Twenty-eight in Taoist magical symbolism is the number of the cosmos as it represents the 28 asterisms that seemingly encircle the plane of the ecliptic surrounding the earth. These in some sense correspond to the 28 Lunar Mansions or Stations of western and tantric astrology.

The disciple magician will stand in the t-shaped step sometimes called Da Yu Bu, the Great Step of Yu. Yu being a shaman king of Chinese lore who among other things controlled the floods of China and discovered the method of the Big Dipper Step. The left foot is foremost, with the left heel nestled into the instep of the right foot to form a t-shape.

Using the left hand to form San Shan Jue or the Mudra of the Three Mountains he holds a small porcelain bowl at the Yellow Court Centre (i.e. level with the heart or middle dantian).

To form San Shan Jue the thumb, index and little fingers are extended upwards to form a three pronged support to hold the bowl. The remaining fingers are folded to the palm. (see chapter 36)

The right hand forms the more familiar Jian Jue or Sword Mudra. Visualising the Purple North Star directly over his or her crown point (bai hui), rays of misty purple light stream down through the bai hui and down the central axis of the magician to gather in a purple ball at the lower dantian. Circulating the purple energy up the right arm and through the fingers of the Sword Hand, he traces the 28 strokes of the Zi Wei Ling on the surface of the water, at the same time uttering the names of the 28 Stars:

JIAO, KANG, DI, FANG, XING, WEI, JI, DOU, NIU, NU, XU, WEI, SHI, BI, GUI, LOU, WEI, ANG, BI, ZUI, CAN, JING, GUI, LIU, XING, ZHANG, YI, ZHEN !!!

Inhale Qi from the North now with the bowl cupped in both hands and blow a visualised purple mist into the bowl. Drink it and feel the power.

This must be a daily practice as the effect is subtle and takes time to manifest. Repeat seven times and for 49 days minimum.

20. Maoshan Fali Meditation The Peach Grove Flowers Of Maoshan Neigong

FALI, means strength, internal power, virtue and skill obtained by cultivation.

Keep your practices to a minimum and engage in Golden Light, and this to prepare for Level 2.

This is a beautiful and positive meditation that will enhance not only your concentration but all five senses. Rather than the intense and often boring zazen style meditations preferred by some schools, Maoshan Taoist meditations should be natural and flowing and unforced.

Do not eat anything for a minimum 30 minutes before and after practice, and drink only cool water.

Sit in your favourite posture, usually some form of panzuo (cross legged, lotus, half lotus etc).

Palms upwards on knees. Back straight but relaxed. Eyes half open.

Set up a natural breathing rhythm but don't force it or make it a big deal.

First relax yourself from head to toes in your favourite method, but they all amount to progressive relaxation don't they?

My sifu advised me to repeat this three times.

Now you must mentally change your external scenery to that of a beautiful day. Let it be like the fabulous Peach Grove. Soft jade-like grass all around you, like a soft quilt increasing your comfort.

The sky is as vivid and blue as Tibetan turquoise. A gentle wind, warm and perfumed.

Now mentally populate this viridian carpet with flowers in bud, not yet open but revealing a hint of the colours that are within. Every colour and shade thereof you can imagine. Reds, blues and yellows, greens, purples, oranges and whites, and even black, silver and gold.

Spend some time on this. Really build a vivid picture.

Imagine this cornucopia of flowers in bud fill your world.

Next, focus on a red sun rising in the East, and the red crimson hot circle stops at the zenith above your head. Feel the nourishing heat and qi.

It's rays scatter around you and fill you with vitality and warmth. The air around you glows with warmth.

At this point the flowers begin to open. You must mentally bond the idea that as the flowers open your skills, your power, wisdom and love are growing and opening too. As the flowers bloom, you are blooming. The more flowers that bloom and the more colours revealed, the more your skill and powers are revealed. Smell their delicious perfume and see their colours.

There you are in the midst of an ocean of flowers.

Now collect all that light and colour into your dantian in any way you choose, condensing the universal power there.

Light, colour, scent, heat all condensed to the lower dantian.

Males put their left palm on dantian and women the right.

Rotate the palm clockwise nine times. Women go counter clockwise.

Finish by rubbing face, neck and waist.

A Qi Flow Health Checkup

Energy flow is incredibly important not only for your health, but for your neigong, meditation and martial arts as well as your magic.

Here is a simple self diagnosis routine to check if the Qi is flowing through your meridians correctly.

At its simplest, health is about balance. Balance is indicated by the flow of energy through a network of channels. These can be 'blocked' and energy 'stagnates' which can open you to ill health and make you vulnerable to disease.

1. Pinch the flesh moderately hard on your thigh. If it hurts there is blockage. In good health you'll hardly feel anything.

2. Hold the wrist of one hand tight enough to restrict blood flow for one minute. Release. If blood flows immediately back, the hand goes red and feels hot, great. The meridians of the upper body are open. If the hand remains white too long, there is stagnation.

3. Lie face down. In good health, the stomach sinks in and the ribs show. Lumps and sagging indicate water damp and phlegm.

4. Lie on your back and press and restrict the groin artery. If you feel blood and heat rush to the toes, you can pat yourself on the back as your lower meridians are free from obstruction.

5. Briskly rub the 8 points on and near your coccyx area. If your feet warm up the bladder and governing meridians are in great health. If just your knees, that's not so great. And if just your coccyx and butt, that's not good.

6. Go to the mirror and check the two main blood vessels under your tongue. If dark, stagnation.

If you drink heavily, do drugs or smoke the results will vary according to damage so far sustained. Smoking and drugs (sorry, even cannabis) is a sure way to ruin your energy body

21. Protection, Condensing And Projection

In common with many if not most systems throughout the world magic must begin with protection and the creation of a space with borders to act as a meeting point between the world of the seen and the unseen.

To create a magically warded space not only offers you protection from minor and often parasitical forces but serves to condense magical energies of Qi.

You could produce massive amounts of Qi, but unless they are contained within a properly bounded circle or other space they will tend to dissipate into space. Thus in Taoist magic we create a space by mental force in which to condense, project and shape Qi as well as affording us protection.

Normally in conventional neigong or its poor relation, Qi gong, the boundary is defined by the body itself. However the practitioner's Qi when attempting feats without the confines of the body tends to peter out and the effect willed for does not occur because of the lack of condensation of the qi within a defined space. This accords with the law of entropy.

Taoism has a number of methods to create such a space and one of them is based on the bagua and another is based on the Four Auspicious Animals of the Four Primary Elements and their corresponding directions.

In taoist magic we call this process Hu Shen, literally, Protect the Body.

In an advanced form of this magic the Taoist magician can create a talisman to instantly have access to such a protective shield, and even carry it around with him or her and/or give it to others that they may benefit from it.

The basic Protect Body Spell or Hu Shen Zhou is fairly simple.

The sorcerer begins facing the South, this is the starting direction for many spells in Taoist magic. In this spell he or she is going to invoke the powers of the Eight Trigrams and create a 'magic circle'. Actually this should be a sphere. If you were to open the ghost eye (clairvoyance) and look at the magical bagua circle it would seem to be a dome or hemisphere over the magician. But the other half of that sphere would be beneath the ground. Or if you were in an upstairs room, the other half of the dome would be seen in the room below.

Begin breathing the Five Coloured Qi. That is, you stand and use the Gathering Heavenly Qi arm motion, with palms turned in.

Then in consciously see the seemingly whole of the cosmos become a light grass green. Let this begin from the East and spread to fill your known universe. Breathe the green particles of qi through the pores of your skin and fill your body.

Repeat the same process with fiery red from the south, watery black from the north, metallic white from the west and earthy yellow from the centre.

You are now filled with the powers of the five Qis. You can condense the five coloured qi at the dantian into a multi coloured orb. Remember TO SPIN THE ORB CLOCKWISE TO CONDENSE IT.

Holding the sword mudra (see Chapter 36) you are ready to draw the QIAN trigram in the air and chant:

YUAN HENG LI ZHEN!!

Then turn eastwards, remember portioning your circle into eight.

Draw DUI and chant: The Lake, the Heroic Army!!

Draw LI and chant: Fire, driving the Wheel of Fire!

Draw Zhen and chant: Thunder, the Vajra Thunderbolt resounds.

Draw Xun Wind, blowing from the lofty mountain.
Draw KAN and chant: Water, rapid great waves.
Draw GEN and chant: Mountain , named the Ghost Road.
Draw KUN and chant Earth, stable and firm O Gate of Men.
Return to the southern position:

O You Bagua Master, manifest your great power, the evil spirits pass away into nothing and cannot move, the Divine Warriors rush like fire.

Ji Ji Ru Lu Ling!!!!

Remember to spend some time as you call upon the powers of the Bagua once you have drawn the trigram. You are invoking the quintessential powers of Nature. Feel the wind of Xun blow on your face and ruffle your hair, feel the searing flame of Li and the vibrations of clashing Thunder.

There is no need to 'recall' this protective circle as it can be your constant companion.

22. Cultivating Jade Wine

The Maoshan magician can further empower himself with a practice known as the Jade Wine by the accumulation of the 'True Qi' or Zhen Qi in the saliva, this is known as Jade Wine among practitioners. Jade is a precious Yang substance in Taoist magic and thus magically and alchemically potenised saliva is called Jade Wine or the Jade Elixir in magical circles.

Saliva in the Chinese tradition is a substance that is a powerful medium for the collection of potent alchemical and magical agents gathered in magical and meditative processes.

Similar practices are found in the Tantric literature of India. Amrita for example is believed to be formed in the head centres, often associated with a mysterious chakra known as Soma. By practice of khechari mudra, the yogin can access a milky essence that is said to bring health and occult powers to the accomplished master. Khechari mudra uses the tongue to pass up behind the nasal passages to access this elixir. Though not as extreme the Taoist masters also consider the tongue as a kind of bridge that links the head centres with the bodily centres, in essence completing the central axial circuit which is broken at the point of the mouth.

I can see no reason why the Taoist Dizi might not use khechari like practices with the Jade Wine.

The mysterious energies that enter the saliva may also include secretions and hormones produced by the head centres but this is conjecture.

The idea of Jade Wine is to condense the alchemico-magical energies (and possible hormonal secretions) and swallow it to be absorbed in the being of the magician. In theory the energies are distributed to his subtle qi body and go towards constructing and crystallising the magical body or ling shen.

In the morning the magician sits facing East and completely empties his lungs several times of all bad air and Qi in a conscious manner. For example, as you exhale, envision all the bad air, Qi, thoughts, stresses and so on as a black cloud that is absorbed and dealt with by nature.

Facing East, envision the whole world right to the horizon as being spring leaf green, inhale and visualise it as entering every pore of the skin and condense it at the lower dan tian.

Turn to, or simply focus on the Southerly direction. Now the whole world is bright fiery scarlet, and breathe the hot red Qi through every pore in your skin, three dimensionally, and again gather it at the Dan Tian.

Repeat this process in the West but the colour is cold, metallic white and then to the North, but the colour is cool watery black.

DO NOT swallow any saliva in the drawing in of the elemental Qi at this stage. Let the saliva build up in the mouth.

By the time you finish you will have a fair portion filling the mouth.

You now use a technique called Drawing the Talisman with the Tongue. Note that in actuality it is nigh impossible to draw a complex design with the tongue on the roof of the mouth. It is enough that you draw the elements of the talisman on top of each other. So with your tongue and without swallowing any saliva, draw the following talisman design on the roof of the mouth or Perfect Heaven:

Once you have drawn it on the roof of the mouth, envision the symbol as emitting 10,000 rays of golden light that reach as far as the dantian. Simultaneously chant the spell:

The Heavens are pure,

The Earth is at peace,

The Sun and Moon are bright,

The Ten Thousand Buddhas come to our aid,
The Hundred Gods protect my body.
Longevity arises from swallowing the saliva,
Dispelling diseases, the true and healthful qi is in my being,
The ten thousand ills are gone from my body.
JI JI RU LU LING !!!!!

Now divide the saliva in your mouth into three portions using your tongue to help this process.

Swallow the first, slowly and absorb its potencies in the dan tian. Repeat two more times and you are finished.

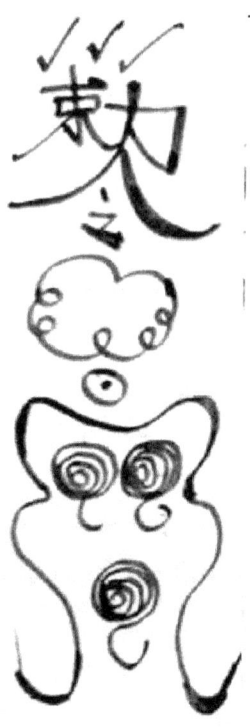

23. Washing The Marrow And Replenishing The Essence

This exercise is called XI SUI BU JING FA, the method of Washing the Marrow and Replenishing the Essence. It is done immediately following the Jade Wine yoga, and in fact they are considered a pair of exercises that are usually worked together.

Marrow or Xi, in Chinese refers to all the matter in your body that is believed to form part of your nervous system, especially the brain and spinal fluid. Essence here is Jing, your sexual energies at their most raw form that is associated with the kidneys.

So still sitting in your meditation posture you again draw a magical seal with your tongue on the roof of your mouth, but there is no need to draw the chinese characters.

The moment you finish drawing the seal let it suddenly blaze up in a sudden explosive burst of golden light.

Let the light fill your body, oozing like warm hot melted butter from the head to the bottom of your feet as if you are filling up the empty vessel of your body. As this golden light oil pushes downwards it is simultaneously absorbing all negativities, mental and emotional toxins and so forth, until ultimately they are pushed out of your feet and absorbed by Nature which can deal with such things better than you.

Recite the following spell three times:

O Ancestral Spirit who can illuminate all things,
Rid my body of all impurity,
Let my whole body be clean and bright,
Increase the Essence and Marrow,
Saving life and building a strong body,

Ten thousand spirits increase my strength,
I return to the spiritual source,
I am reborn into a long life,
I accomplish this by Heaven.
JI JI RU LU LING

Swallow the saliva that has built up and absorb the essence at the dan tian.

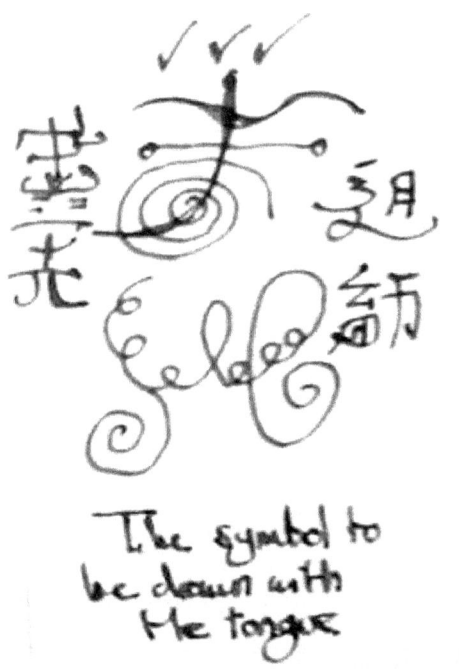

The symbol to be drawn with the tongue

24. Basic Qi Gathering

To work with energy you must gather it. You cannot use what you do not possess. The main function of Qi is in fact to keep you alive and in balance. It is a serious mistake to use your own reservoirs of Qi in magical work and healing. That is why if you look at many pictures of so-called Qigong masters they look old before their time.

Rather than drawing from the ample reservoirs of pure Qi from the universe, the Earth and the stars and planets, they have drawn on their own Qi. Instead of becoming rejuvenated they have lost years of vitality. This is particularly the case of the Qi practitioner who relies purely on their own jing or sexual root essence. They compound the problem by forced and unnatural celibacy. In Maoshan you cannot work with one sided forces. Without the Yin from the sexual yoga, or the Yang in the case of females, they dry up and shrivel in the disharmonious gathering of forces. You cannot work with the dragon alone or the tiger alone constantly.

Cosmic Qi and the Qi of the Earth has less limitations. Though of course you should work with both to be in harmony.

The first exercises in qi are therefore to learn to mentally tune in to the vibrations of Heavenly Energy (Tian Qi) and Earthly Qi (Di Qi), the macrocosmic Dragon and Tiger.

In the first exercise you gather Qi and cleanse the body.

In the second exercise you gather Qi and store it for use in inner (alchemical) and magical work.

1. Gathering Celestial Qi To Wash The Spirit

Ideally you will want to do this exercise in the early hours of the morning. However if this is impossible you can do it at any time.

Stand upright with your spine erect and gazing forwards. RELAX. Your feet should be naturally spaced at about a shoulder width apart. And the arms hanging at the sides with palms resting on the outer thighs. BE NATURAL. If you ever see Qi practices that are forceful or use strenuous stances like deep horse stances ... that is NOT Dao. Many of the martial arts that have come from Shaolin for example, were developed in times of national emergency and war. Thus martial artists had to take many shortcuts to force the Qi unnaturally and with forced breathing and tension. This is not true Dao AND CAN LEAD TO SELF DAMAGE ... In their investigation of the occult forces of the universe, the Taoist sages have discovered that muscular tension is a death knell to the flow of Qi. Mentally scan your body from head to toe looking for every tension. Even micro tensions such as tense eyebrows, tension in the knees and so on.

Next, become aware of the space around you. Visualise it peppered with a mist of purple light. This represents the Heavenly Qi. Purple represents the spiritual vibration of the Heavenly Qi as near as human consciousness can perceive it.

Inhale slowly with natural breathing without force or tension. As you inhale the abdominal muscles push outwards WITHOUT FORCE OR TENSION.

As you inhale your arms, slightly bent rise upwards, turning palms up. Envision gathering some of the purple mist in each palm as if it clings to your palms.

When you reach above your head, pause the breath for one second. Then the palms turn toward the ground, still holding the purple mist.

Exhale and push the purple mist through your head and body. Let it cleanse you. Carrying away negativity, worry, tension, emotional toxins and so on. Continue exhaling until you push down to the maximum extension. Pause in breath and let the purple Qi descend through your feet into the Earth. Repeat 21 times.

2. Gathering Celestial Qi To Build The Store

This exercise accompanies the above exercise. Once you have cleansed the spirit body, the adept must now gather the celestial energy and store it for future use.

Learning to gather power has three distinct components.

1. Posture and bodily movement.

2. Visualisation with a focus on Colour.

3. Breath.

In Daoist magic there is no denial of the body or an imagined split between the body and spirit as in Abrahamic religious paradigms. Rather there is a continuum. The body is qi too albeit in a highly condensed form moving at a slower vibration and subject to more laws of time and space. However whereas western scientists of the old school tend to (and have to) centre their analysis of the human experience in the gross matter of the body, the spiritual science exemplified by the Tao sees a continuum of increasingly higher vibrations of energy that make up the human entity. The higher we go the less laws that energetic level is subject to and the more connected it is to the whole cosmos.

The control of the body and its use to guide energies is a frequent tool in Daoist yoga and magic. These can be in the form of hand seals or mudras or stances and footwork as well as the movements used in various kinds of alchemy. Bodily movements are a language by which we make known intention (YI).

Visualisation is also a highly developed art in Daoist magic. An adept can construct whole palaces filled with symbolic architecture, colours, spirits and gods.

At a basic level, in Daoist alchemy we make use of colour. Like all magical systems, Daoism accepts the law of correspondence. Colour has a vibratory rate and a definite psychological effect as has been proven by experimental psychology. The colours used in Daoist meditations have a definite meaning. For example the most well known are the colours of the Five Elements and by default these are identical to the colours of the Five Planets and the Five Directions and so forth.

In these basic exercises the colour purple is used as it is the colour most representative of the Celestial Qi. Purple is itself a mixture of RED and BLUE. Two primary colours that represent Fire and Water, Yin and Yang. Purple thus represents the perfect equilibrium of the polarities and by association, purple is the colour of the Dao.

The third component is breath. Breath is one of the few bodily functions that works unconsciously and yet can also be consciously controlled. Breath is intimately linked to consciousness. Different rates and qualities of breath can reveal or even induce certain states, either inhibitory and trance like, or excitatory and stimulating.

Breath and its rhythms are thus a key to control consciousness and furthermore breath is used to inhale not only air but Qi, the subtle and cosmic power of life force that impregnates the whole of Nature. By breath control and visualisation, the adept can control and direct and even mentally colour this Qi power.

As was already indicated in our teaching materials, Daoism distinguishes between Pre-Heaven and Post-Heaven.

Pre Heaven is an ideal perfect pre manifestation state that kind of equates with the Neoplatonic idea of the Archetypal World. It exists in, to paraphrase Keats, in perfect truth and perfect beauty. It is beyond time and space and because it is in perfect equilibrium, it is effectively non-polar.

However the moment something is born into manifestation, be it a human or a galaxy, it enters the Post-Heaven State, which, due to the limitations imposed on it by time and space, exhibits CHANGE and MOTION. Thus polarity is born, and of course the cycles of change such as life and death. The moment the spiritual essence that represents say me or you is incarnated in the realm of time and space, the operating ground of the Post-Heaven Bagua, we begin the inevitable process of temporal existence, change and decay. Physicists call this process entropy, as stated in the third law of thermodynamics. That is, in layman's terms, complex organised structures will tend to become disorganised over time and space.

However, the Daoist can in a sense, through his understanding of these processes achieve a certain immunity to post-heaven entropy. One way is to build a body that is not subject to the laws of change and by default corruption. This is the idea behind the infamous alchemical pill of alchemy. To build a consciousness capable of surviving the trauma of death and an immortal body capable of acting as its vehicle.

The replenishment of lost Jing essence is the first step in this process of immortalisation. Jing or Kidney Jing is in a sense the sands of time in the hourglass of the human lifespan. Jing is passed down from our ancestors and is in essence a sexual creative force at its most raw form. As we pass through time and space (age) we lose jing and become more and more prone to surrender to cosmic entropy.

One way to slow this process is to restore our jing and to fortify it with Qi from Nature.

In Gathering Celestial energy we assume the same stance as before and breathe in the same way and even gather the purple mist in the same manner. The difference is in the intention. This time we do not push the energy into the Earth, but we end at the Dan Tian with the palms facing inwards over the DanTian and fix the purple energy at the lower Dan Tian. Letting it form into a purple ball about the size of a golf ball. Then stop.

Do this 21 times.

25. An Exercise To Gather Qi From The Soul Of The Earth

In this exercise the dizi draws on the qi inherent in Nature to replenish their store of internal Qi.

The practice is quite simple in essence but relatively hard to master.

It is best to stand outside with bare feet planted on the grass, rocks or wherever you find yourself. The point is to have a genuine connection with nature.

If circumstances don't permit it, you can try and visualise yourself in a beautiful natural environment with green meadows, mountains, forests, lakes etc.

You must now visualise around you the following pattern with the colours shown (see diagram).

Chant the mantra:

YI HE REN, ER HE DI, SAN HE TIAN, SI HE DAO.
WU HE ZIRAN !
(Meaning:
FIRST UNITE WITH MAN, SECONDLY UNITE WITH EARTH, THIRDLY UNITE WITH HEAVEN, FOURTHLY UNITE WITH THE DAO, FIFTHLY UNITE WITH NATURE!!

Inhale deeply and slowly and envision all the powers of Nature and its powerful energies flowing into your breath and into your Dan Tian. Hold your breath.

Recite the power mantra:

LI ZHI HOU TIAN ZUN SHENG

Then release the energies back into Nature letting it carry all your accumulated toxins, tensions, and bad Qi etc. The residual nature energies will remain with you to further empower your practice of magic and alchemy.

You will notice at this level there is no standard nei gong as you would expect in most martial or other traditions.

This is simply because you are not ready. The focus here is on infusing yourself with and learning to connect with earthly and cosmic energies of the Dao.

You will also be focusing on the Six Healing Breaths to connect with the energies of the Elements/Planets and learn to communicate and put your consciousness into the relevant organ.

The real secret of Daoist Yoga is that your body is a gross manifestation of the Cosmos. Though it is seemingly 'you' it really isn't. The body is a vehicle by which you experience and grow in matter. Furthermore the body consists of thousands if not millions of life forms that have coalesced and work in harmony together. The Daoist student must learn to communicate with the intelligences that make up his body.

When a Maoshan adept speaks about the Spirit of the Liver, this isn't metaphorical, it is a fact. The Daoist can communicate with his liver, his heart, his kidneys and so forth. To this end the initial exercises of Maoshan are a little different from the standard Qigong of most other schools that focus on the Dan Tian, though that will come later.

If you cannot communicate with your own body and understand it, if your body doesn't speak to you, all the microcosmic orbits in the world will not do very much if anything at all.

Initial practices such as the Golden Light, Jade Wine and Spirit Water help prepare the ground, and Golden Light itself if done to perfection would be in itself enough to bring all the results of 'dan tian' nei gong.

So how do we learn to communicate with our bodies so we can speak to it and it can speak to us?

This is the practice of the Inner Landscape. Usually we identify the major solid or Yin organs as being attributed to certain elements, planets, images and names.

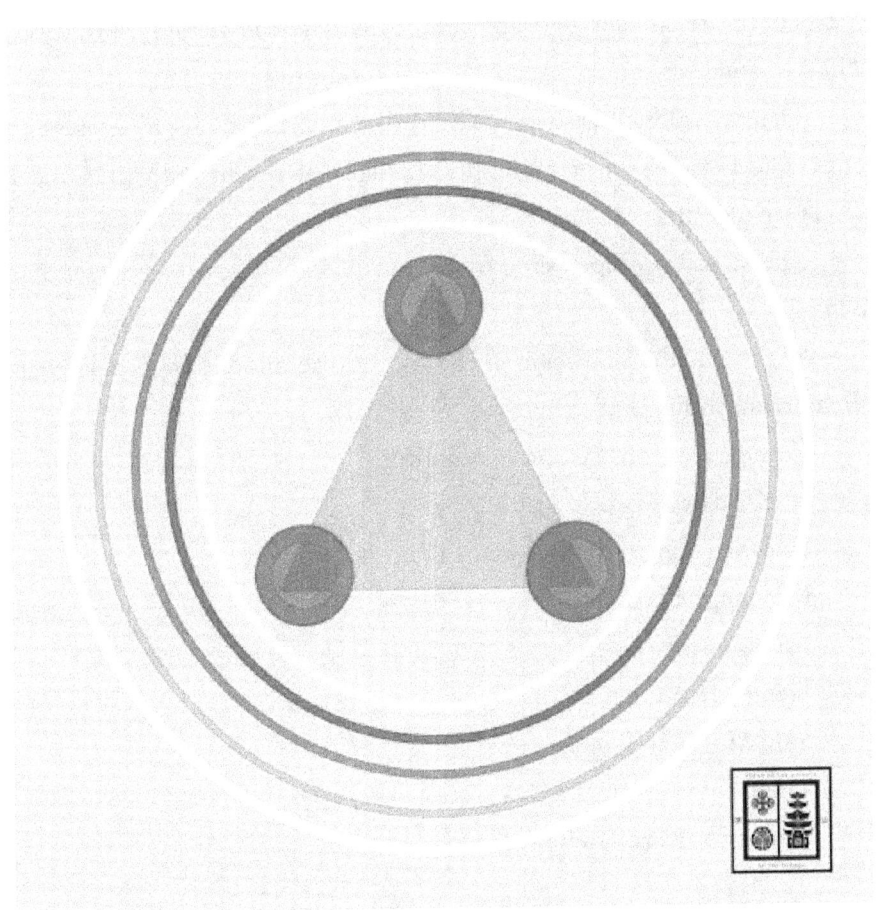

Daoist Qi Absorption Circle

26. Jian Jue
Activating The Sword Finger

The most famous Daoist mudra is the Sword Finger, you'll even find it in martial arts, but what is less known is that it is 'dead' until activated.

Not even qigong or thirty years of martial arts can activate it for spiritual purposes.

There are in fact two activations. This is the Lesser Activation. The Greater Activation is a spell and a Gong fu in itself.

That would include oaths, a kind of Gong fu leading to telekinetic effects and studies in acupuncture. In light of recent oath breaking I won't divulge this yet.

The sword is empowered by the seven stars to create a Seven Star Sword.

With your thumb, begin at the top of the middle finger and then the corresponding finger creases.

O the Heavenly Sword is beautiful.

The Earth Sword is Truth.

Encapsulating Thunder and Lightning.

Moving the North Stars.

All is auspicious.

Heng Zhen Qian Yuan Hengli!

Sun, Moon and Stars.

Their light removes all dangers.

Sword to heart. Bow.

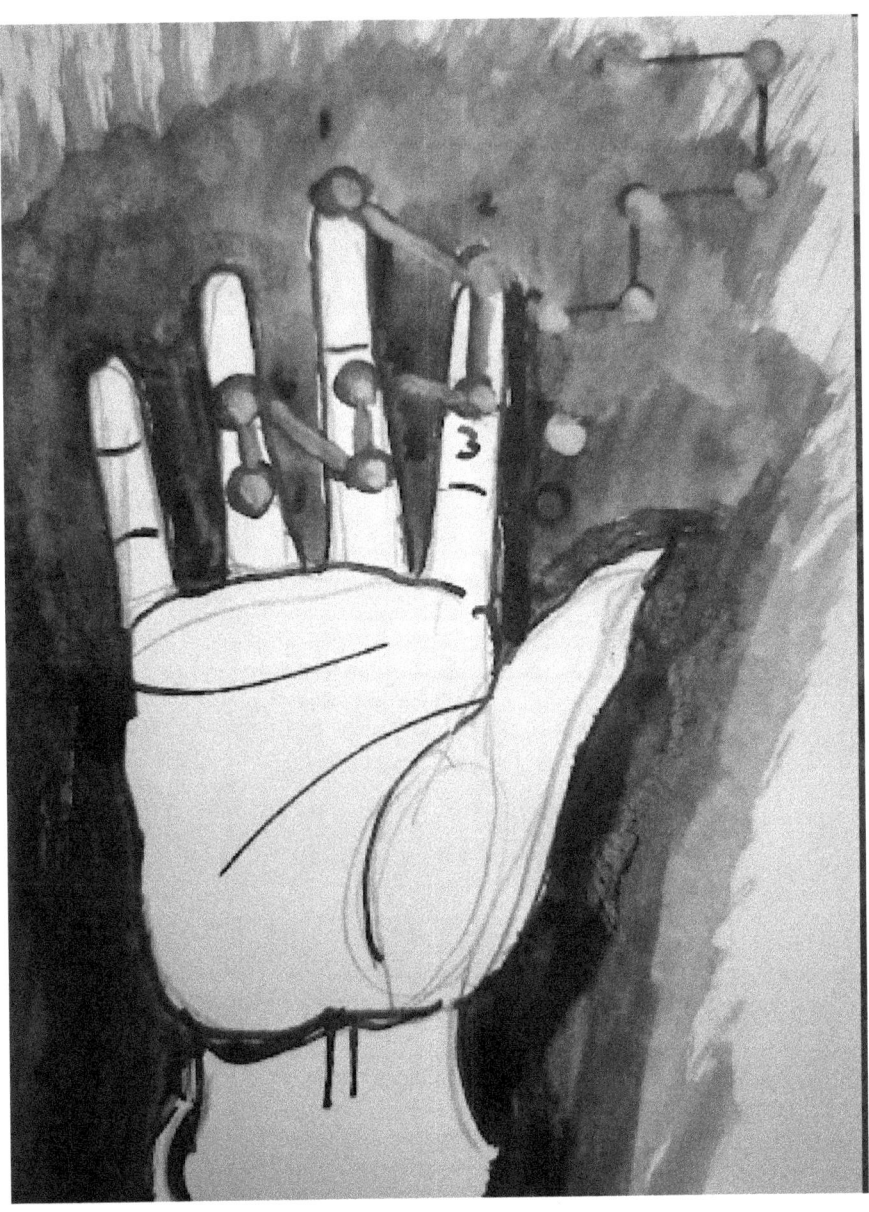

The Big Dipper Pattern used to consecrate the Sword for use

Part III
Ritual and Spellwork

27. Basic Spell Work 1

With all the basic energy and internal work, the student is now ready to engage in basic spell creation.

For our first spell we are going to use a basic BaGua Protection talisman.

The Bagua will be well known to you as it is the central holy symbol of Taoist magic. The history of the Bagua was given earlier in the introduction volume.

In your learning how to construct a simple bagua talisman you will learn the basic procedures of how to construct a talisman according to Taoist magical principles.

Paper talismans are the most visible and obvious manifestation of the magical intention. Some readers may have seen them on tv shows or movies or even in your local Chinatown or a temple you have visited. Yet, most talismans you will see are from orthodox schools and will have not quite the same function as those of Maoshan, nor the same working procedure and so on.

Maoshan talismans are, if properly constructed, extremely powerful.

Many students also confuse the magic with the talisman itself. One student complained that "But all Taoist magic is are loads of talismans!"

At this comment I chuckled to myself. It isn't as easy as simply drawing some signs on paper. There is a whole process behind each and every of the few thousand talismans used in Maoshan magic. While most people see the outcome, a simple paper talisman, what they do not see is the magical process and inner work that goes into it, nor do they understand the supernatural processes that go into making each talisman.

So, I would recommend the student begins the talisman making art some 3 to 6 months after beginning the Golden Light practice. Without at minimum, the gathering of energies to hold some magical capability, talisman making will be a useless pursuit.

So what is a talisman? In Maoshan teaching, a talisman or FU is a relationship, connection and communication between Heaven and Earth.

No one can be quite sure when the first talismans appeared in China, but scholars in China generally plump for the Xia Dynasty (2070-1600 BC) with increasingly complex development in the Shang and Zhou dynasties.

There are a number of considerations the student needs to make before constructing talismans, some of these points include:

Zhi.

Fingers or mudras as they are called in Sanskrit (see chapter 36 for mudras). Certain hand signs or hand seals are used in conjunction with talismans.

ZHOU.

Spells, the spoken word that encapsulates the intention of the operator.

FU.

The talisman itself.

BU.

the steps, or Bu Gang, the step or pace in time and space used to invoke the powers.

RI.

Time. Understanding the correct times for constructing talismans. The Taoist magician needs to be well versed in the knowledge of time and space. For Daoist magicians this is indicated by the Chinese Lunar Calendar and the combinations of the Heavenly Stems and Earthly

Branches in a cycle based on the number 60. As well as lunar phases and solar considerations. The Taoist magician can know for example a Noble Day (Guiren Ri) is good for money and career and a Sanhe or Three Harmonious Day is good for marriage, partnerships and romance as well as healing.

Some days it is forbidden to make talismans such as Clash Days.

The student will learn these step by step.

The Four Treasures Of The Scholar

The Four Treasures are well known to all Chinese and are iconic in representing the revered essence of the scholar. It is in fact still a common practice to give as a gift a boxed set of the Four Treasures to friends or even business acquaintances

The Four Treasures are

1. Pen.

Though translated as pen it is in fact a very fine brush.

2. Paper

Paper of course originated in China and truly is a great treasure. Generally the paper used for Chinese talismans is made of rice or straw, sometimes with added herbs and mostly dyed a particularly bright yellow known as Imperial Yellow, which is the most common colour for the majority of talismans. Yellow as a colour is associated with Chinese royalty and hence was deemed suitable as the main colour for royal commands and edicts, which, in essence, is what some talismans are.

3. Ink

Ink is another famous product of China. Recipes for the finest inks are closely guarded secrets in families who have held the best recipes. Some inks include medical herbs.

The best inks are believed to be made in Anhui.

In practical terms you shouldn't be cheap in your choice of ink. Keep away from cheap ink or ready made bottles except for practice.

Real talismans should use fine quality ink. Ink is produced in sticks, some of which have beautiful designs.

Generally the Taoist will have two kinds of ink, red and black. Occasionally white will be needed and silver and gold. However the red and black are the two most important.

The black ink is usually sold in sticks and made from refined pine soot, herbs and gums. The red ink is usually made from cinnabar. Cinnabar of course should be treated cautiously as it contains poisonous mercury. Another ink, golden in colour, is made with the equally toxic realgar.

4. Ink Stone.

The inkstone is a special piece of stone, often in a rectangular or oval shape. Usually the Daoist magician will use a tiny spoon to scoop water into the inkstone. The ink stick is then pressed on the stone and grinding begins in small circles. Tiny particles of ink fall into the little pool of water and ink is produced. This grinding process is very important in itself as during this time spells and incantations are said to empower the ink.

Without these tools, the production of talismans is quite difficult, though it has been known that in a pinch, an adept can use any paper and any pen in an emergency situation.

To write talismans therefore, the first step is to acquire and, to borrow a western magical term, consecrate your tools of art.

The first thing you must consecrate are the pens. One pen is not enough. You should have at least two such pens. However most Taoist magicians have at least twenty to thirty, some of which are not yet consecrated and remain in storage, and some are used for practice only.

NEVER PRACTICE WITH A CONSECRATED PEN !!!!

Now, you will need two basic pens for the Art. One is used for red ink and is associated with the South.

The other is for the black ink and is associated with the North.

The red pen will be stored and wrapped in red cloth and the black pen will be wrapped and stored in…..yes you guessed it … black cloth.

Before you purify and consecrate a pen, make sure you are clean and pure yourself. And furthermore choose a good day to buy the pens and to consecrate them.

There are a few Pen Consecration Spells, but this one is not only effective, but simple:

> Heaven is calm and Earth is Spirit,
> The Sun and Moon Travel Together,
> The Pen is connected to the ten thousand spirits,
> The Pen uses magical power given by the Warriors!
> JI JI RU LULING!!!!

Generally we will need to consecrate a pen over a period of seven days and ideally three times a day, though once a day is acceptable, but in which case it is better to extend the period to 21 days.

You will breathe on the tip of the brush, holding the pen in your left hand and commanding it with the sword finger and stamping the right foot on the ground.

Or you can place the pen on your altar and use the left thunder and right sword hand seal over the pen and chant the spell above or this following one:

I receive here the Five Thunder Gods who shall assist me,
The Upper Lords restrain the ghosts,
Subduing the evils that lie below,
Saving life, and all fate aids me in living long in the Dao!
JI JI RU LU LING!!

Then wrap the pen in the correct colour cloth. Repeat as according to the instructions above.

After seven or twenty one days the pen will be ready for use. Do not use them for anything else, even for practicing drawing talismans.

Some Rules On Talismans

1. Talismans should be made on auspicious days. Do not make them on inauspicious days. The absolute best time is at the Dragon Boat Festival on the 5th Day of the Fifth Lunar Month. Each year has 4 days when you cannot make talismans or there will be ill fortune.

    The 9th day of the 3rd Moon.
    The 2nd day of the 2nd Moon.
    The 6th day of the 9th Moon.
    The 2nd day of the 12th Moon.

2. The best hour or Shichen is Zishi (11pm to 1am) and Haishi (9pm to 11pm). Zishi is the best hour because the Yin and Yang energies are changing, Yang is waning and Yin is waxing a state known as 'Yin and Yang exchanging Heaven and Earth'.

3. It is wise to factor in personal considerations such as Tai Sui Xing Jun, that is, your relationship with the great Star Monarch of the Year. For example those born in the year of a particular Tai Sui Xing Jun will be safe or afflicted according to their birth year.

4. You cannot make marks on a talisman or they will be ineffectual.

5. You cannot imbibe alcohol or eat garlic, duck, eel or frog.

6. According to the hour of birth, when constructing talismans certain hours are not ideal: Those born at the Zi hour should not make talismans at Wu hour.
   Hai, Mao and Wei should not use Wu.
   Wu cannot use Chou.
   Si, You and Chu cannot use Chen.
   Shen, Zi and Chen cannot use Wei.

7. Before drawing you should brush your teeth and rinse the mouth, shower, bathe or at minimum wash the face and hands. Sit for a while, in a quiet atmosphere without distractions. Meditate on the Gods, Immortals and Buddhas who will assist you.

8. When drawing talismans write with confidence and power. Write the whole talisman in one sitting.

9. Before drawing a Fu talisman, face the East and draw in Qi by conscious breathing.

10. If you are just practicing drawing talismans make a declaration that is your intention to avoid accidentally creating a powerful talisman:

    I Disciple xxxx am only practicing drawing this Fu,
    Spirits, Gods, Buddhas do not come!!
    Do not listen!

11. When you have finished drawing a talisman, even a practice one, DO NOT throw it in the trash. Burn it sandwiched between two pieces of gold money. (See the chapter tools of the trade)

12. Different colour papers are used for different kinds of talismans. RED PAPER. Money, luck and fortune.

YELLOW PAPER. Protection, kill evil, peace, protection of an unborn child, peace and calm.
ULTRAMARINE. Collecting debts, vengeance and attacking.
BLACK. Protection, especially against fires as black is the colour of the element of water.

13. Before drawing, use the tip of the pen to tap the paper three times from bottom to top.

When you have finished drawing the talisman use the tip of the pen to tap the talisman from top to bottom.

Talisman Structure

The talisman structure or Jiegou. We can look at the structure of a talisman in a number of ways. The first method is by visually and practically dividing into three sections. (see diagram).

A. Tou. Talisman head

B. Shen. Talisman body.

C. Talisman Gallbladder or FUDAN.

The futou or talisman head will often give you a clue to the stream, branch or school from which the talisman comes from, though not always.

Also on the head will be the Zhu Shen or the Host God.

The Host God is the main source of power for the talisman. The most popular being the Jade Emperor or the Mysterious Girl of the Ninth Heaven. In our own tradition you will often see the Maoshan Patriarch in that position.

The body of the talisman usually contains the main spell itself and sometimes the name and birthdate of the subject.

The final part is the Fudan or Gallbladder. This seals the talisman as will be explained in more detail later.

It is no accident that the talisman parts are named for the parts of

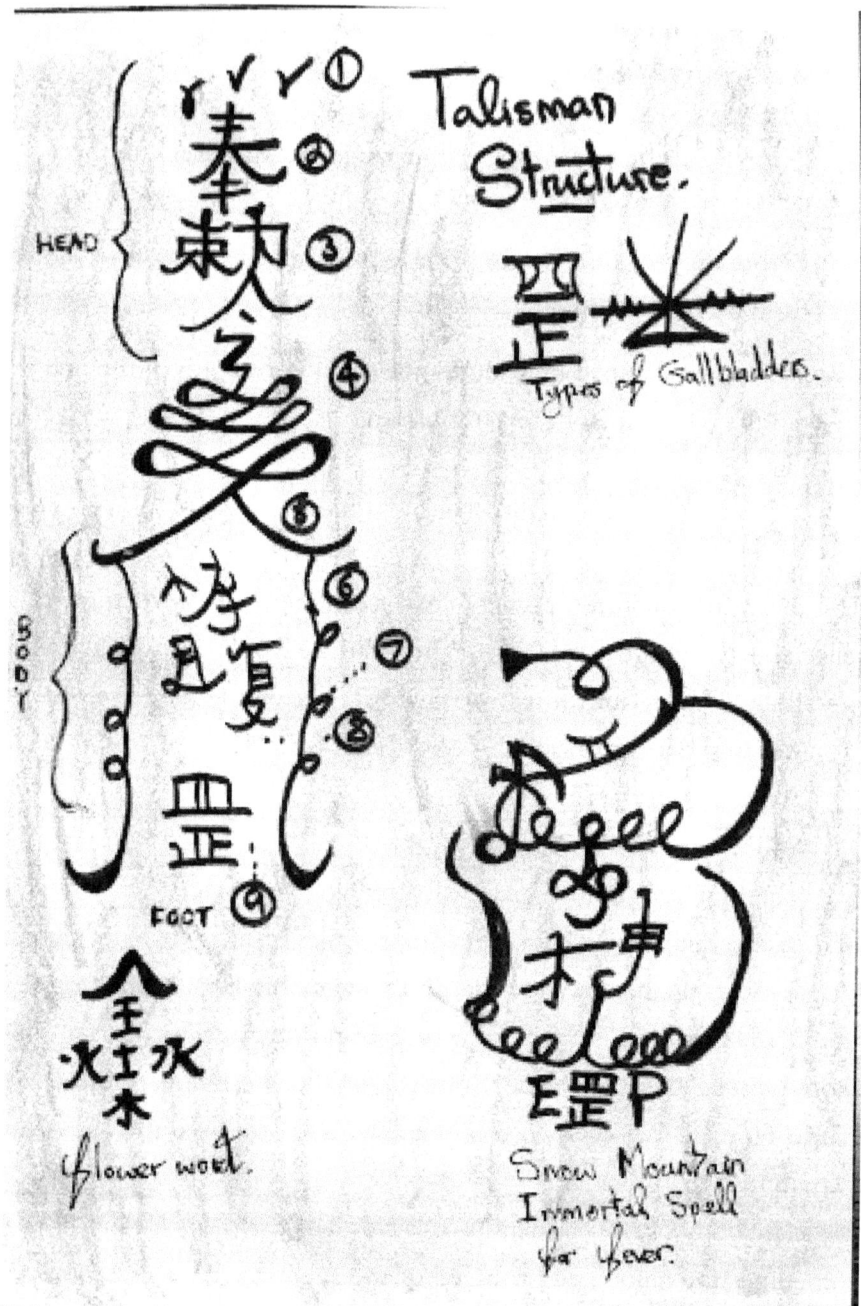

Talisman Structure

the body. In Daoist magical theory the talisman is a living being, an embodiment of the will of the Three Powers of Heaven, Earth and Man. In Chinese thought, the gallbladder is the source of strength and courage and a source of power. The magician will draw a special Fu Dan symbol on completion of the talisman to activate and complete the talisman. The Chinese Masters also explain that the Fudan Seal or sigil will lock in the power as well as preventing the power from leaking from the talisman as a whole.

Talismans also have certain features which are shown in the following diagrams. Not all talismans have every feature it should be noted.

The Key to Talismanic Structure

1. Three Stars of the Three Pure Ones.
2. Feng. Command of the Host God, Immortal or Spirit.
3. Chi Ling. The Command character.
4. Immortal Rope or Rope of Law.
5. Heaven's Beam.
6. Earth Pillar.
7. Fire Star or Coin.
8. The written purpose of the spell.
9. The Talismanic Gallbladder or Fudan.

In the above diagram you can also see the Flower Word or Hua Zi. This is like a small fortifying spell that consolidates the power of the spell. The Flower Word shown in the diagram relates to the Five

Elements, a common use being for spells of health and medicine.

The Flower Word is usually written over the Fudan, one character superimposed on the other so eventually it often looks like a blot of dark ink without discernible characters.

The diagram also shows another form of seal talisman, in this case the Snow Mountain Talisman for curing fever and lowering the bodily temperature of the patient.

We will now discuss the individual elements of the talisman.

1. The Three Stars Of The Pure Ones

The three stars were originally just three points but over time have come to resemble ticks or checks because of the nature of the Chinese brush pen. When finishing the point a quick upward and oblique finishing stroke gives rise to the tick like mark.

There are in fact three major forms of the three stars whose meaning differs according to the function of the talisman.

In the most common form, the three ticks are the first thing drawn on the talisman and are used to draw on the most abstract hidden forces known to Taoism, the trinity of the sublime Pure Ones that were the initiators of creation and the evolution of the spiritual path of Nature and mankind.

The order of operation is thus. With the pen loaded with ink at the ready and one hand in the Sword Mudra (see chapter 36 for Mudras), and visualising the bright white or golden light in which the three Pure Ones are seated. Make the first point quickly and without hesitation, finishing with an upward flourish angled to the upper right, he invokes:

One Stroke and the world is shaken!

He or she then makes the second stroke:

The second stroke and the Ancestral Sword strikes!

Finally make the third point and utter:

The third stroke and the evil ghosts flee a thousand miles!

This form of the Three Stars is known in Chinese as

SAN TIANZUN SANQING FUTOU.

The Three Revered Holy Ones Talisman Head.

See A. in the diagram.

The second form of the Three Stars is nearly always under the Command Character or Chi Ling (see the following section) and is said to refer to the San Jiangjun, the Three Generals of Thunder, Fire and Wind, or Lei, Huo and Feng.

The order of the writing is the same but the invocation will differ. With each stroke recite the Chinese names of Thunder, Fire and Wind in that order. As you do so you must visualise and feel each of the elements in question. Naturally the sharp magician will quickly realise that they refer to three of the Trigrams of the Bagua ... Zhen (Thunder), Li (Fire) and Xun (Wind). These are the so-called Three Mobile Powers of Nature symbolised by the Three Yang Generals. This form is used in more forceful spells that require gathering more elemental power.

These, as previously stated, are always drawn under the character of command.

See B in the diagram.

The final form of the Three Stars or Three Points are those of The Three Officials (San Guan), sometimes called the Three Kings or the Three Powers. This form is called the SAN TAI. Again they are always drawn under the Chi Ling.

In Daoist theology the Three Officials are very high deities directly under the Jade Emperor and are responsible for translating his commands into reality in the universe.

They are:

Tian Guan The Official of Heaven

Di Guan, The Official of Earth.

Shui Guan, The Official of Water.

They can be assigned to the trigrams

Qian, Kun and Kan respectively.

The spell to write these is:

On the first stroke: SAN TAI CREATES ME!

On the second stroke say: SAN TAI NOURISHES ME!

On the third stroke; SAN TAI PROTECTS ME!

2. The Command Character

The command character is known as Chi Ling. In ancient times it could refer to both a mandate from heaven or his representative on Earth, the Emperor who was meant to have been a kind of go-between transmitting the will of Heaven to Earth. Or it could refer to the command of a general or commander to his troops in battle.

In Daoist magick, the sorcerer or fangshi is himself the medium between Heaven and Earth who issues an order, usually on behalf of a host deity, immortal or spirit. The Chi Ling is composed of three characters which are often blended together or stylised in the talisman

Ⓐ ① ...... TAI QING TAISHANG LAOJUN
   ② ...... ③ LINGBAO TIANZUN.
   ...... YUANSHI TIANZUN

Ⓑ ② ① ③ = SAN JIANG-JUN

Ⓒ ② ① ③ = SAN TAI.

The three major forms of San Dian or San Xing

Practical Chinese Magic 215

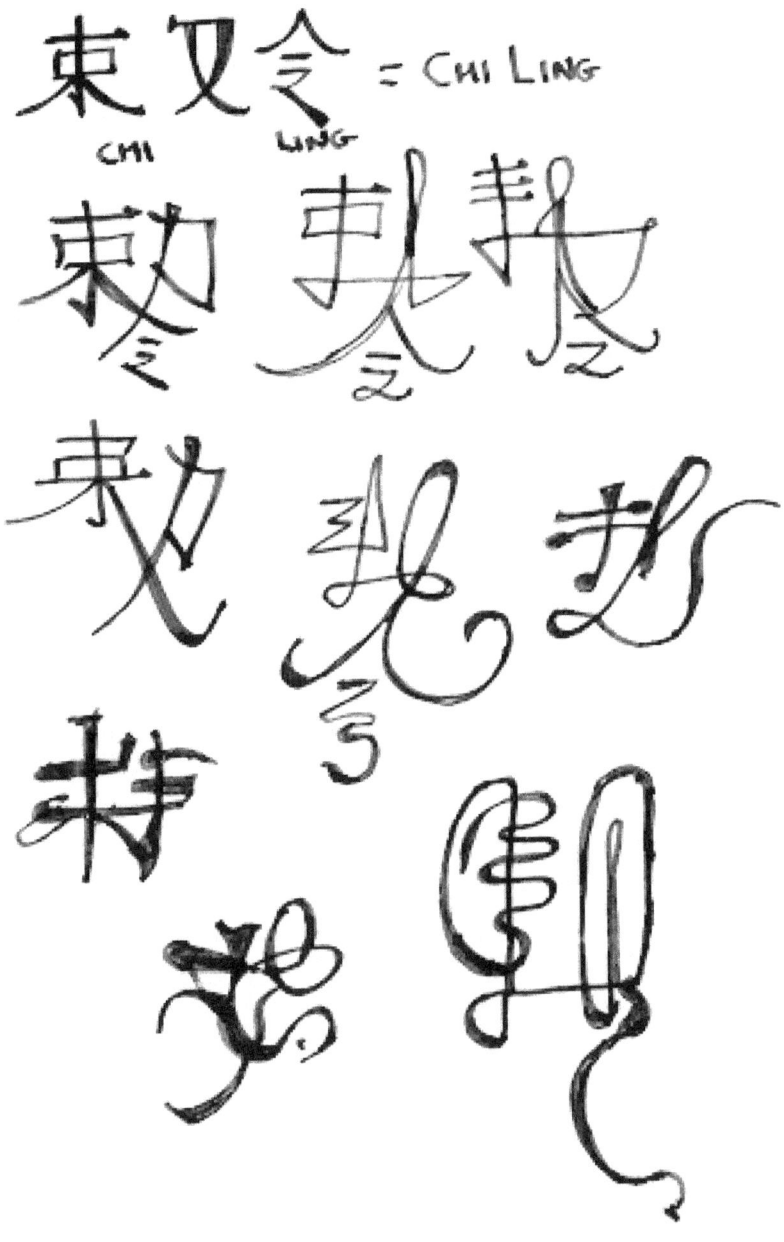

Different forms of the Chi Ling Character.

head (fu tou).

The Ling part of the character, the part that to westerners looks like a triangular roof with a kind of 'z' character is often incorporated into the framework of the talisman itself, usually on the horizontal Heaven's Pillar so as to encompass the spell in the spirit of absolute command.

For this reason, in drawing the Chi Ling there must be absolutely no doubt or hesitation in its creation. Firm and confident strokes with eyes blazing with the fire of absolute and confident will.

Before committing the brush pen you invoke:

O the Sphere of Heaven decrees by the Nine Chapters,

Today I write and the ten thousand ghosts cower.

Ji ji ru lu ling!!!

The Nine Chapters referred to here are of course the nine sections of the DaodeJing. In causing 'ghosts' to flee we can interpret this as banishing all interior and exterior obstacles and doubts to the spell work at hand. See the diagram for different forms of the chi ling.

3. The 'Feng' Character

Another component of the FuTou is the Feng character which in essence activates and opens the character by inviting a God, Goddess, Immortal or a Master of a school. In Maoshan we might for example invoke the Root Master of our school, Maoshan Fa Zhu for example.

In drawing it, we simply have to call the name we are invoking as we mentally communicate and connect with the deity or Master in question. For example we say FENG JIU TIAN XUAN NU NIANG

Practical Chinese Magic ᓚ 217

Forms and usage of the Feng or Invitation Character.

NIANG if we invite the Mysterious Girl of the Ninth Heaven to empower our work.

4. Fu Shen

The Fu Shen or talisman body will contain the actual spell. This can include the spell intention and even names and birth dates of the target of the spell, extra empowering characters or sigils and even drawings of relevant objects like celestial objects, animals, deities and spirits. These spells are most often written vertically from top to bottom. Obviously in writing the spell, the intention is held one pointedly in the mind without any distractions.

5. Immortal Ropes, Fairy Ropes, Law Ropes

In some talismans you will see twisting coils often forming stacks of loops. These quite often are at the top of the talisman and their function is a little like electronic wire, transmitting and intensifying the power of the spiritual entity invoked and guiding it into the body of the spell intention. In Taoist thought, Qi travels in curves, in sinuous lines like a coiling dragon. Thus in drawing fairy ropes this intention of leading energy must be held foremost in mind. There is a purpose behind them. You may notice the coils have odd numbers of loops such as 3, 7 or 9, though occasionally there may be 8, 10 or 12 to represent other factors such as the Bagua, the Ten Heavenly Stems or Twelve Earthly Branches, though this is far rarer in practice. The invocations used in drawing are the same as for the Fire stars given below.

Fairy Ropes are always drawn from top to bottom. Take note of the direction. Is it beginning left (yang) or right (yin)?

6. Fire Stars Or Coins

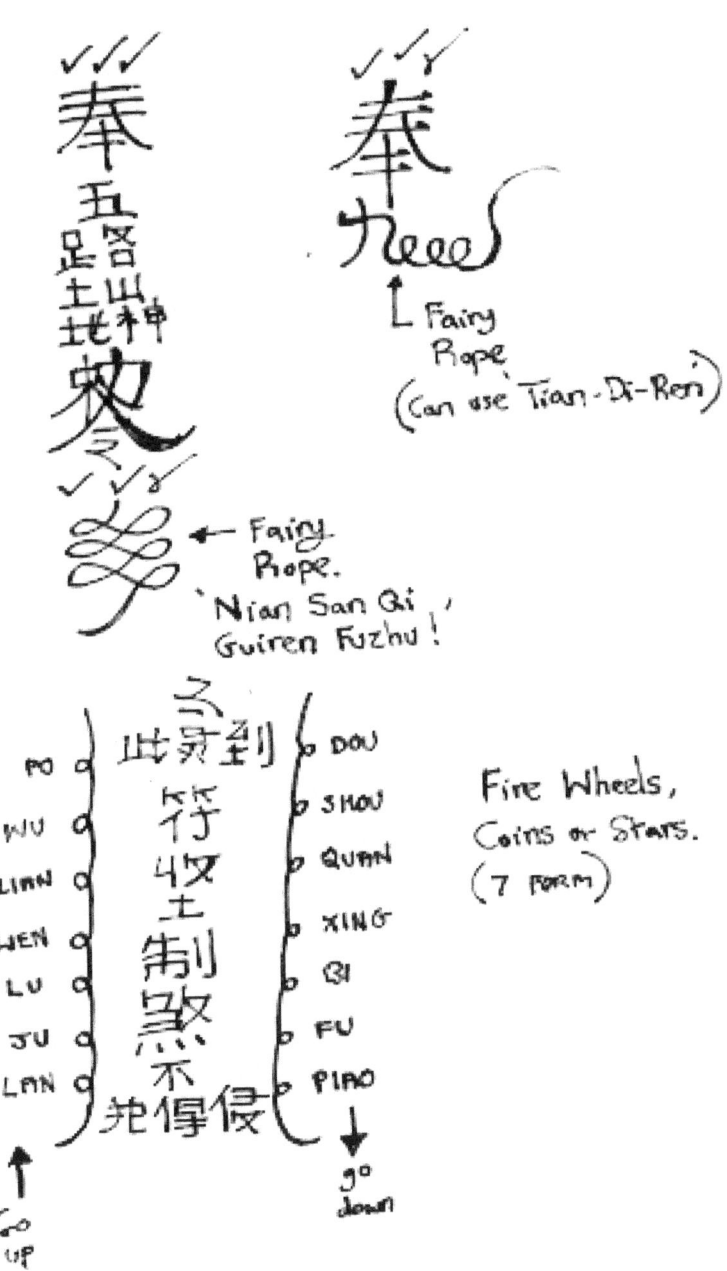

The seven stars of the Big Dipper plus the left and right 'dark stars'.

In drawing the Earthly Pillars one may see little loops or circles incorporated into the design. These are not just for decoration but have a definite meaning and purpose and even their own little spells and procedures.

In drawing a talisman you should count the loops. Again they will be an odd number such as 3, 5, 7 or 9.

For 3 loops or 3 fire stars: Use the Spell of the Three Officials or San Guan or the Three Powers Heaven, Earth and Man.

If for Three Stars , the left is invoked UPWARDS thus:

TIAN, DI, REN !! (HEAVEN, EARTH, MAN)

The right is invoked downwards:

RI, YUE, XING!! (SUN, MOON, STARS).

For five loops invoke the Five Elements:

JIN MU SHUI HUO TU!!

(METAL, WOOD, WATER, FIRE, EARTH!!)

For five fire stars on left and right sides:

Left, going upwards:

QIAN YUAN HENG LI ZHEN!!

And right going downwards:

JIN MU SHUI HUO TU!!

For seven loops invoke the mantric names of the Seven Stars of the Big Dipper:

DOU SHOU QUAN XING BI PU PIAO!!

For seven fire circles, left and right:

Going upwards on the left the names of the Stars:

LAN, JU, LU, WEN, LIAN, WU, PO!!

Going downwards on the right:

DOU, SHOU, QUAN, XING, BI, FU, PIAO!!

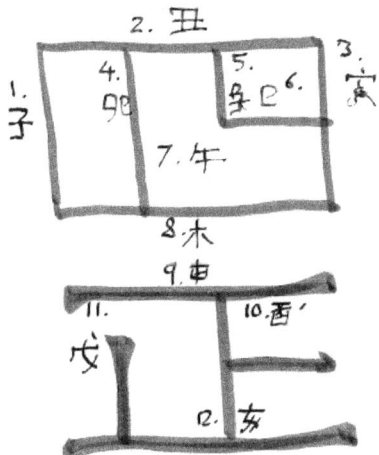

Liu Jia: 子, 寅, 辰, 午, 申, 戌
Liu Ding: 丑, 卯, 巳, 未, 酉, 亥

The above diagrams show two methods of drawing the Gang symbol. Either is good. The important thing is to get twelve strokes and name the Twelve Branches in order

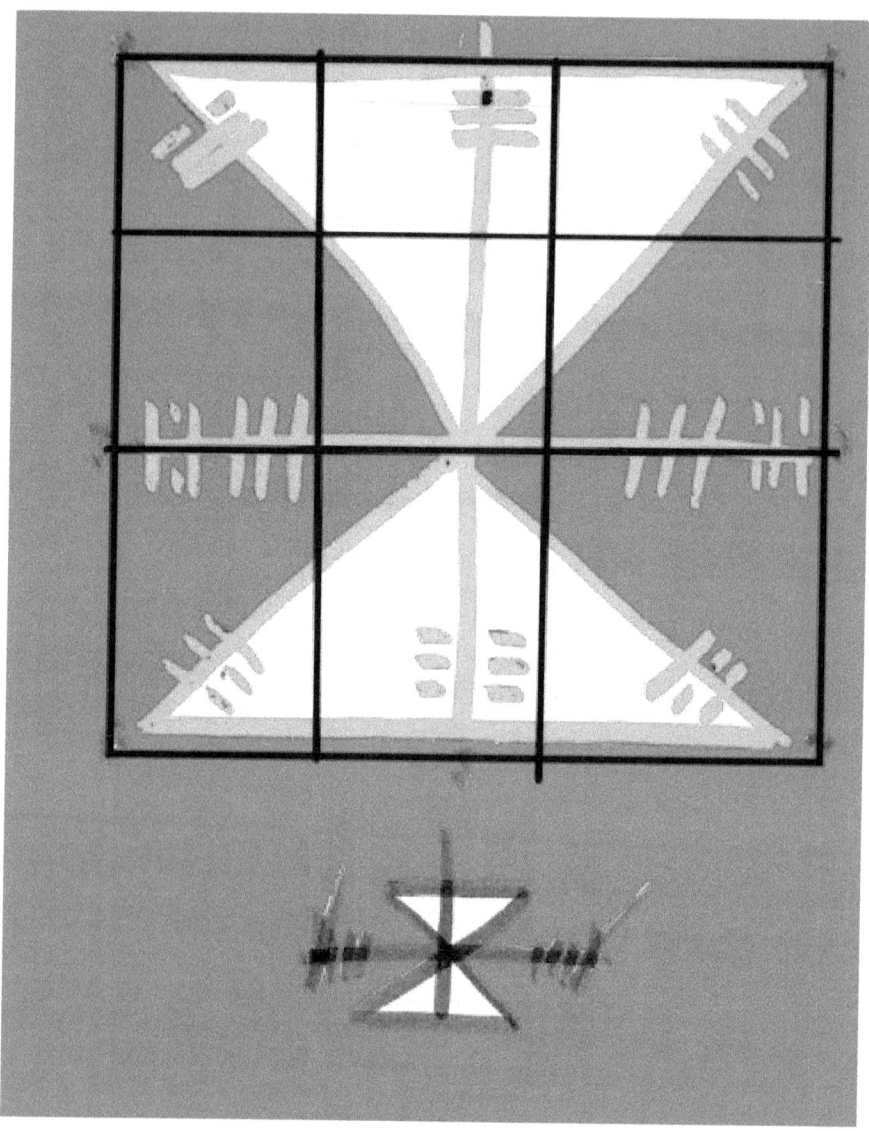

Fudan showing the derivation from the Pre Heaven Bagua and the Nine Palaces of the Yellow River Diagram. Among other purposes it can also be used to empower Bagua Mirrors as well as talismans

For 9 loops or 9 fire stars for the stars it will be going up on the left.
YI BAI, ER HAI, SAN BI, SI LU,
WU HUANG, LIU BAI, QI CHI, BA BAI, JIU ZI!!
(First White, Second Black, Third jade green, Fourth Green,
Fifth Yellow, Sixth White, Seventh red, Eight White, Ninth Purple!!)
NOTE: Colours of the Nine Palaces in Chinese Cosmology.
Going down on the right:
LAN, JU, LU, WEN, LIAN, WU, PO, ZUO FU, YOU BI!!

7. The Talismanic Gallbladder

The final part of the talisman is set right at the foot or jiao of the talisman. When everything else has been completed the gallbladder or FUDAN is drawn. This will empower the talisman and seal it. It will guard it from exterior influences getting in and power leaking out.

There are many fudan designs that can be used for different purposes. Generally, at least in the Maoshan and Lushan schools of magic there are two basic forms. The crossed triangle and the Gang (Strength) symbol).

Let us deal with the Gang symbol first. Gang literally means 'to be strong' or 'strength'. The Gang symbol represents the Twelve Earthly Branches of Chinese cosmology and is drawn with 12 strokes as you name the twelve branches out loud to invoke their power. Those who in know that these also represent those occult powers known as the Twelve Generals composed of the Liu Jia and Liu Ding.

Gang is also a sly reference to the Commanding General of the Big Dipper. Nothing in Taoist Magic is quite what it seems.

In the diagram shown below the Gang symbol is drawn, the box shape drawn first, then the sorcerer completes the Gang with the lower symbol.. With each stroke he names the Twelve Earthly Branches.

ZI, CHOU, YIN, MAO, CHEN, SI,
WU, WEI, SHEN, YOU, XU, HAI!!
Another spell for empowering the Gang Fudan is a s follows:
Open The Heavenly Gates,
Slay The Ghost Road,
Open The Underworld,
Kill The Ghost Soldier!!

The above diagrams show two methods of drawing the Gang symbol. Either is good. The important thing is to get twelve strokes and name the Twelve Branches in order

The second major type of Fudan is the triangle, usually with a horizontal and vertical slash. This is a more complex design than the Gang and has a number of variations which are used for different purposes. Some are for specific kinds of spells, for example there are triangle fudan designed for invoking ghost warriors, some are for yang magic and some for yin magic.

The design is really an occult rendering of the Ba Gua as rendered onto a Nine Palace Square.

There are several ways to draw and empower this style of Fudan which we shall have a look at now.

Remember however, that this is the last part of the talisman that you draw, apart from, sometimes, if you need to add flower words, Hua zi.

A popular and reliable method is to draw the whole double triangle in one stroke beginning at the top left saying:

THE ARMY OF HEAVEN AND EARTH IS RIGHTEOUS!

Then from left to right draw the horizontal slash saying:

ONE HORIZONTAL STROKE

AND THE DIVINE SWORDS ASSEMBLE!

Draw the vertical stroke and say:

ONE VERTICAL STROKE

AND THE GHOSTS ARE TERRIFIED!

Draw the first slash on the horizontal line on the left side and say:

THE FIRST STROKE OPENS HEAVEN AND EARTH.

Draw a stroke on the right hand side and say:

THE SECOND STROKE,

THE FIVE THUNDER COMMAND!

Add final strokes on the left and right
as shown in the diagram and say:

DIVINE WARRIORS URGENTLY RUSH LIKE FIRE

TO COMPLY WITH THE COMMAND!

Method two is as follows:
Draw the first line, the top of the double triangle:

OPEN THE GATES OF HEAVEN!

Draw the second line going top right and diagonally down to the bottom left:

OPEN THE UNDERWORLD!

Draw the bottom line:

SAVE THE PEOPLE'S GATE!

Draw the final line going from bottom right to top left:

BLOCK THE GHOST PATH!

Draw the vertical line from up to down:

IMPALE THE GHOST HEART!

Draw the horizontal line:

BREAK THE GHOST BELLY!

Draw three small vertical slashes on the left:

METAL, WOOD, WATER!

Draw three slashes on the right :

FIRE AND EARTH!!

There are other methods but these will suffice for most purposes. Other methods will be discussed in future publications with talismans more deeply analysed.

While the standard Fudan as shown above is suitable for most purposes, there are other specialist kinds of Fudan for all kinds of

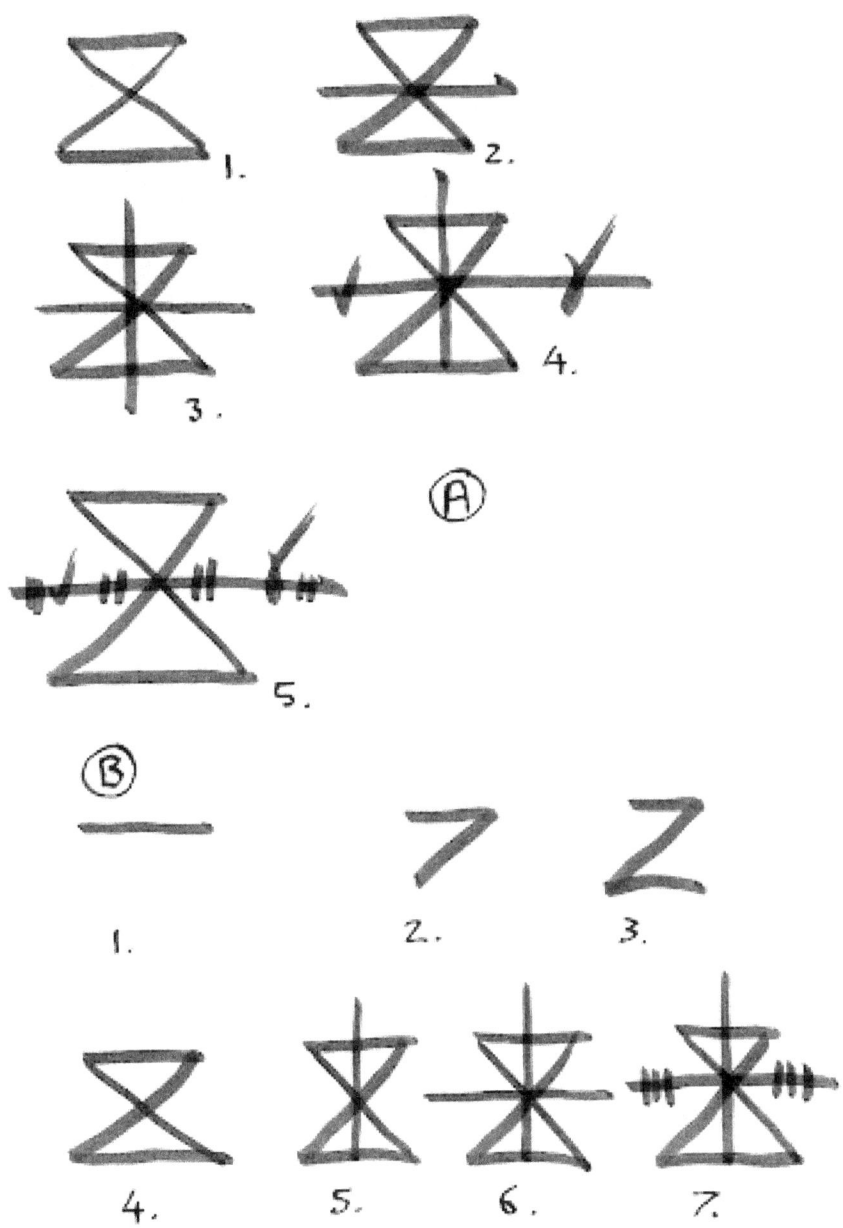

Methods for drawing the Fudan of the double triangle

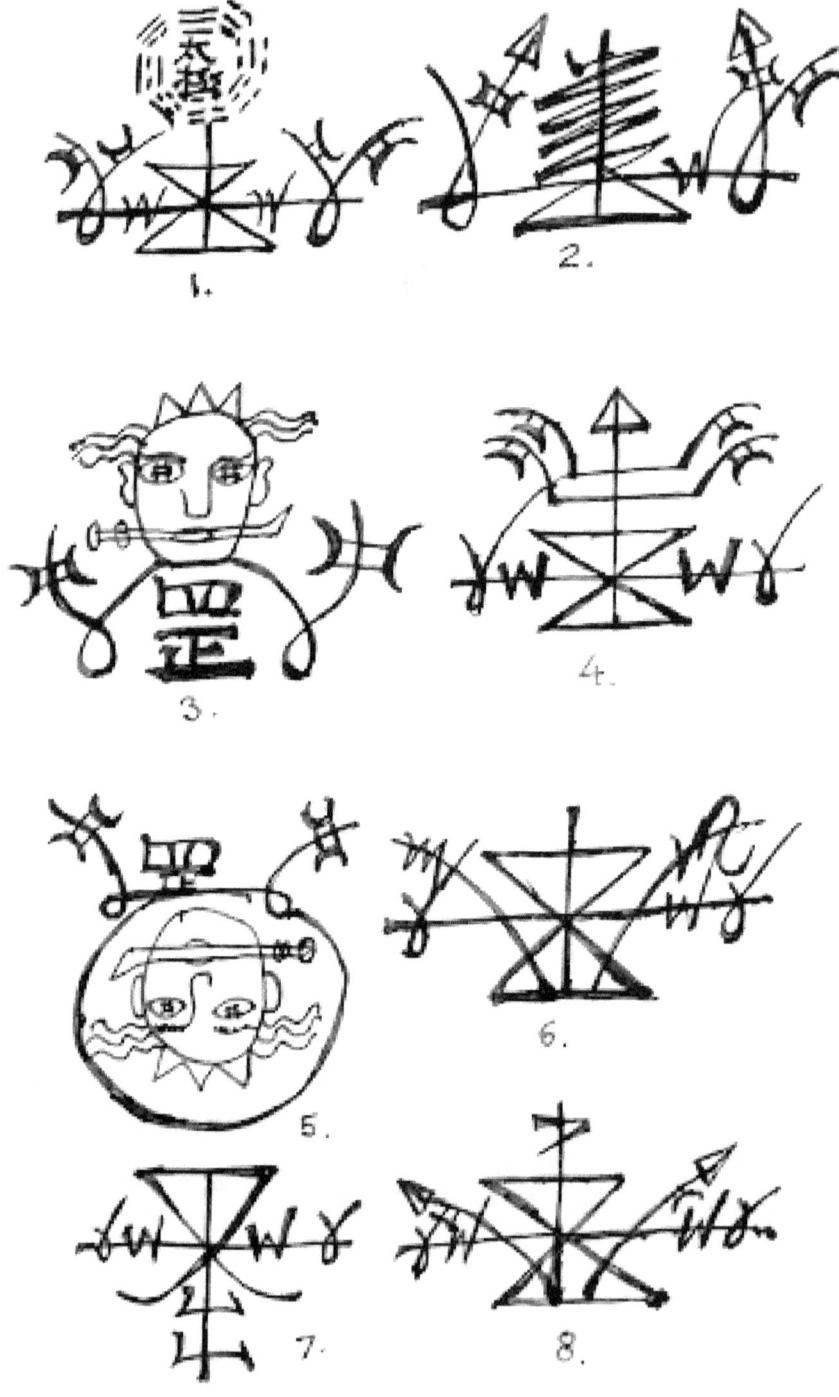

purposes and are in essence magical seals in their own right.

Some of these are shown here:

1. SWORD KILLING FUDAN. Is used for killing evil yin influences which can be a negative environmental qi called yin xie, or evil spirits.

2. SWORD AND SLASHING FUDAN: Like the first it is used for stopping and dissolving yin evil.

3. CHASING SOUL FUDAN: Is used to rid of evil thoughts, whether your own or those of another.

4. CHASING YIN AND EVIL DEMONS FUDAN: Used to get rid of demons.

5. CATCH SOUL FUDAN: Used to place a magical influence on a person.

6. HEHE FUDAN: This is used in love and sex magic and for repairing a failing marriage or relationship.

7. SENDING THE YIN SOLDIERS TO FIGHT FUDAN. Speaks for itself, used to send Yin Spirits to perform a particular task.

8. CUT THE EVIL YIN SPIRITS: For talismans to destroy powerful evil spirits or sorcerers.

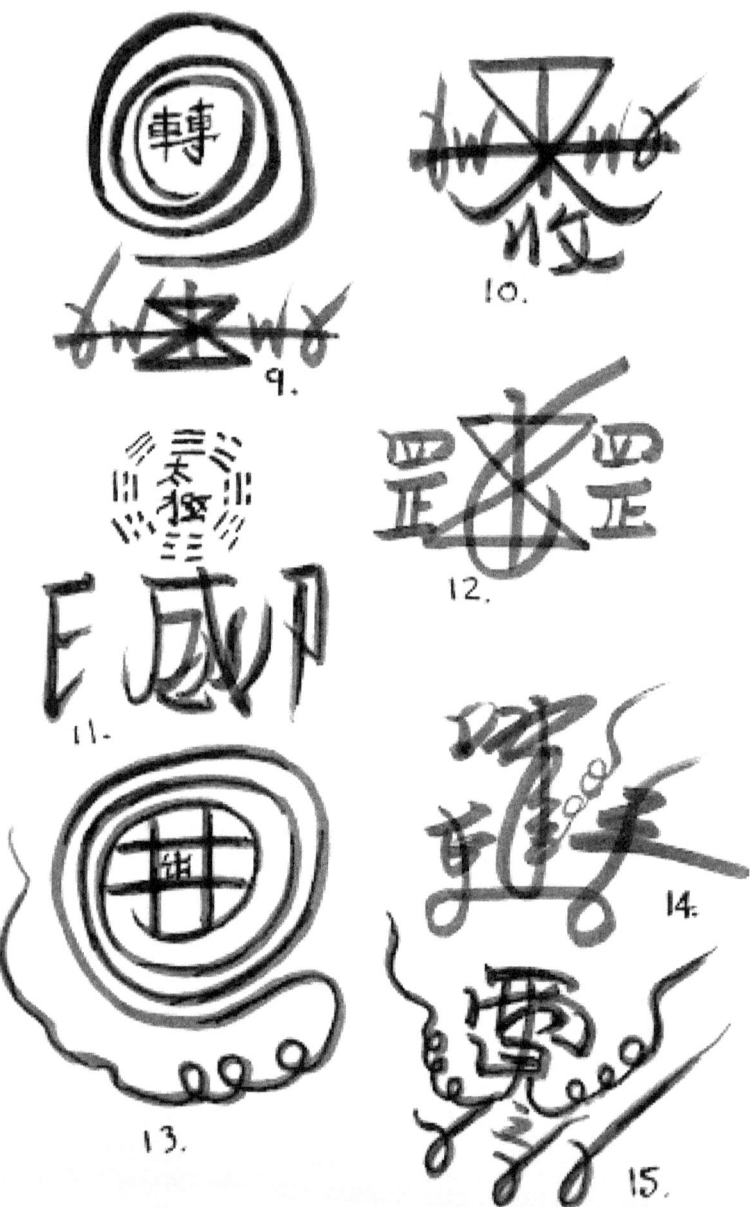

9. CHANGING LUCK FUDAN: Can be used to remove obstacles to one's path of prosperity, to change your luck.

10. CALLING BACK THE DIVINE WARRIORS FUDAN: Used to call and gather astral warriors.

11. BAGUA PROTECTS THE HOME FUDAN: For protection of a home or business premises.

12. RECALL THE SOUL FUDAN: Used in recalling a soul.

13. SENDING THE MAGICAL WARRIOR FUDAN. Sending a magical astral warrior on a specific task.

14. THE PEACE AND PROTECTION OF BUDDHA FUDAN. For the luck and protection of Guanyin or Buddha.

15. THUNDER BLASTS THE DEMONS FUDAN. Calling upon the powers of the Thunder Gods to destroy a demon or evil influence.

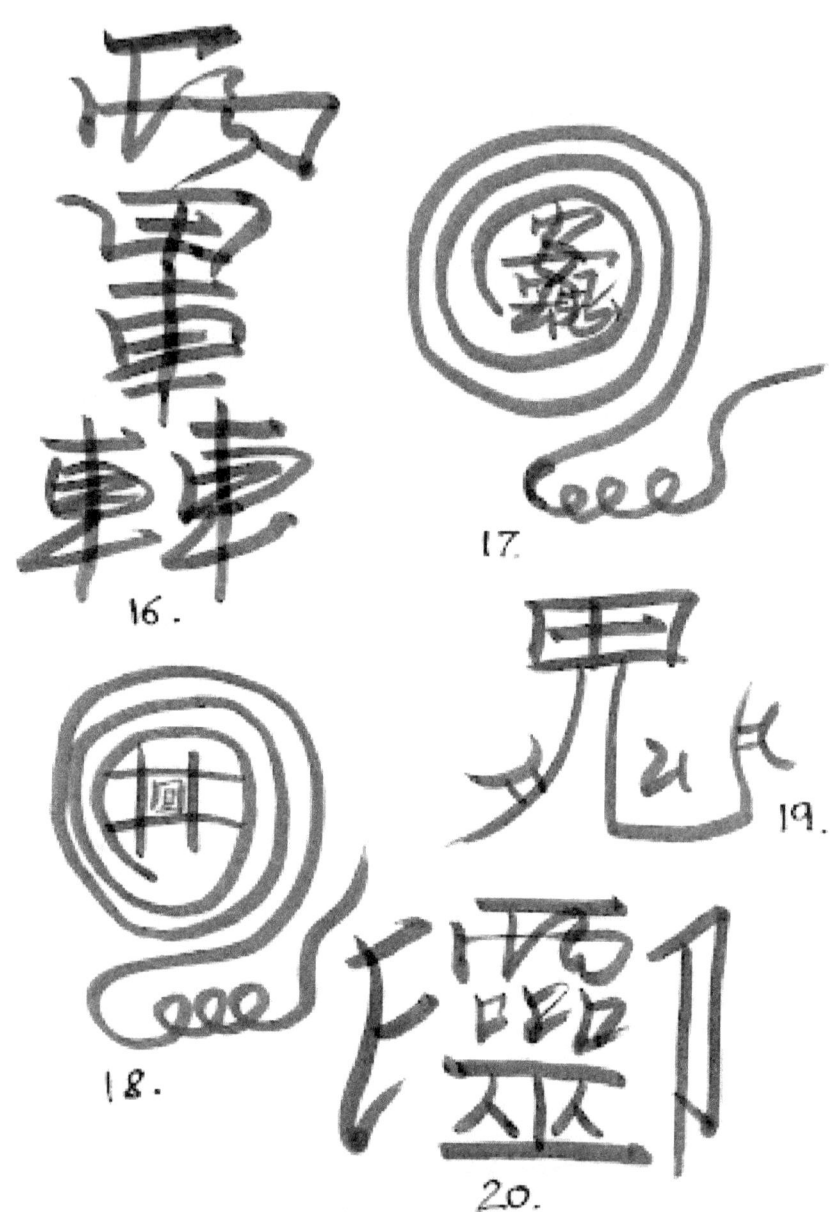

16. FIVE THUNDERS DESTROY EVIL FUDAN: Destroy an evil power by virtue of the Five Thunders magic.

17. SOUL GATHERING AND CALMING FUDAN. Regathers a scattered soul or lost soul fragments and brings calm to nervous and mental conditions.

18. CALLING BACK WARRIORS. Recalling magical warriors.

19. REVEALING AND DRIVING AWAY THE HIDDEN GHOST FUDAN. Speaks for itself.

20. SEND MAGICAL WARRIORS TO DESTROY EVIL SPIRITS. Again the title of this fudan speaks for itself.

Flower Words

Flower Words or Hua Zi is a final spell consisting of words and/or symbols that are superimposed character by character over the fudan. Different spells have different and often unique flower words.

Because the Hua Zi is written, each character on top of each other the end result cannot be read, rather it looks like a blob of ink.

When we write it we can, if we wish, utter the spell under the breath as we write it.

A common one as we noted earlier consists of the Five Elements and is frequently used in healing and medical spells.

If there are flower words to be written in the fudan of the talisman, the normal convention in Daoist spellbooks is to write them next to the talisman, but in practice they should be written on the fudan in the manner mentioned above.

Once completed we need to take further steps to fully empower the talisman. There are a number of ways to do this.

A quick and effective method is to draw the Seal of the Golden

Light over the talisman envisioning the liquid light poured into the talisman.

Another method is to use the sword finger to write Chiling in 'astral' or Qi writing and Ling or Spirit on the base of the talisman.

Nearly always the completed talisman is held over incense and circled through it in three or seven passes. The talisman is then deemed ready for use, whether to be incinerated to ash, carried or pasted on a door or bed.

28. Making Your First Basic Talisman Step By Step

1. Decide possible, three days before, an elected and appropriate day and time on which to draw the talisman.

   On these three preparation days you should observe all the taboos as far as foods and sexual activity are concerned. The sexual fluids should not be spilled. This is not a moral injunction, rather it is about building the magical force. However sexual intercourse without ejaculation and with dual cultivation is fine and may in fact intensify the power.

2. Gather all the materials necessary.

   The pen, ink, water, inkstone and any other materials necessary or unique to the spell.

3. Set up the altar as necessary, with incense, candles and images necessary to the spell. These can vary.

4. Ensure you are using pens properly consecrated as related above.

   Remember to use the correct pen for the correct colour. There is the black pen for general purpose talismans and specifically Yin magic. The Red Pen will use cinnabar ink and is specifically for Yang magic or for Kai Guang, the Ceremony of Opening the Eyes of altar statues and images. The White ink pen is used on black paper or cloth talismans.

5. Even though your pen is consecrated you must still activate it before you immediately use it.

   In this way. Make a powder composed of agarwood, amber and pearl and add to the incense burner.

   Pass the brushes through this incense smoke and utter a spell:

   O the Ancestral Master commands the Magical Pen,

The Immortals command the Magical Pen,

The Jade Maiden saves us with the Magical Pen,

The drop of vermillion, a ray of light banishing evil spirits into darkness.

One stroke and the people thrive in longevity,

On two strokes the magical pen evaporates evil ghosts,

On three, the Gods save us, wealth and prosperity come, the eyes of the God open in light,

JI JI ru Lu Ling!!

Then raise the pen so the brush end is at the height of your third eye and then tilt it so it faces the mouth of the incense burner and write the character JING 淨 (to cleanse or purify) in the centre of the incense burner.

Raise the left sword finger and write on the brush tip the word GUANG 光 (Light or Ray of Light).

The pen is now ready to use.

6. Before drawing the talisman it is wise that the sorcerer sits in meditation for a minimum of twenty minutes.

Let him contemplate the Gods and Buddhas, especially those who are involved or invoked in the operation. Make sincere prayers for success. It is highly recommended you go through the Eight Spells. At minimum use the Cleanse Heart, Mouth, Heart and the Golden Light Spell in its energetic form. For some spells you may need to invoke protection or perform magical concealment.

7. The magician now will need to purify and consecrate the ink, water and paper.

There are a number of methods to do this but we shall keep it simple in this introductory process.

8. Consecrating the Ink (Chi Mo Zhou)

The consecration of the ink differs slightly according to whether you are using normal black ink or cinnabar ink.

For black ink a standard and common spell is thus, with sword finger of the right hand pointing at the ink stick utter:

The Jade Emperor has the power of Divine Command,
The spirit of the form of this ink must obey,
Cloud and Mist, above are the Nine Stars Gods,
When this simple ink comes to be ground,
The Vajra Thunderbolt is issued!!
JI JI RU LU LING!

Cinnabar ink is consecrated in a different manner. You can obtain cinnabar ink in convenient sticks just as for black ink, but many magicians prefer the powder form. If using powder a little is added to Chinese Rice Wine with a starch such as wheat juice and shaken in a small bottle.

Pointing the right sword finger at the cinnabar in whatever form you choose, the spell is:

The White Official Creates,
The Red Official saves,
A point above, Heavenly Warriors come,
A point below, the Five Elements come,
The righteous point, Heaven and Earth,
With two points the ghosts are startled,
With three points the man is victorious.
By the command of Taishang Laojun,
JI JI RU LU LING!

Another spell that can be used is far more involved:

O the Divine Cinnabar originated from the Yang Power,
The Root Master brought to us in his very hand,
Cinnabar frightens demons and evil ghosts,

That which consecrates the eyes, the treasure of the Sages,

O Rise divine treasure that possesses the Divine Spirit,

The Master welcomes us coming with cinnabar concealed in his palms,

QIAN KUN!! The Divine Mirror Comes,

The Stone of the Way does not have the taint of falsehood and is admired by all the Gods,

O worship the Treasure of the Law from ages unto the ages,

And evil is stopped at the Altar and demons are frightened,

Evil is so exorcised!!

By honour of the Maoshan Method Master's command!!

JI JI RU LULING!!

9. CONSECRATING THE INKSTONE (CHI YAN ZHOU}

The inkstone has been previously described in the chapter on the four treasures of the scholar. As with all magical tools it must also be consecrated, again with the Sword or Vajra Mudra: Repeat this spell when you grind the ink.

The Jade Emperor commands the Spirit of the Inkstone,

I invoke the Four Directions and Metal, Wood, Water, Fire and Earth,

The Divine Inkstone will grind,

The Vajra Thunderbolt crackles with electrical radiance!!

JI JI RU LULING!!

10. Consecrating The Water. (Shui Zhou)

Taoist magic recommends that you use water that has never touched the earth as the best water, ire rainwater which you have collected in a bowl at the Hour of Wu.

Second best is water gathered from a mountain stream or a spring. You then make Yin-Yang Water by blending equal parts of hot boiled water and cold water. In fact this may differ according to different spells. Some add more cold or more hot according to whether the spell is more Yin or more Yang. It can be as complex as dividing different temperature waters into five bowls and adding say 2 parts of hot to 3 parts of cold and so on.

The most common spell, pointing with the Sword or Vajra hand seal is this:

> This is not ordinary water, it is a precious water,
> The Northern Ren Gui Water, One drop in the Inkstone,
> Clouds and Rain arrive,
> If the sick shall drink of it they are healed of a hundred sicknesses,
> A hundred ghosts are dissolved by it, exorcising the Evil Ones,
> If the evil should drink of it they are shattered into fragments.
> JI JI RU LULING!!

11. The Consecrate Paper Spell (Chi Zhi Zhou)

The paper is laid flat on the sacred altar or table where you are writing the talisman. Again it is a simple process of holding the correct hand seal, be it the Sword Seal or the Vajra Seal, pointing at the paper and uttering the spell as follows. Note that in all such spells there must be genuine feeling and intent. Study the words of each spell correctly to conjure a vivid mental picture of the imagery implied in the spell.

> O Ye, the Northern Emperor commands it,
> That this paper is for the working of talismans.
> Is banished of all evil ghosts,
> Those who have enough strength to survive shall be cast into the Underworld!
> JI JI RU LU LING!!

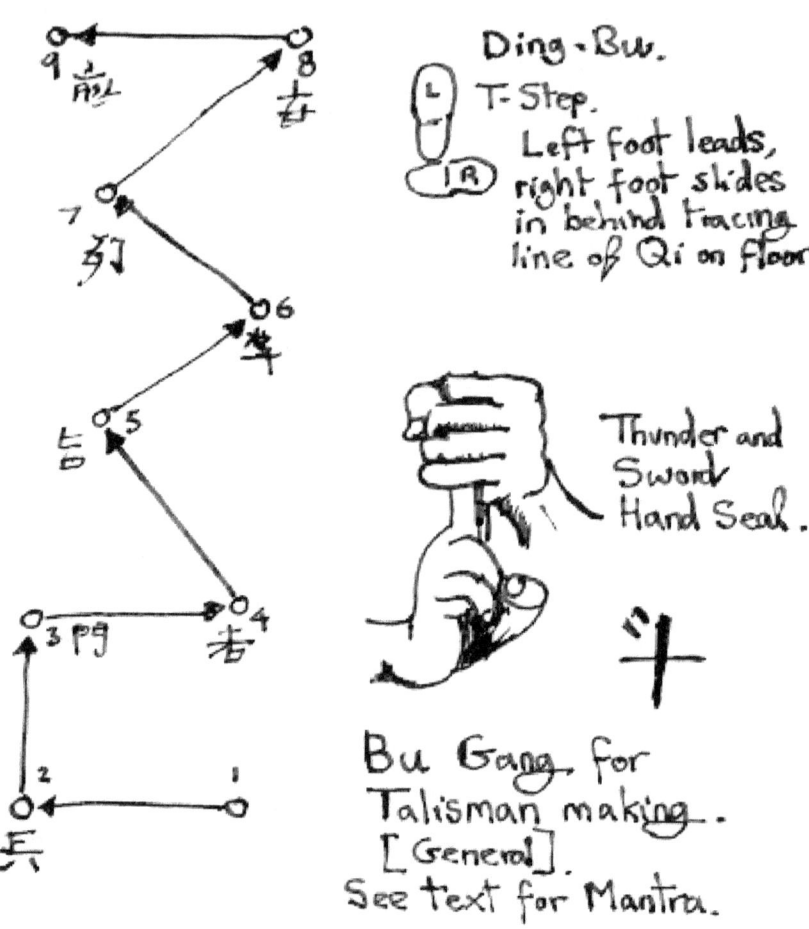

Bu Gang for Talisman

12. Now the magician can leave the altar room and prepare himself with actual physical washing with cold water and incense himself with hemp smoke if he or she wishes.

13. To enter the room he must tread the Big Dipper Step or Bu Gang. He or she should recite the Seven Star Spell and have the right Sword Finger held in the hollow of the left (Thunder) fist.
    I tread on the Seven Stars, Step by Step, Ascending to the Heavens where are the Three Wonders,
    the Sun, the Moon and the Stars,
    Opening Heaven and penetrating the Earth,
    The Ghosts and Gods are startled,
    the Demons seeing me must bow their heads,
    Closer to Heaven I am followed by the Twenty-Eight Stars who are bound to me,
    I request the Mysterious Girl to slay the Evil Ones!!
    JI JI RU LU LING!

    Now you are in the altar chamber or Quiet Room as we call it in Daoist Magic, you can light the incense.

    Three sticks is the normal number, though five, seven or nine may sometimes be used.

14. Before the Altar you should recite one of the many REQUEST GODS INCANTATIONS (QING SHEN ZHOU) to invite the Gods, Immortals and Buddhas to the Altar.
    Choose any of the following according to what
    you feel fits your needs:
    Qing Shen Zhou 1.
    Burning sweet fragrance,
    Heaven and Earth shall assist,
    Open the Kingdom Law,
    The distant Ocean hears,
    The distant mountain where the journey is long

and the road is far,
I request the Six Ding and Six Jia,
To accomplish the House of Treasures and climb the Golden Stairs of the Temple,
Holy symbols in the furnace rise in waves of auspicious smoke,
The clouds of incense pass beyond the Void,
And so I request all the Gods to descend, the Spirit Warriors rushing like fire by this command!

Qing Shen An Zhou. The Secret Spell Of Requesting Gods
This can be used alone or in addition with any Qing Shen Zhou and invokes further power by way of the Thunderbolt.

The Thunderbolt Vajra command is quick,
The Ten Positions and the Three Kingdoms must listen,
The Wheel of the Year turns, the Moon revolves, the Sun is precious, and so as time moves the work is accomplished,
Communicating with the Spiritual Power, Tudi listens.
By command come quickly!!
Quickly descend unto this Altar!!
JI JI RU LU LING!!

Qing Shen Zhu Fu Bing Gan. Requesting The Gods To Assist In Empowering A Talisman.

I the Disciple xxx burn incense and ask you, the Northern Dipper King, the Mysterious Girl of the Ninth Heaven, Taishang Immortal Master and all the Heavenly Gods and Sages, the Ten Directions of the Universe, East and West, South and North, High and Low, the Void, the Omnipresent Nothingness that cannot be reached or comprehended, I invite the Immortals to quickly,quickly descend and arrive here at this altar,the Disciple xxxxx today requests all the Gods and

Buddhas, Ancestors of the Dao, Gods and Spirits to bestow on us your assistance, Let your Disciple xxx make effective magical talismans, the writing of spirit charms, O kind Zhuwei Immortals, Buddhas and Ancestors of Dao, Gods and Sages, the Daoist Law protects and confers blessings, the talismans are powerful, Disciple xxx asks ever and ever again, knocks and requests you!

15. With the end of the pen tap the bottom, centre and top of the talisman three times saying Earth, Man, Heaven.

16. Before the first stroke of the pen, pen held ready and above the paper say:
Heaven is a circle and Earth is a Square,
By the command of the Nine Chapters I today put pen to paper and the ten thousand ghosts flee!
Ji Ji RU LU LING.

17. Write the spell according to the rules of art already noted as far as the three ticks, the Chiling, fairy ropes and fire stars are concerned as well as the fudan and flower words.

All talismans should be completed in one sitting. You cannot start a talisman and not finish it. On completion of the talisman press it with the Sword Finger or Vajra Finger and say:

I honour the Mysterious Girl of the Ninth Heaven,
You are my Empress,
The Big Dipper, the Supreme Immortal Master, the Sword of Heaven Master, I have the pen of gold, iron and steel, pointing to the Heavens, to the Earth Spirit, rescuing the people and giving longevity, and so this talisman is good to use.
By the honour and command of Taishang Laojun.
JI JI RU LULING.

18. The power of the talisman is further consolidated by this spell, CHI ZAO FU ZHOU, THE SPELL THAT BUILDS THE TALISMAN. It should be said three times.

> The Root Ancestor builds the talisman,
> The Root Master builds the talisman,
> The Celestial Immortal Jade Maiden builds the talisman,
> O come and build the talisman,
> The Seventh Ancestor Immortal Master bulbs the talisman,
> Building the talisman head, purifying,
> Building ten thousand spirit talisman heads,
> Purifying it of evil spirits,
> The talisman base is purified of all evil demons,
> The talisman head point allows all living beings to enjoy longevity,
> The talisman base stops power exiting, it cannot move,
> The spiritual talisman changes to ten ways,
> Ten ways change to a hundred ways,
> A hundred ways changes to a thousand ways,
> A thousand ways change to ten thousand ways,
> All the Ways possess the Spirit Way,
> The Way possesses the Talisman of ONE DAO.

(Here the magician inserts the intent of the talisman, of which some examples are as follows)

A. To Banish Evil Spirits:

Evil spirits and demons quickly begone, power pursues you and stops you!!

B. To Ensure The Safety Of An Unborn Child.

Keep safe this unborn child, protect this pregnancy, the mother and child shall not experience mishap.

C. For Use In Soul Loss And Soul Shock.

Quickly I call the three immortal souls and seven mortal souls of xxxxxxx, return to the root palace , return to the root of life!

D. To Purify, Cleanse And Bring Calm And Tranquility.

Five Dragons spit water, rays of light and peace, the essence of auspiciousness descends.

E. To Punish And Cut Off A Wicked Person.

This person, xxxxxxx, shall quickly leave, forever and ever, and we shall never meet again,

>Then end the spell by declaring:
>By the honour and command of Taishang Laojun, the Heavenly Warriors rush like fire! Quickly!!!

19. With the end of the brush click or tap the talisman from top, middle then bottom three times. Heaven, Man, Earth.

20. With the Sword Finger write Chi Ling three times at the top and Spirit, three times at the bottom.

For extra power you can draw the Seal of the Golden Light upon it to further fill it with fali.

21. Hold the talisman with the sword finger and circle it through the incense three, five, seven or nine times. Most magicians will do the 'rounds' seven times.

The talisman is ready for use.

Disposing Of A Talisman

One cannot simply throw a talisman in the trash can. This is a great taboo in Chinese magic. Every talisman, even those considered 'evil' are holy symbols that connect with the Gods and spirits, thus they cannot be indiscriminately thrown away. There are various taboos that can cause a talisman to be contaminated and in this case it will need to be disposed of. Or there is a mistake made when the talisman is written, for example a wrong character or ink damage. Sometimes you may be called upon to destroy an evil talisman or to deactivate an old one or one that is no longer needed.

The process is fairly simple and should be committed to memory. Talismans that were written for practice and not empowered would have, if you recall, been preceded by an invocation to the spirits as given earlier, and sandwiched between two sheets of spirit money and then burned.

So what are some of the situations that can occur that make a talisman not effective or worse still, dangerous and/or impure?

Let us look at one traditional aspect known as the Qi Jinji, The Seven Taboos:

1. When drawing a talisman the mind is not correct, there is confusion, worry, fear and so the writing is ineffective.
2. The hands and mouth are unclean, a euphemism for the fact that a talisman writer cannot lie or steal.
3. When writing a talisman you cannot use broken, second hand, incorrect or unclean instruments.
4. When writing a talisman you cannot fidget or cross the legs.
5. When writing a talisman you cannot say one thing and then act in contradiction to the idea. For example in writing a talisman for wealth but in your heart you are thinking about some other thoughts like how long it will take, your lovely girlfriend, what is on tv later etc.

6. Avoid alcohol, the so-called 'coloured by wine' (Jia se) in Daoism.
7. Never correct a symbol or character by attempting to overwrite it. If it is written incorrectly, the talisman is broken and you must start again.

If any of these factors are in play, the talisman is po, broken, and must be disposed of.

There is also another set of Six taboos to be observed, the LIU JINJI.

1. A talisman can never be given directly to a pregnant woman but must be given to her in a red sachet, packet or pouch. If she has been pregnant for over five months she cannot handle a talisman at all except in the case of the Protect Foetus Talisman.
2. Girls or women cannot write or handle talismans during their periods.
3. Talismans cannot only not be written when the mind is confused, tired or disturbed, they cannot be given either.
4. If the incantation does not match the nature of the talisman it is invalid.
5. The talisman cannot be written or given in a place that is unclean and not in a state of tranquility and quiet.
6. If the talisman is not clearly written, or it is damaged it is invalid.

A talisman that has been found and is designed to direct ill will or evil forces at a client are usually, though not always of an ultramarine or greenish colour. Some foreign talismans such as those from Thailand and Indonesia can be thin metal plates, cloths or white paper.

Now concerning the ritual to dispose of and deactivate a talisman. One can use the sword finger to this, or you can use a cinnabar loaded brush. Both are effective but the beginner may find using the cinnabar brush more effective.

1. Lay the talisman down on the altar.

2. Draw a clockwise circle around the talisman declaring:
   Yi Yuan Yi Taiji!!
   (One Circle, One Taiji)

3. Draw a line through the middle of the circle:
   Yi Bi Zu Shi Dao!
   (One Stroke And The Ancestral Master Comes!)

4. Retrace the line through the circle and declare:
   Er Bi Zu Shi Lai Dao
   (Two Strokes And The Ancestral Master Arrives!)

5. Note that the top half of the circle is Yang,
   and the bottom half is Yin.

6. The Master of the Art must now draw four tick shapes similar to those drawn in the futou.

7. First we draw the Yang ticks in the order of 1,2,3 and 4.
   With each tick we say:
   Fu Tui!
   Fu Tui!
   Fu Tui!
   Fu Tui Chu!

8. Finally we repeat the process for the Yin cycle in the order of 2, 1, 3, and 4. Repeating the same ticks and the same incantation. Fu Tui means 'Remove the talisman' and the final chu means 'destroy!'

9. Finally we again sandwich the talisman between two sheets of gold or silver money and bury, burn or throw into a running stream.

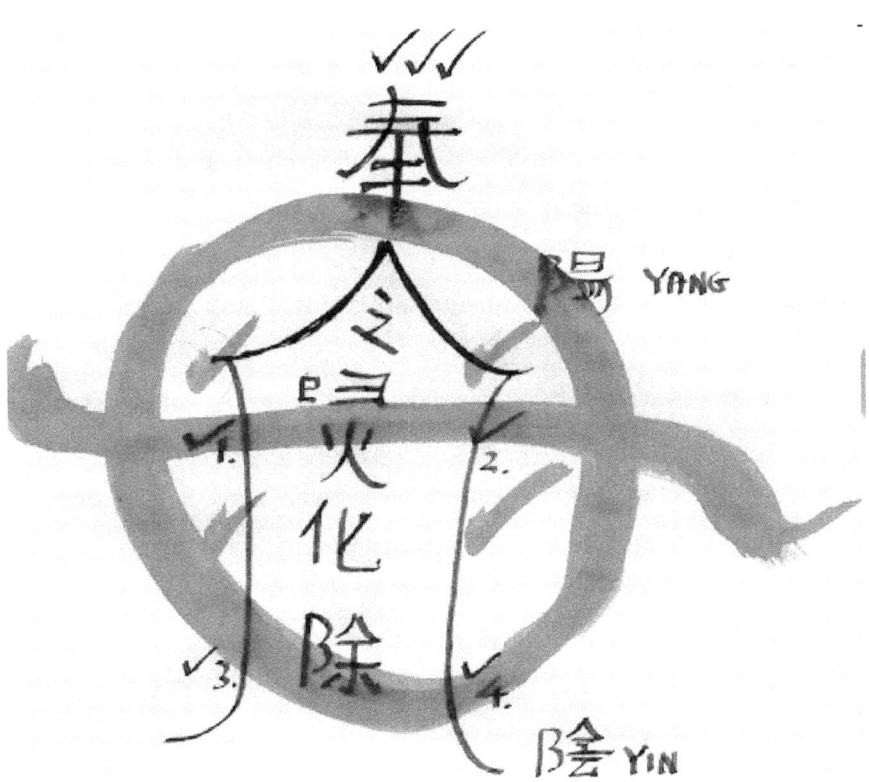

29. The Talisman Of Protection (Hu Shen Fu)

The principle idea of this talisman is to create a powerful talisman infused and radiating with a three dimensional, multi-directional sphere of protection wherever it is placed or worn on the body. As well as protecting the owner who wears it, or the home it is in, it will cause forces that dissipate opportunity to be held in check and so apparently increase the luck of the individual and his family.

Essentially a protection bag is made of red material and filled with five very powerful talismans that are infused with and radiate with the energies of the bagua.

The apprentice will have guessed we will be using yellow paper for this one and the ink will be black. You will also need red material to make the protection bag. If you are handy with a needle you can sew the talismanic design on the bag, otherwise use textile paint to draw the special power symbols on the front and back of the bag of power.

Now let us go through this step by step.

You will need the Black Pen of Art, sewing needle and thread, five standard imperial yellow papers on which to draw the five talismans of power, incense and an image of Fu Xi is useful.

Now let us proceed with the spell step by step as it will be one of your first attempts at Taoist magic in a practical and full sense.

The Apprentice or Dizi should prepare an altar with a red or yellow altar cloth. Yellow is the most ideal colour in protection and exorcistic spells. Red is second best, the colour of yang force and carrying the idea of 'birthing' a magical force into manifestation on Earth.

Say the BUILD PEN spell three times. This is a little different from the consecration spells given earlier. The Build Pen or ZAOBI ZHOU, is said immediately before using the pen in important operations. Holding the pen in your hand, visualising golden light pouring from above, through the crown centre (baihui) down the central channel and through your hand and into the pen, say:

> The Ancestral Master builds the pen,
> The Root Teacher builds the pen,
> The Immortals build the pen,
> The Jade Maiden builds the pen,
> The Seven Ancestor Immortal Master builds the Pen,
> Quickly, quickly! Come and build the pen.
> Build the head of the pen and purify it! Purify!!
> O up rise the ten thousand spirits,
> Removing the evil spirits from the pen head,
> From the base of the pen remove the evil spirits,
> The tip of the pen shall give longevity to all living beings,
> The base of the pen removes, stops
> and banishes evil without a trace,
> This is a divine pen wrought to build talismans, talismans,
> Talismans of power, effective in their application,
> O the Warriors of Spirit descend to guard the talisman at its centre,
> O you Divine Warriors!!
> JI JI RU LU LING!!!!

Consecrate the ink, inkstone and water.
The paper should be consecrated three times.

Utter any of the Request God Spells (Qing Shen Zhou) holding three incense sticks at the level of your heart.

Protection Bag

With the three incense sticks draw the Rain Ghost Power symbol in the air over the altar and all the gathered instruments. This symbol is shown in A. in the accompanying figure.

Yu Gui, or Rain Ghost is commonly used in Daoist magic as a carrier of magical power. The character consists of Rain, representing the power of heaven descending, and beneath, the Ghost character, representing spirit. Usually the Rain Ghost forms a kind of 'cartouche' that carries further magical characters.

> Draw the Rain Ghost five times, consciously invoking the power.
> Now read the Fu Zhou Zao Fu Zhou or Build the Talisman Spell:
> The Chief Ancestral Master builds the talisman,
> The Root Teacher builds the talisman,
> The Celestial Immortal Jade Maiden builds the talisman,
> O come and build this talisman!!
> The Seven Ancestor Immortal Master comes
> and builds the talisman,
> Build the head of the talisman, purifying,
> Build and there arise ten thousand spirit talisman heads,
> Purifying it of all evil spirits,
> The base of the talisman is purified of evil spirits,
> The talisman head allows all living beings longevity,
> The talisman base is stopped, power cannot be leaked ,
> The spiritual talisman changes to ten ways,
> Ten ways turn to a hundred ways,
> A hundred ways become a thousand ways,
> A thousand ways become ten thousand ways,
> All ways possess the way of spirit,
> The Way possesses the talisman of One Dao.

I should note here, that some practitioners, to build even more power, will do the Build Talisman Spell over a period of seven days.

It is now time for the Apprentice to invoke the powers of the Bagua, the elements of energetic change represented by the natural forces of nature ... the wind, the sky, the earth, fire, water, thunder, a lake and the lofty mountain.

It is wise to hold the Bagua Hand Seal when calling upon these powers in the following spell. Remember, do not merely read it out like a grocery list, but allow the imagery to arise vividly and use it.

Ba Gua Zhou (Bagua Spell)

Qian ☰

Yuan Hengli Zhen!! (Origin! Penetrating! Righteous! Loyal!) Note that this phrase is from the I Ching and is a potent mantra. It begins the esteemed Book of Changes. Thus it frequently appears in Taoist magical

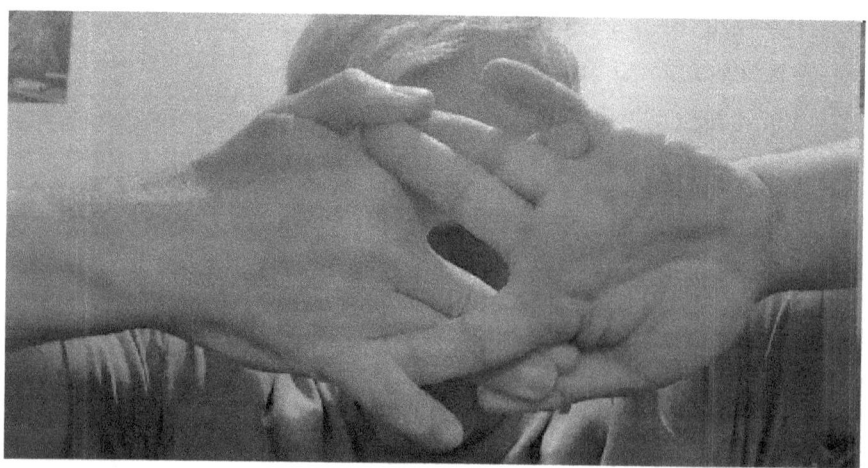

Ba Gua Hand Seal. Sometimes called Ghost Eye
when used in clairvoyance methods.

invocations. It can be translated From the Source, Creating Success, Consistency brings forth the fruit.

Most spells can be said in English, but in this case, say it in Chinese.

DUI !	☱	The Lake, the Army of Heroes!
Li !	☲	Fire, driving the Fire Wheel!
ZHEN !	☳	Thunder, the Vajra Thunderbolt resounds!
XUN!	☴	Wind, blowing from the lofty mountains!
KAN!	☵	Water, rapid and great waves!!
GEN!	☶	Mountain, named the Ghost Road
KUN!	☷	Earth, stable and firm, the Gate of Men

O Bagua Master, display the great power, the evil spirits pass away and cannot move, the Divine Warriors rush like fire!! Ji Ji Ru Lu Ling!

Repeat the above Ba Gua Spell in the Hu Shen Form. Begin facing South and use the sword finger to draw Qian three times, and turn in place to draw a complete circle of the eight bagua around you to form a sphere of protection. See the chapter called Protection, Condensing And Projection for full details.

Next in our lengthy spell, we say the following spell known as DA SHA ZHOU or Stopping Strike Spell. This spell calls upon the protection of the Heavenly Warriors, sometimes called the Ghost Soldiers. They are the souls of fallen heroes, soldiers, policemen, and others who through cultivation and/or altruism have chosen to serve humanity.

Da Sha Zhou (Stopping Strike Spell)

I request this, Heaven quickens and Earth Quickens,

The Three Heavens commands the lower,

Great Heavenly Emperor Tian wang True Master,

The Heavenly King supports the lower world beneath,

O gather from the left O Warriors,

Gather from the right O Jade Knights,

By this command I call together ten thousand warriors,

Who by foot come, O you Ghost Soldiers, over thousands of miles,

In this world are many ghosts and demons,

Thus the true gods descend to slay the demons,

I request the Mountain Path Heavenly King General,

in whose right hand is raised and poised to strike the demons

again and again, a flying strike, beating the demons,

Heaven stops them, the demons pass away,

Earth stops them and they pass to the Underworld,

In this year of xxx, in the month of xxx, on the day of xxx in the hour of xxx, they are stopped in the Four Directions, by Metal, Wood, Water, Fire and Earth, the Five Elemental Lords and spirits return by the Five Directions,

The demons and spirits are blocked, the evil is stopped.
Yin and Yang Spirits and Evil Gods are stopped,
They cannot move.
Quickly, quickly, banished a thousand li, you cannot meet me.
By the Maoshan Master's command.
Shen Bing Huoji Ru Lu Ling!!

This is quickly followed by the invocation of Tong Gong Taiyi, a warrior fire God of Mars.

I call upon you Tang Gong Taiyi Jun (Jun means Lord or Monarch), having the appearance of Mars, stepping on black clouds, in your hand the Seven Star Sword which, on descending cuts the evil spirits of the Yin World, a hundred gods and ghosts, a thousand demons, a hundred monsters respond and the spiritual water of power leaves nothing.

At the first point in the East, Yi, Wood, the river of purifying water, calming, purifying the sight, all is clear.

At the Second Point in the South, Bing, Fire, the Ten Palaces of King Yan see all, and lock in metal.

At the Third Point in the West, Geng, Metal, fortune, day after day the Parents come and protect us.

At the Fourth Point in the North, Gui, Water, conquering demons, slaying goblins, cutting the monstrous spirits.

The Fifth Point is the Centre, Wu and Yi, Earth, opening the Gate of Heaven, Shutting the Door of Earth, by Tang Gong Taiyi Jun, slay the Yin evil influences, quickly, so they cannot move and they shall leave no trace.

SHEN BING HUOJI RU LULING!!

The occult protection continues by invoking the Five Thunders. For more insight into this consult Thunder Magic.

Wu Lei Shen Zhou (Five Thunder Gods Spell)

I request the City of Heaven, the Great Thunder God Thunderbolt Spirit, together with a thousand million warriors to assist in this spell. In the centre the evil ones cannot hide, the Five Thunders blast them and no trace is left.

I command it by the order of Taishang Laojun!

Ji Ji Ru Lu Ling!

Next the invocation of the Lord of Mars and Fire,
HUO DE SHEN JUN.

Huo De Shen Jun Zhou

(The Mars Or Fire Lord Spell)

I call Guanyin Bodhisattva to come.

One gathers, two transforms and three is the True Fire of Samadhi!

The Power of Fire, Cinnabar is that which gives birth to Hou de Xing Jun, the Lord of Mars, vermillion cleaves to and penetrates the evil spirit who cannot thus remain.

O you, the righteous God, I request Huo Shen to assist me!
JI JI RU LU LING.

The next power invoked is the Iron Official, Tie Gong, a powerful warrior made of iron and brings invulnerability and protective powers like an iron shield to the talisman.

Tie Gong Zhou
(Iron Master Spell)

Iron headed, iron faced, Iron General Brother, most wonderful in his methods of power, Heaven and Earth, Great Heaven listens, Sages descend to this Altar to manifest magic, I am troubled and assailed, the Three Doctrinal Ancestral Masters are strong in the ways of magic, the Iron Master emits fire, the fire is eaten, the sword comes, Iron head, iron face, iron general, iron foot, iron skin, iron hand, iron bone, iron intestines, iron belly, iron heart, flames emitted received in the soul, the spirits and ghosts are startled, the hand that grasps the sword cuts the evil ones.

Iron lips, iron teeth, iron mouth swallowing, the great call resounds and opens the Three Kingdoms,

The lesser call resounds and rises to the mountain gate, Yin is the home of the demons, go to the Southern Mountain, they die and cannot understand or stay, the emitting of Fire of Heaven relieves the suffering, the male ghosts perform magic, male ghosts flee, female ghosts work magic
but cannot look back.
I command it by the order of Taishang Laojun.
Shen Bing Huoji Ru Luling!!

The final invocation employs a tactic in Taoist magic known as Cang Shen or 'hide the body'. It literally hides the presence of the talisman wearer or magician from the sight of evil spirits or those sending black spells.

Cang Shen Zhou
(Hiding Body And Life Spell)
QIAN YUAN HENG LI ZHEN!!
Sun and Moon hide my body,
Big Dipper hide my body,
All plants, hide my body,
Like grass on the verges of a path hiding the deer,
Longevity to all beings!
I cannot be seen, ghosts cannot be aware of my presence.
By the command of Taishang Laojun!!
JI JI RU LU LING!!

The Masters say we should repeat all the above invocations three times daily for seven days.

On the second day, the apprentice should write the five talismans that will go into the red bag.

Using the methods taught previously, paint the talismans according to Daoist protocols. When finished, fold them into a square and then into an octagon. The octagon of course represents the bagua. This folding is to be done on the seventh day.

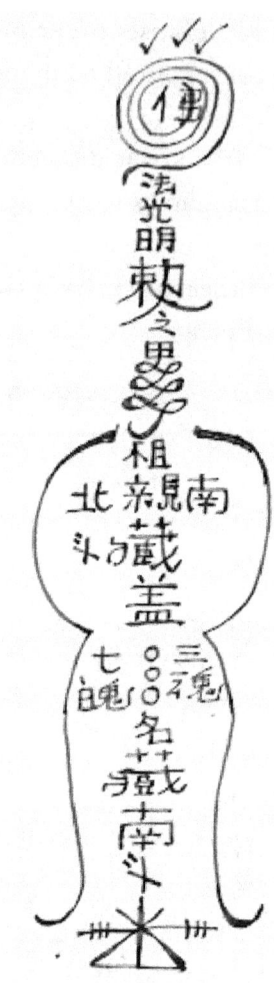

Five Talismans to be folded into octagons and put in the bag.

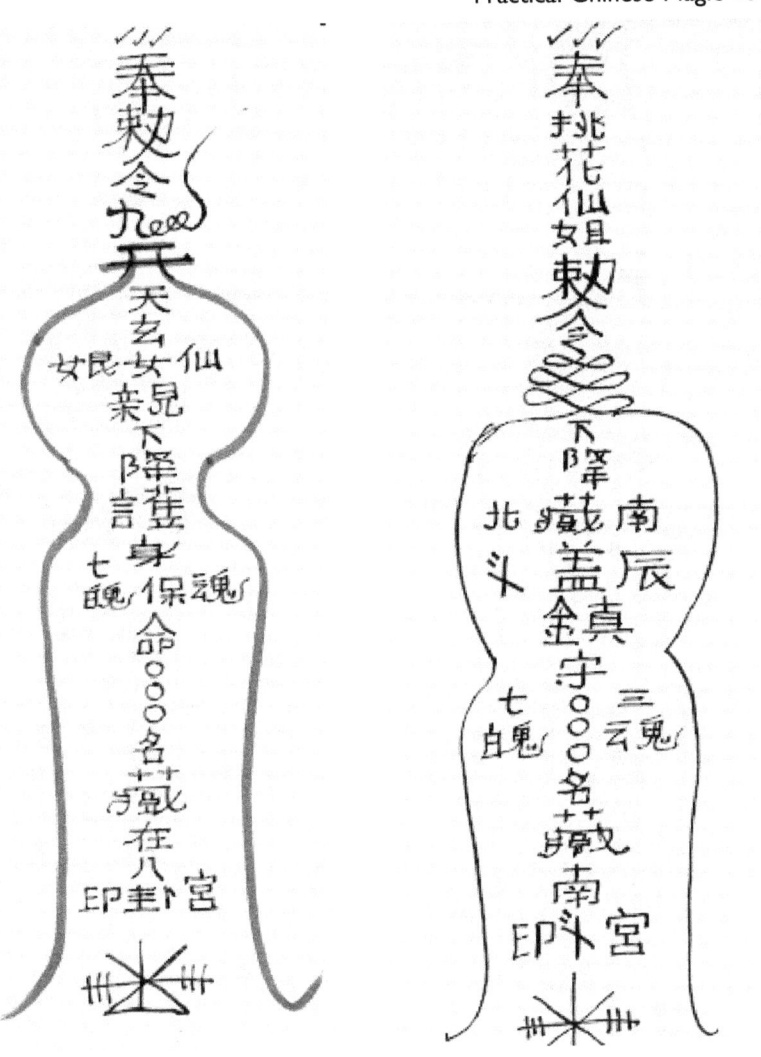

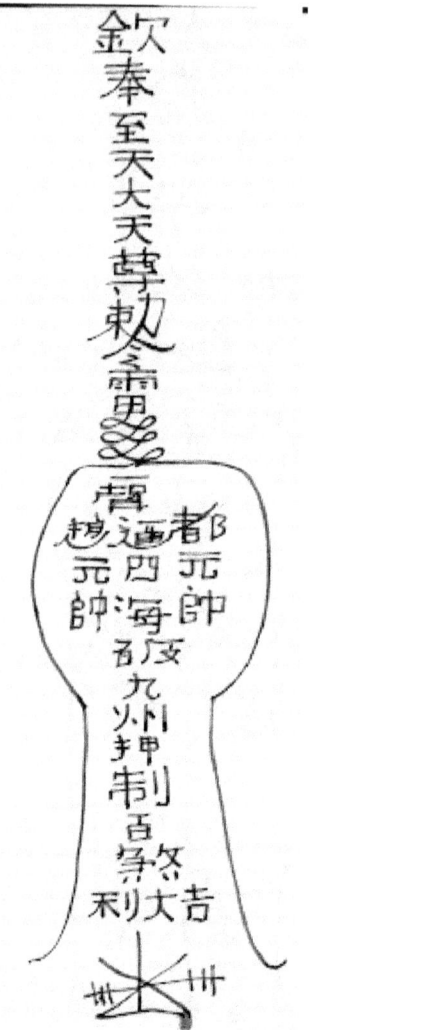

You must now prepare the red cloth bag. Sew this yourself leaving the top open.

Insert the five talismans which are now convenient octagon-like coins. With the black brush paint the symbol B on the front and the symbol C on the reverse of the red silk, cotton or brocade.

> Read the spell:
> Bagua Master descends and protects life and body, defending his/her destiny.
> As you say this point with three sticks of incense or sword finger to the centre of the Ba Gua.
> As you paint, read aloud the names of the individual Trigrams, Qian! Dui! LI! Zhen! Xun! Kan! Gen! Kun!
> On completion again point to the centre of the Bagua and recite the following:
> BAGUA ZUSHI JIANG LAI LIN HU SHEN BAO MING!!
> (Bagua Master descends and protects life and body, defending his/her destiny.)

With the three sticks of incense or the sword finger, use the Xu Shu style (writing in the air above the object to be blessed) the name of the person to be protected.

> Write a triangle fudan and a gang symbol
> and Taishang Laojun Ji Ji Ru Lu Ling!!

太上老君 急急如律令

This is done on a separate piece of paper and inserted into the bag. Bind up the bag and the spell is complete. The spell is finalised by binding up the bag with a red or yellow string where it can be carried by the client.

NOTE: When drawing the gang symbol don't forget to recite the names of the 28 Stars.

30. The House Protection Bagua Talisman Of Defence And Fortune (AN BAGUA FU)

This is another powerful and well known method used in Chinese magic and is often one of the first spells learned by apprentices in the art. Yet we should not for a moment think that this spell is in any way less powerful or easy to manufacture.

At the heart of the spell is the holy Bagua, the timeless cosmogram of the inner workings of the universe and man in one simple diagram. It is the key symbol of not only magic in China but in surrounding countries like Japan, Korea and Vietnam.

The talisman itself can be as simple as a bagua or a more complex design with reinforcing spells and talismanic designs that can be breathtakingly beautiful.

The altar for this spell should have two candles in candlesticks on the left and right and a bowl with three incense sticks, three small chinese style cups with tea , a plate with three or five pieces of fruit, some spirit money and the bagua design of your choice. For the beginner, choose a simple design. One of the best is the simple design that has both Pre-Heaven and Post-Heaven designs incorporated.

You will also need a brush and cinnabar ink to fully empower this particular talisman.

Choose your Bagua design, and preferably one you have painted yourself on paper or cloth, both of which must be yellow though white or 'buddhist' orange will suffice.

After the Altar is laid out and you have done the preliminaries, you pick up the bagua and pass it in clockwise circles through the incense smoke and recite the Spell of Purification and Calm known as Qinjing Zhou:

The Ancestral Master purifies,

The Root Master purifies,

The Immortals purify,

The Jade Girl purifies,

The Seven Ancestor Immortal Master purifies,

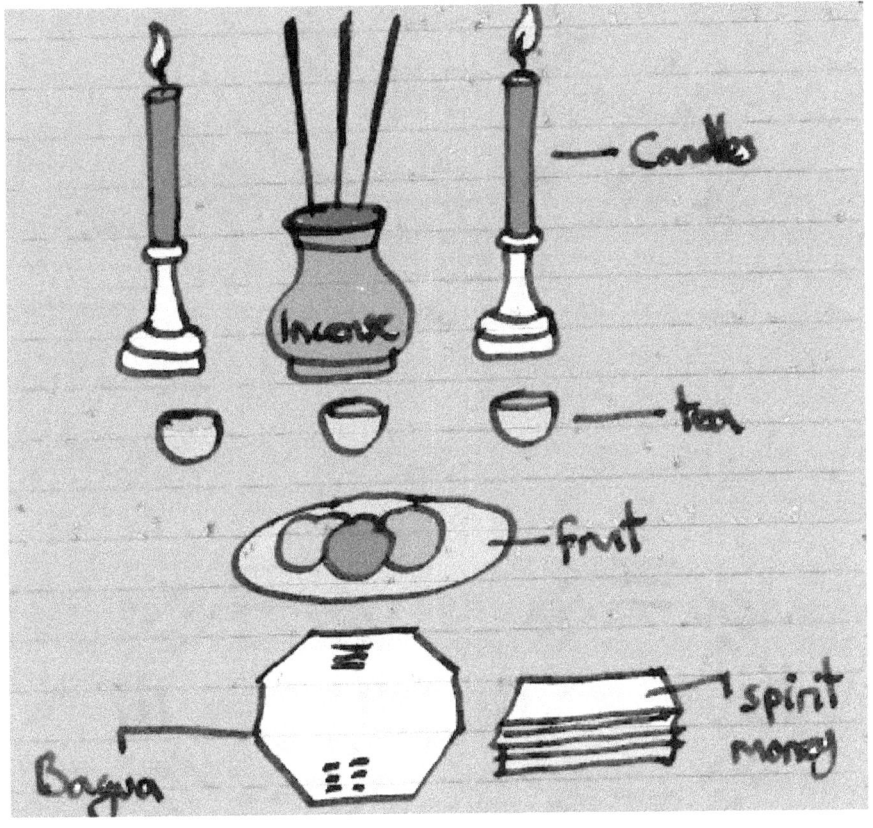

Altar used for consecration of the House Protection Bagua Talisman. Note you can use this ritual for any bagua imagery such as feng shui bagua mirrors and jewellery. The Altar cloth should be white, yellow or red.

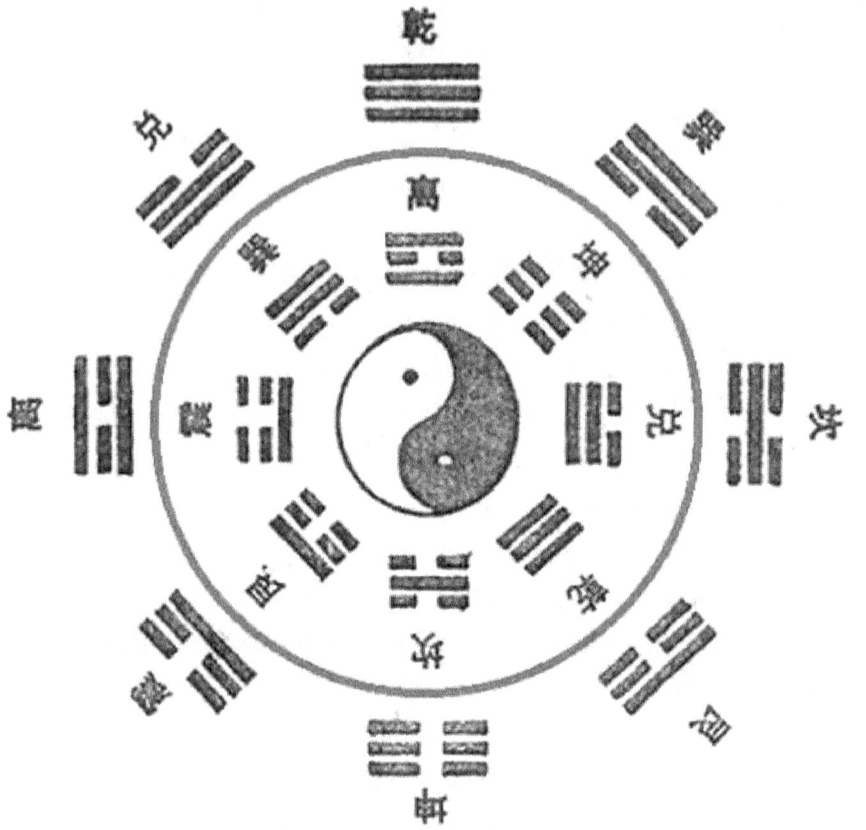

Pre-Heaven Bagua   Post-Heaven Bagua

Commanding purity,
The Three Masters and the Three Children,
The Five Dragons spit water and golden rays of light,
Divine warriors descend rushing like fire,
It is commanded!!

Pick up a stick of incense and draw this character in the air above the Altar:

The character is one of the key magical symbols of Chinese magic and signifies Fire and Battle, rushing fire of spiritual and magical heat known as Samadhi Fire in the Chinese magical tradition.

Holding the three incense sticks the magician must first call the powers of the Bagua. We use a special request god spell specifically designed to invoke those powers:

I present to you this incense. The smoke rises to pass through the gates of the Heavenly Palace.
I ask the Southern Dipper Lord and the Lord of the Northern Dipper to descend to this mortal realm.
And you, the 28 Star Kings, the Sun and the Moon, who work to illuminate all things, forever shining inner palaces so all things are clear. O come!!

With incense, I honour and humbly ask you O Jiu Tian Xuan Nu, True Immortal Guanyin, Fuxi, Shang Di, Wen Wang

Zhougong, Kongzi Yanggong Zushi, O come!!

I give honour to and ask the Root City God Master who serves this area, Tudi the Venerable Emperor and illustrious Xukong who shall always be venerated, all Gods come!

Come and support your disciple named ………………..,
O come, the incense is offered.

I request the Root House Family God, Venerable and Respected to receive the incense, and the Door Gods, the Dragon God of the Well, the Kitchen Star Lord and all Gods to assist me in performing this magic, arise O you Symbols that forever shall exist, rise dark blue presence, there is peace in the Hall of Art, supporting life and saving life and purifying. The Five Mountains and Nine Kingdoms, the Temple Gods, Yin Ghosts and you the lesser demons, evil energies and black magic, you the greater demons, follow the Yin-Wind Steps, the Wind Steps, the Metal God Seven kills the demons and evil spirits, the Earth God and Water stops the evil demons and ghosts, a wall gathers from every direction!!

Come O come to me, the Symbol diagram centre and quickly extinguish the evil forms.

I honour Buddha Sakyamuni, Buddha Wen, and open the An Bagua!!!

JI JI RU LULING!!

The next step is to load your brush with cinnabar ink, then to say the Xiantian Bagua Zhou (Pre-Heaven Bagua Spell). This will consecrate the bagua of the Pre-Heaven Sequence. With each statement put a tiny point of cinnabar on the relevant trigram on the talisman.

QIAN, three lines.

KUN, six are broken.

LI, the middle is empty.

KAN, the centre is full.

DUI, the top is open.

XUN, the bottom is broken.

ZHEN, the rising one.

GEN, the upturned bowl.

Bagua Ancestral Master descends here now,
Comply with the strokes of the brush.
The turning circle of the Bagua, focusing on the circle,
Protect body and protect destiny,
let there be peace and calm,
QIAN acts as Heaven,
KUN acts as Earth,
Heaven and Earth are in order,
Li acts as Fire,
KAN acts as Water,
Fire and Water mutually exude their power,
DUI acts as a lake,
GEN acts as a mountain,
Mountain and Lake open the Qi energies.
ZHEN acts as Thunder,
XUN acts as Wind,
Thunder and Wind are together strength.

This invocation is a crash course in the essentials of the essence of the trigrams and the dynamic of their interplay. The first part is a mnemonic device allowing you to mentally recall and construct the visual form of the trigrams or yao. We then call the Bagua Ancestral Master Fu Xi. The magician then recalls the ever flowing cyclical nature of the bagua, and then pairs each of the trigrams into pairs. As with all Taoist magic nothing is truly a thing in itself unless paired with its opposite and all things reduce to one and then, paradoxically the Absolute of Formless Wu Ji.

What then follows is a process that sets the Lo Shu magic square into the bagua talisman. You can read about this square in a previous chapter but will be covered far more deeply in a future book on Magical Astrology and Magical Feng Shui.

Again with the brush loaded with cinnabar, a tiny point is placed at each imagined square:One is white,

> Two is black,
>
> Three is jade green,
>
> Four is green,
>
> Five is yellow,
>
> Six is white,
>
> Seven is red,
>
> Eight is white,
>
> Nine is purple.
>
> The Nine Steps alone,
>
> The left three, the right seven,
>
> Two and four are the shoulders,
>
> Six and Eight are the legs!!

(Note that the last part refers to the Lo Shu as the Turtle hence the mention of the shoulders and feet)

The Pre-Heaven part of the Bagua Talisman is complete, and now the magician must invoke and actualise the powers of the Bagua as it manifests in physical reality, the so-called Post-Heaven Bagua.

With the brush again loaded with cinnabar he recites the HOUTIAN BAGUA ZHOU (The Post-Heaven Bagua Spell):

Again dot with a tiny point of cinnabar ink on the appropriate point:

The Supreme Great Thunder! Zhen.
Its equal the Wind. Xun.
Meeting in Fire. Li.
Labouring. Kun.
The speech and words of DUI.
The warrior might of QIAN.
The effort of KAN.
Accomplishing the words, GEN.

Where in the spell the Pre-Heaven sequence uses the Lo Shu Magic Square, the Post-Heaven is consolidated with the Yellow River Map or He Tu. Loading once again the cinnabar brush the sorcerer points the River Map:

One and Six, All the Ancestors.
Two and Seven, All on the same path.
Three and Eight are friends.
Four and Nine are companions.
Five and Ten are the same road.

Quickly follow with the second Post-Heaven Bagua Spell again pointing whenever the appropriate trigram is invoked:

The armies of the Nine Kingdoms come!!
First is KAN.
Li is the ninth post of Nangong,
On the left is three, ZHEN, the post of Yan Zhou,
On the right is seven, DUI, the post of XI Liang.
KUN is two the Yong Zhou nation.
GEN is eight is the coldness of Yang Zhou,

QIAN, six is Bing Zhou, the territory of the Master.
Four is Xun, the post of Jing Zhou Nation!

(Quickly dot the trigrams in a circle)

I fear no evil spirits by virtue of this method,
Demons and ghosts cannot walk here,
By Taishang Laojun's command,
SHEN HUOJI RU LULING!!!

(A final point in the centre)

We now pick up the Bagua talisman and read the ZAO BAGUA ZHOU (BUILD THE BAGUA SPELL):

Heaven quickens, Earth quickens,
I call Pangu the Great Emperor,
I call Fuxi, Shennong, Wen Wang the Duke of Zhou,
Come and open the points of the Bagua,
of the 8, 8, 6, 14, 64 Gua,
Spirits of renown,
open the point of QIAN YUAN HENGLI ZHEN!!
The Second point opens that of DUI,
the Lake of the Heroic Army,
The third point opens KUN, the Earth, solid stability and the Gate of Men,
The Fourth point opens LI, driving the flaming wheel.
The Fifth opens the point of XUN, the wind blowing from the lofty mountain,
The sixth opens the point of ZHEN, Thunder, the sound of the spiritual Vajra Thunderbolt,
The Seventh opens the point of GEN, the Mountain named the Ghost Gate,

The Eighth opens the Point of KAN, Water that is the rushing waves.
In the centre is the Taiji.
All descend to support the power of the Gua Shen King.

I call the Teachers, the Five Buddhas to come and open the Sword Point, Gua, fate and life are changeless, Let Fo Shijia Wen Fo assist me in this method and support me to perform this magic, open the Gua Point with magical authority, banish the evil spirits, come O you who are marching over the Land under Heaven , leading ten million warriors, Buddhas and Spirits, the Bagua turns to the Assembly of the Gods who in turn assist the Gua Spirits, I ask you to remain here.
Masters come to the Gua and remain, let the Gua spirits rid of the ghosts and demons, I ………………..call you to come to me, from the Yunmeng Mountain Peak, the Ghost Valley Master, Chen Bo Xiansheng, Sun Bin Xiansheng, Kongming Xiansheng, Baihe Xiansheng, Guangguan Guo Pu Xiansheng, Guanyin Xiansheng assists me, City God defends me, Zuo Xiansheng, Baihe Xiansheng, Youxi Xiansheng, I the disciple named………….. ask you to aid me in my work, Gaoyou Fu Xiansheng, Zhou Fa Yu Xiansheng, Zuo Fu Tongzi, Pai Fu Tong Lang, Liu Ding and Liujia, assist me to guard and defend!

Heavenly Warriors guard! Spirit Warriors guard the people with sincerity and authority. Answer us, by the magical command that is the equal of Heaven, the Great Marshal,
SHEN BING JI JI RU LU LING!!

The talisman is complete and is usually hung or pasted in the home. Choose the place according to need or by the rules of Feng Shui.

The Following Plates Show Several Designs For More Complex Forms Of Bagua An Talismans

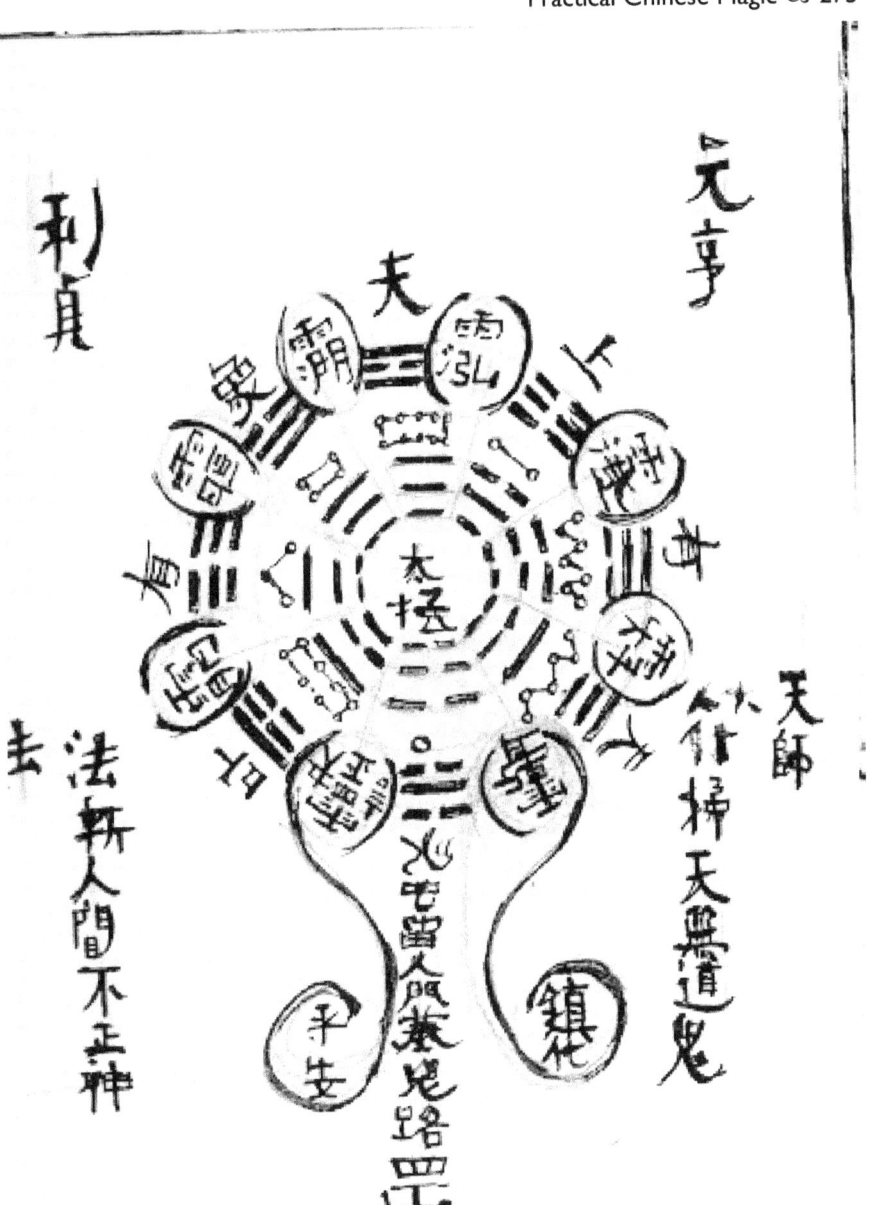

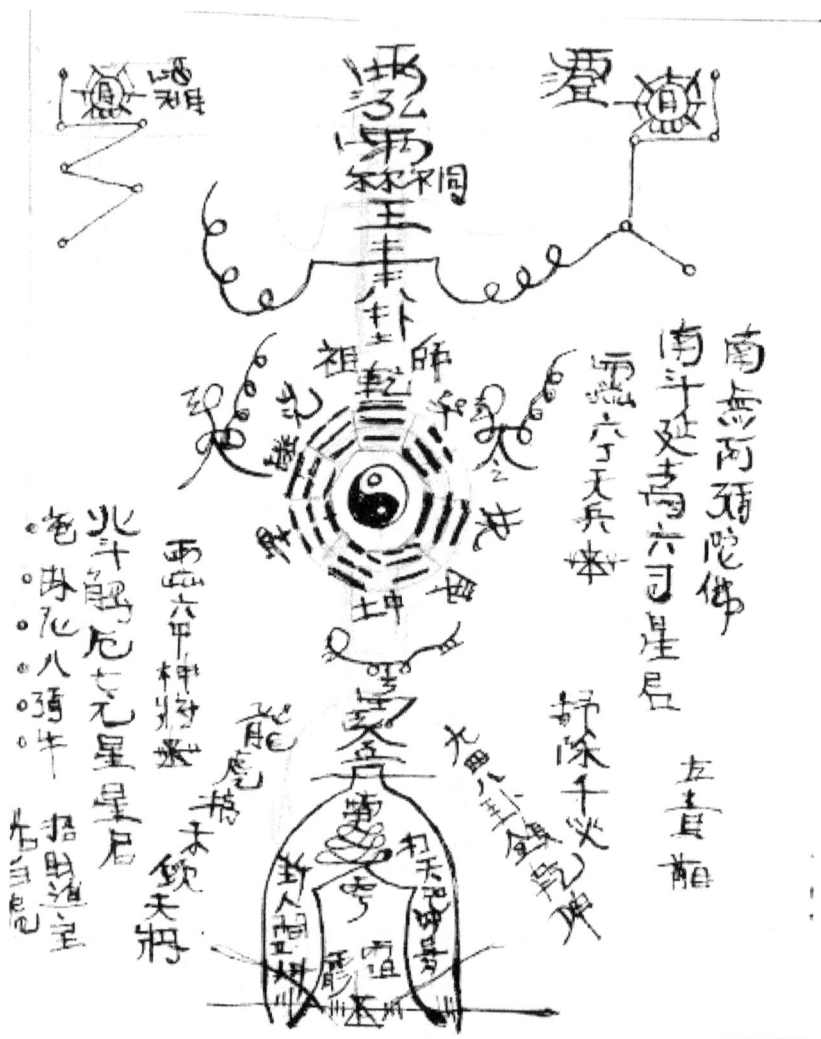

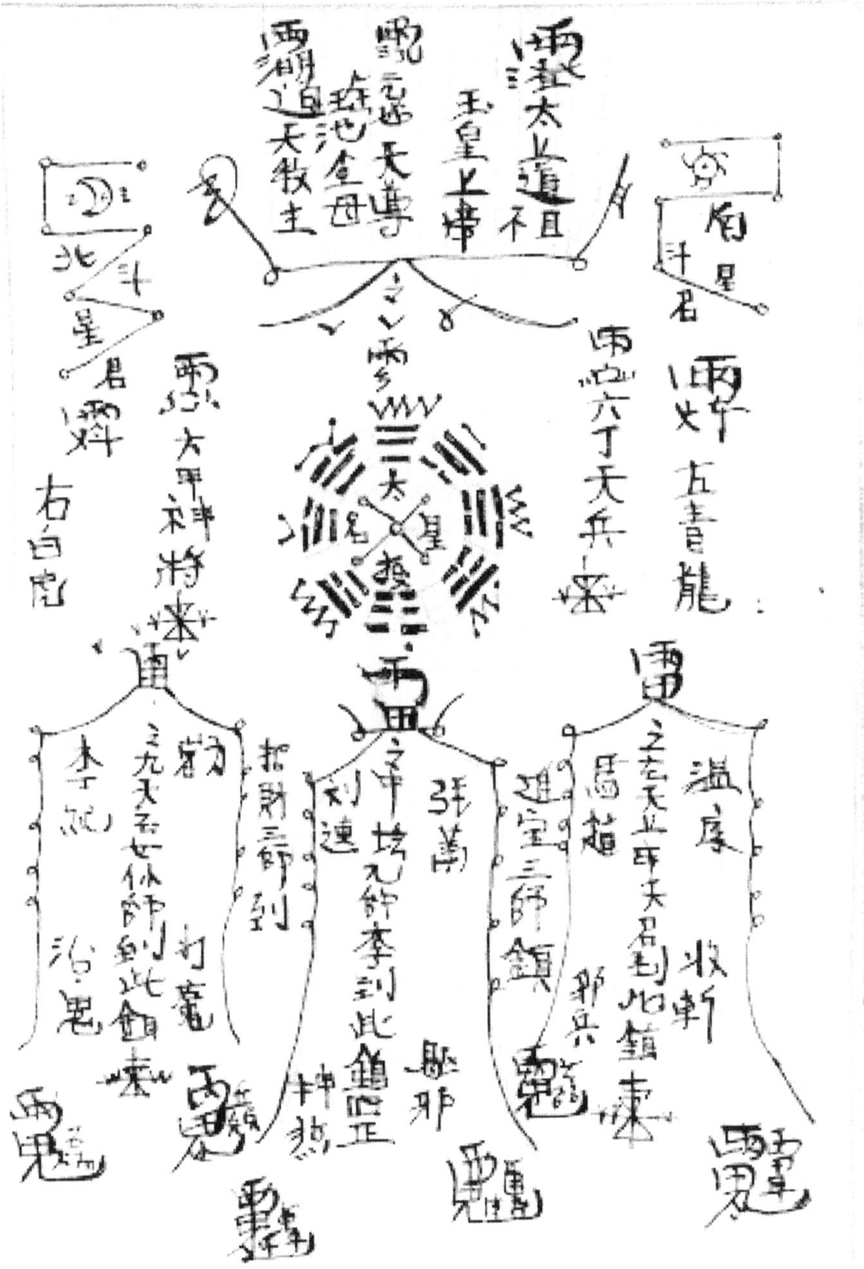
太上道祖
玉皇上帝
元始天尊
瑤池金母
通天教主
北斗星君
六丁天兵
右白虎

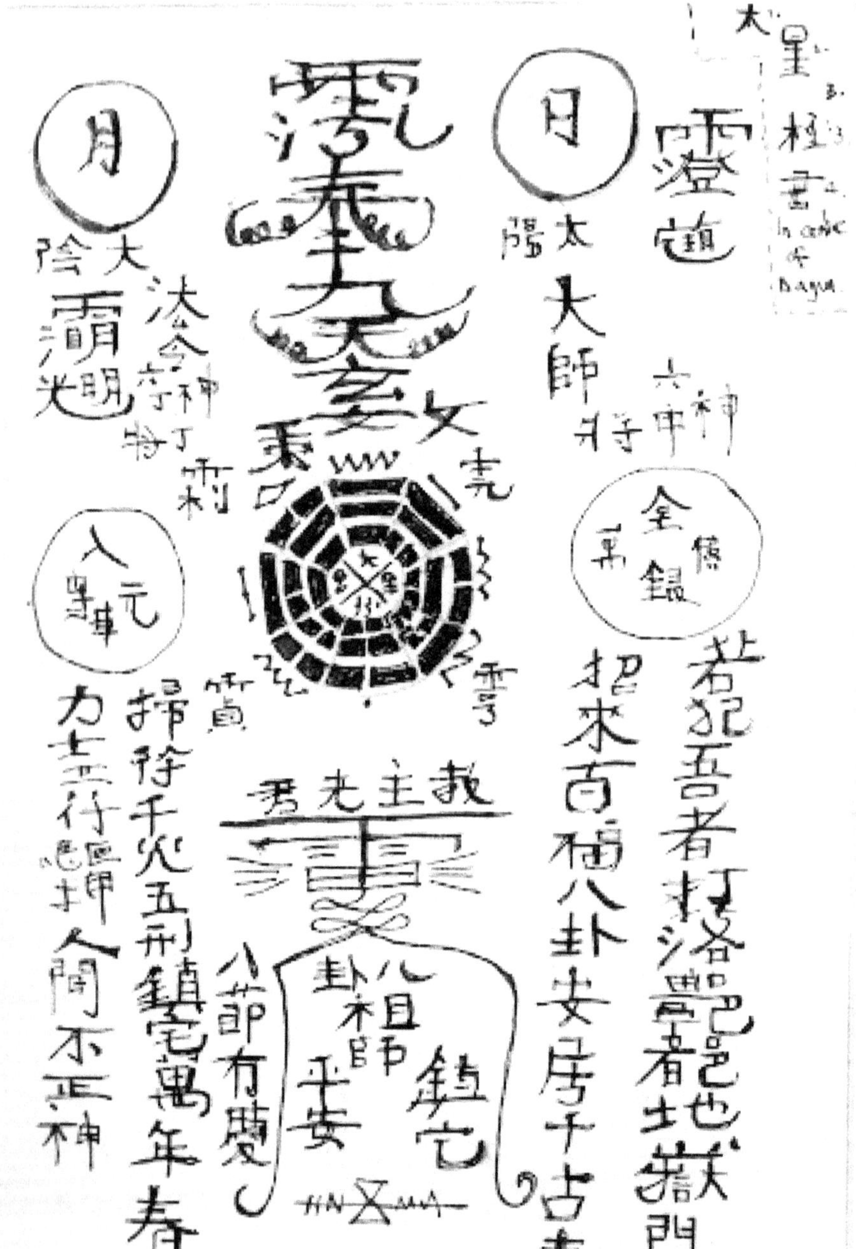

○月 陰大 光明 法令斬神丁莉

亂秦九玄女乘

○日 陽太 大師 六甲神將

○入元畢

○金銀 財寶

若犯吾者指落豐亂者地獄門
招來百福八卦安房千古泰

力士無行□甲人間不正神
掃除千災五刑鎮宅萬年春

我主光君
八節有慶
八卦相助平安
鎮宅

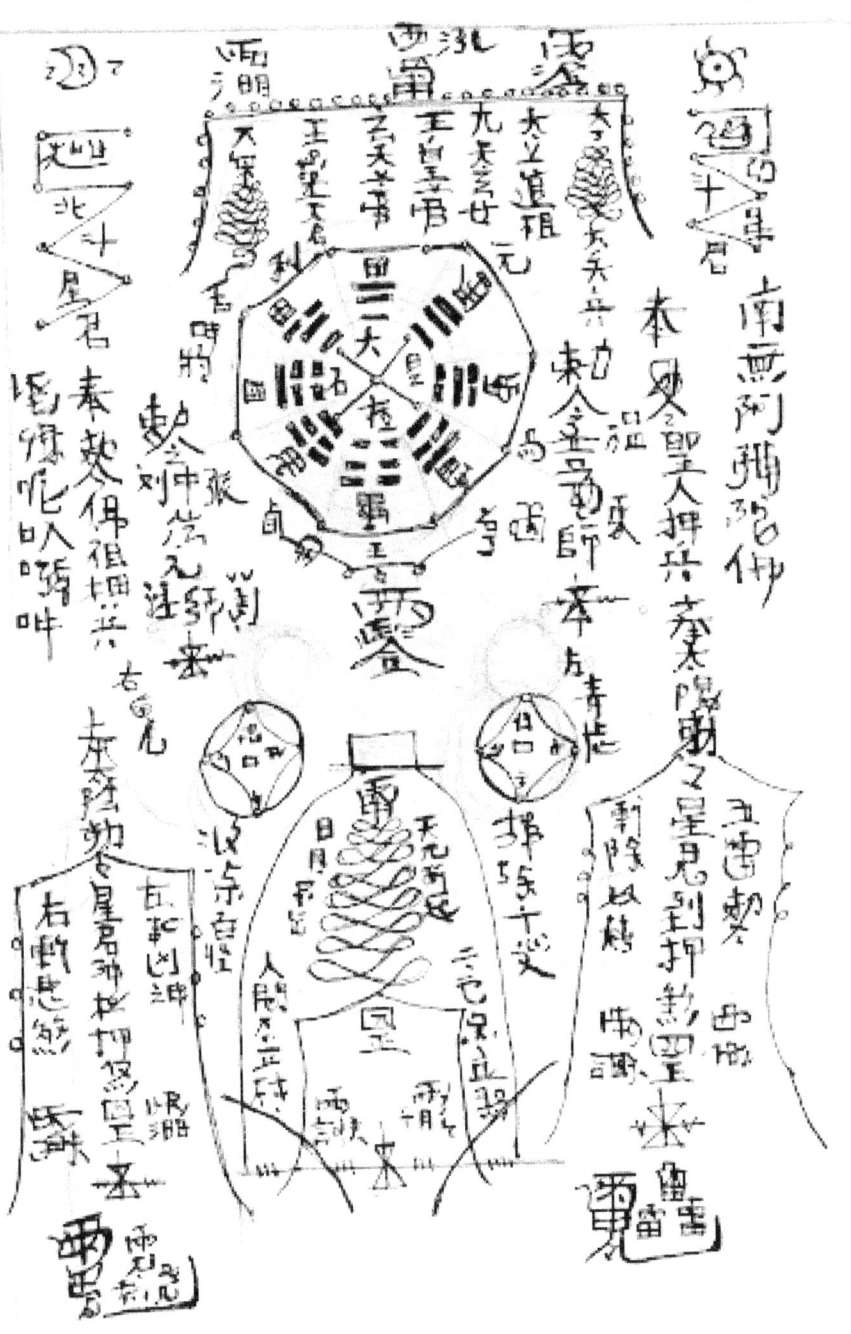

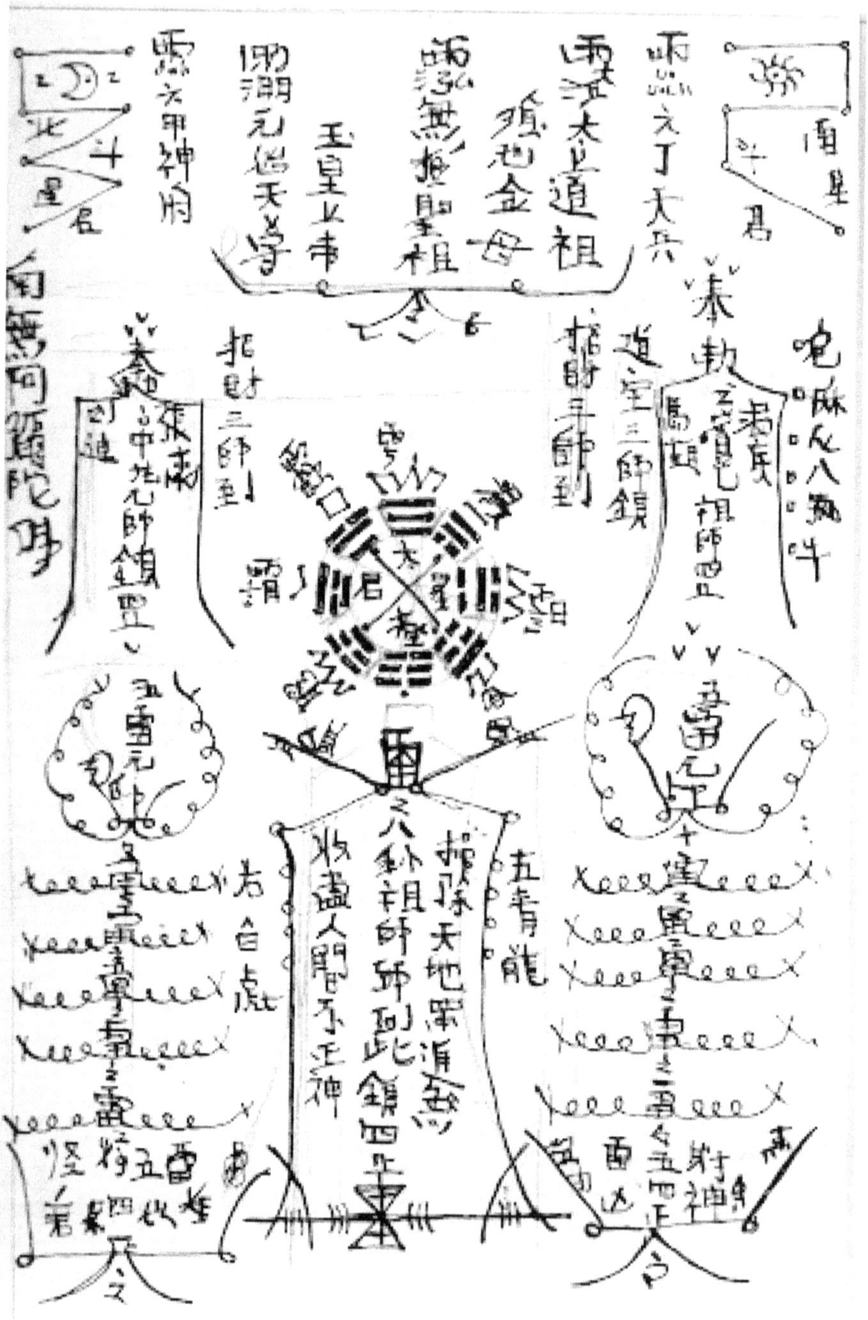
南斗星君
北斗星君
玉皇上帝
南無阿彌陀佛

Practical Chinese Magic

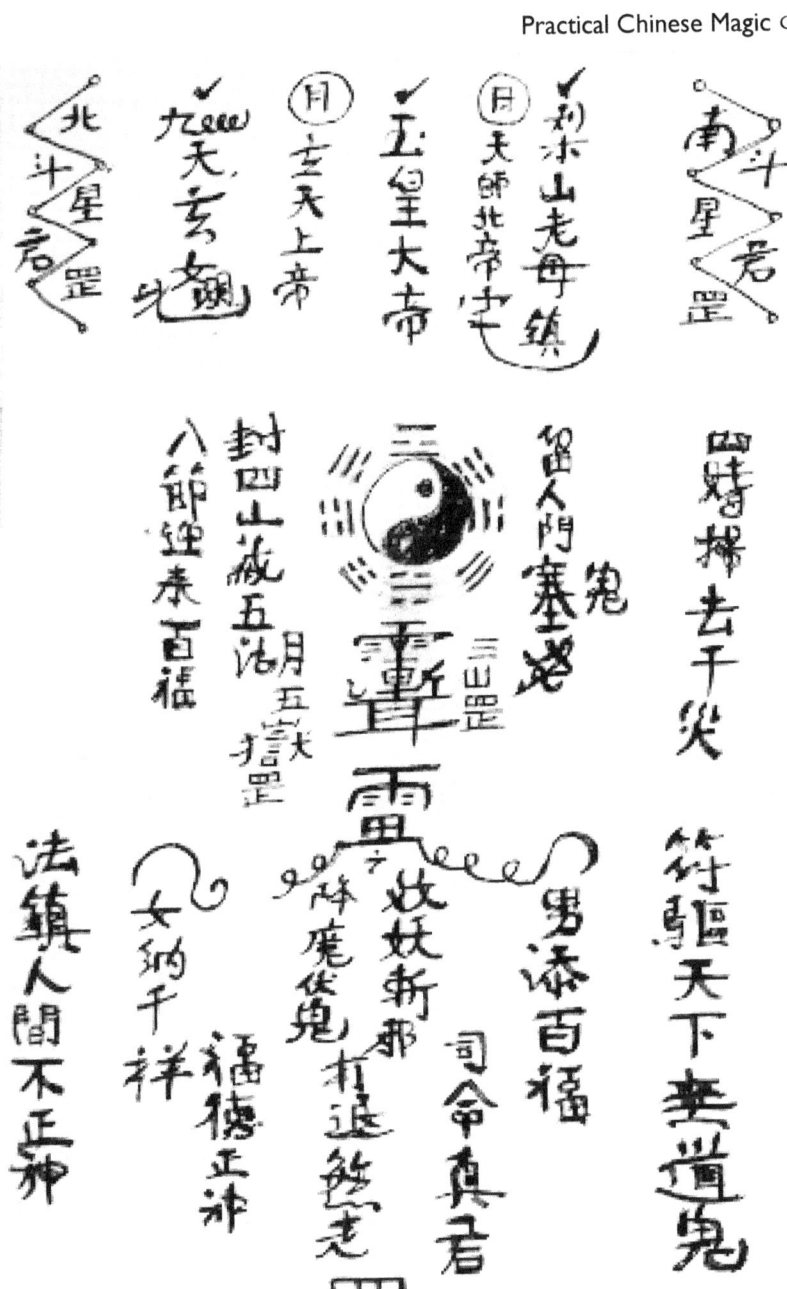

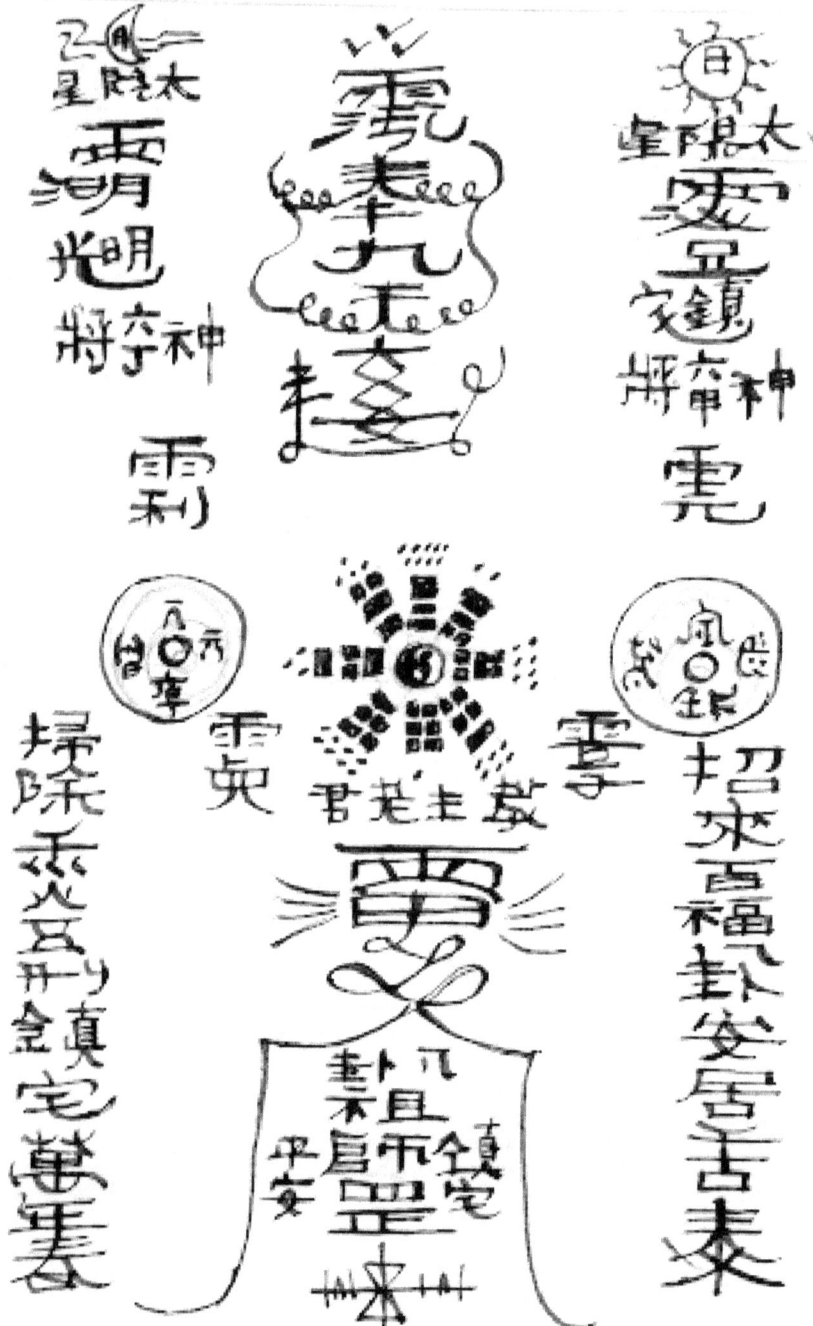

31. QINGJING FU (The Talisman Of Bringing Peace, Calm And Purity)

This is an important talisman used whenever purity is needed. For example in cleansing an altar, a room or even the self by washing it in water in which the ashes of this talisman has been deposited. It is also used to purify your pens, ritual tools, water bowls, icons of gods and so on.

This symbol uses black ink on the standard Imperial Yellow paper. You will need to draw three of them.

Once the talisman is drawn according to all the standard rules, utter the invocation as follows:

QINGJING ZHOU (SPELL OF PURITY)

The Ancestral Master purifies,
The Root Teacher purifies,
The Immortals purify,
The Jade Girl purifies,
The Seven Ancestor Immortal Master purifies,
Commanding purity,
The Three Masters and Three Children purify,
The Five Dragons spit water and golden rays of light,
SHEN BING HOUJI RU LU LING!!

Trace the character as follows with the Sword Finger or three sticks of incense:

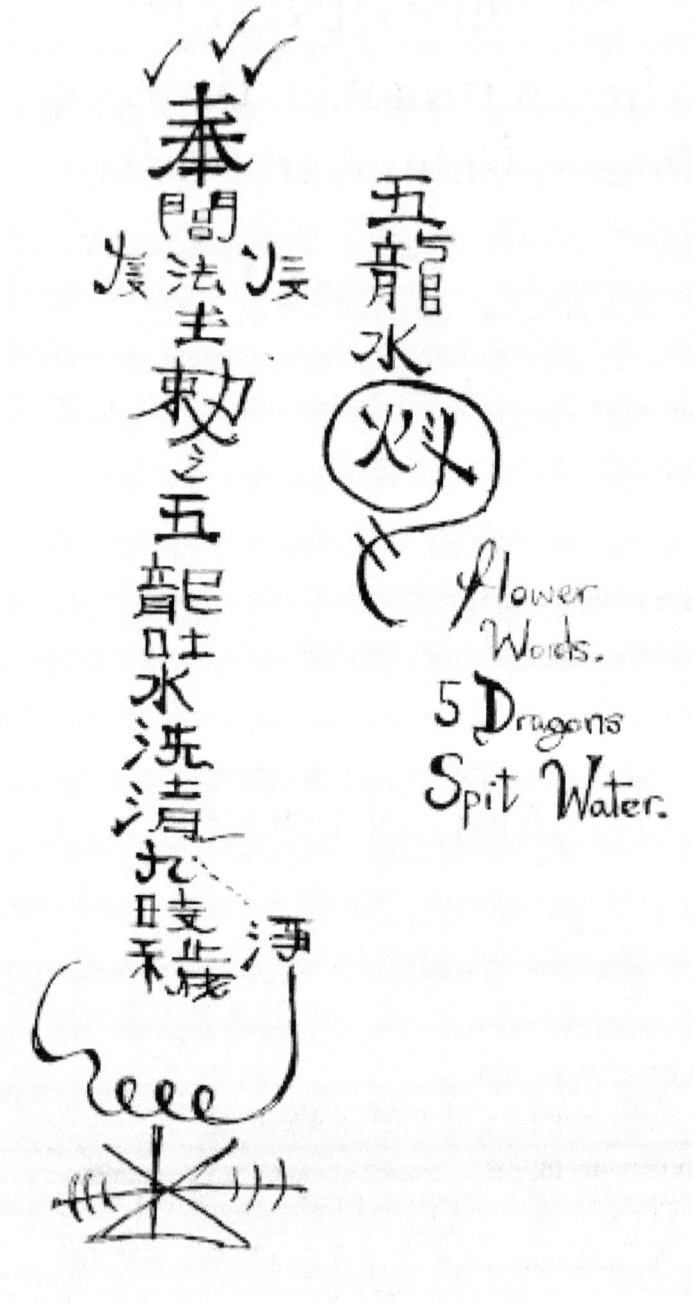

Qingjing Talisman

When you have finished writing this talisman, fold it. Then burn the talisman over water letting the ashes drop in it and wash the body, the object or whatever is to be purified.

You can use seven pieces of Shoujin, or longevity money to dip into the water and cleanse the self, altar and so forth.

The Qing Jing Fu is shown below.

32. ZHAOCAI CUI KE WANG DIAN FA
(Ritual Of Money And Prosperity Inviting Prosperity And Customers For A Prosperous Business Technique)

This is an interesting ritual and obviously one that is highly sought after by clientele in Asia and I can attest to its effectiveness.

In the West there is a certain hesitation to spells that call for money and material prosperity. No such quandaries exist in Chinese culture. A

Safflower the flower of prosperity

lack of prosperity or money is considered a disharmony, a sickness and a blockage in one's life that has a root cause that needs to be solved. The ancient peoples of Europe and India also had no reservations using the aid of the supernatural realms to improve their financial situation and open the roads to further opportunities.

Fate and luck in Chinese magical thought is associated with the Big Dipper, those seven stars that seem to be an ever turning handle ladling out the blessings or wrath of the heavens upon the earth blow. Thus in this ritual the Big Dipper features prominently.

The disciple needs to acquire seven tea light candles or seven candles in candlesticks, or perhaps seven oil lamps. The choice is yours. We will be arranging these into a seven star pattern in the ritual format known as the QIXING DENG or Seven Star Lamps.

The idea of the ritual will be to change your luck and 'open the way' for blessings and fortune to favour you.

Also needed are seven safflowers. The reason is that this flower represents wealth and prosperity in the Chinese tradition. Some may use chrysanthemum in place of safflower, with red, the favoured colour as representing the yang forces of birth and fortune..

The diagram below shows the items that are needed for the altar.

1. A red card with the name of Tudi, the Lord of the Earth written on it. This is a shen pei or God Tablet that invites the God of the Earth and stands at the end of the Altar.
2. Red wax altar candles in twin candlesticks.
3. Incense pot and joss sticks.
4. Three small chinese cups with green tea.
5. Five small chinese cups with rice wine.
6. Spirit Money or Joss Money. Do not use the so-called, gold paper

Caishen And Wealth Children

money, Hell Money burned for ancestors. It is best to use shoujin or longevity money or jiama money.

7. Three tea lights on the left and four on the right hand side.
8. Seven eggs in a basket or bowl.
9. Three kinds of fruit.
10. The prepared talismans.
11. An unwashed item of the client's clothes, usually a shirt with incense sticks nearby, seven or nine in number.
12. Safflowers or chrysanthemums.

The main lamps are arranged either on the side of the altar or on the side using both Yin and Yang Dipper formations as shown.

Preparing The Lamps

The lamps are prepared by having three red talisman papers placed under its base along with seven pieces of shoujin or gold paper money.

With a consecrated brush, write the kui character shown in figure A. in the diagram.

As you write the Kui character say:
The cloud head,
Ghost Foot,
Big Dipper!

B. in the diagram shows an alternative form.

Place the papers and money under the lamps and arrange them into position.

The Sparse Text

The sparse text is really a letter of request to the gods summarising

The Wealth Gods of the Five Directions

the details and request of the client. On it write the client's name, birth date, address and nature of the business, occupation etc.

Finish with I sincerely pray for the road of fortune and prosperity, let extensive riches come.

The text is shown in Chinese characters in the diagram as F.

In pinyin this reads:

QI BIU YUN LU HENGTONG CAIYUAN GUANG JIN.

The Ceremony

1. The magician and the client are at the altar. The client holds three incense sticks and faces the host god. Let the client bow three times and say his most heartfelt prayers for prosperity and a change in his fortunes.

2. The magician then reads the Qing Jing Zhou spell for purification as previously given. To purify the Altar.

3. Light the three incense sticks near the client's clothes that are folded at the front of the altar, and with the right sword finger draw in the air above the clothes the Qiu Cai Fu or Request Money Seal shown in C. on the diagram.
   As you do this utter the words:
   Cloud head, ghost foot, ten thousand gold!
   (YUN YOU, GUI JIAO, JIN WANWAN)

4. Lay the sticks down horizontally on the clothes but be cautious ... potential fire hazard. You may want to use a metal plate or tin foil here.

5. Make the Dao Mudra with the left hand and let the right hand lights a match, and recite the Three Wonders Open the Fortune Spell (SAN QI KAI YUN ZHOU):

Diagrams For Wealth Rituals
Note the talismans are black ink on red paper.

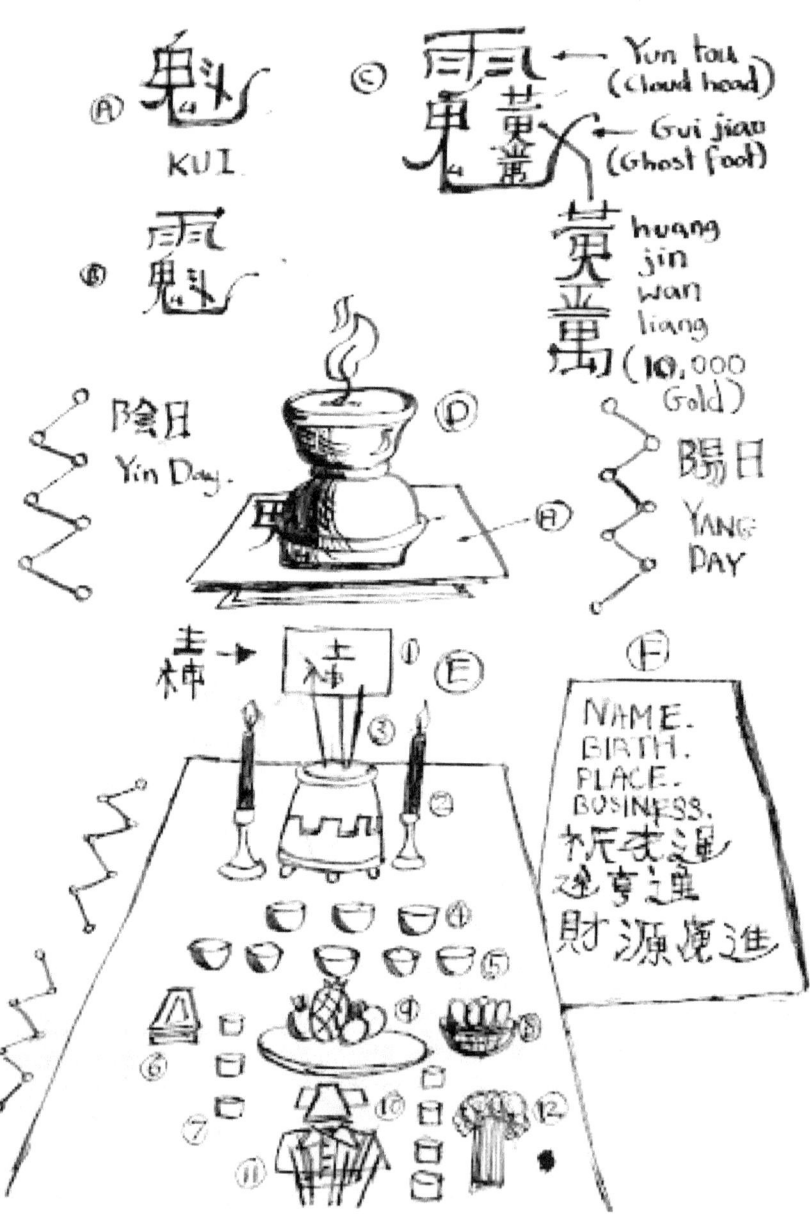

The Zhaocai Altar for Prosperity and Wealth

Zhaocai talisman 1

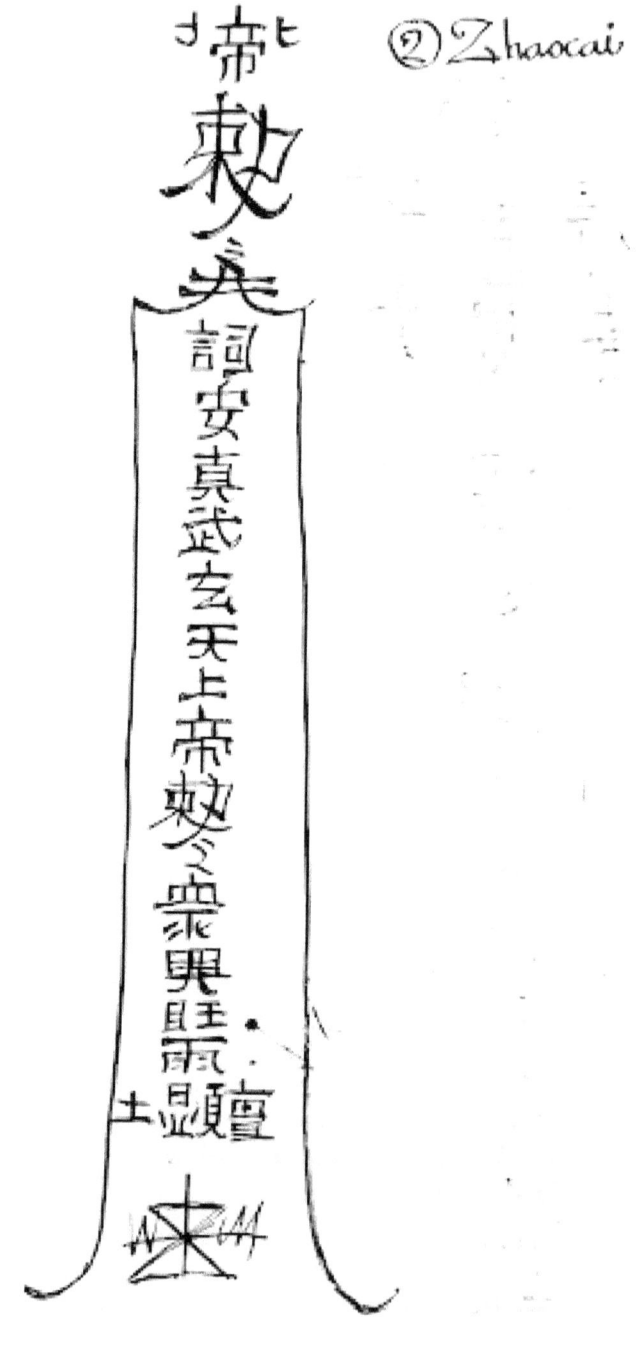

Zhaocai talisman 2

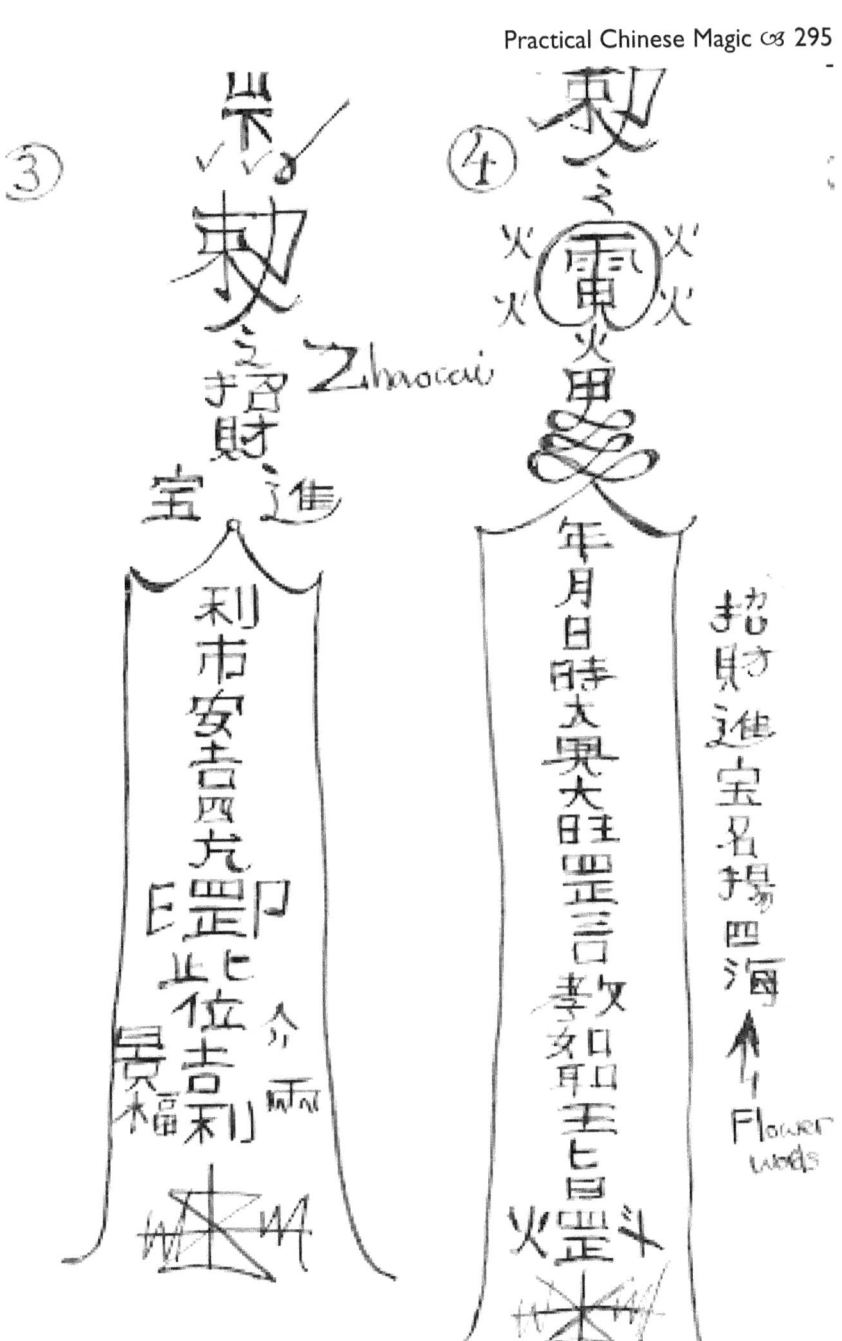

Zhaocai talismans 3 and 4

Above in the Heavens are the Three Wonders, the Sun, the Moon and the Stars. O I request the Star Lord and the ghosts are frightened and demons are forced to bow their heads in respect. The evil ones depart and leave without a trace.

The 28 Stars listen to my command, the Liu Ding and Liu Jia, the Shining Five Elements, the Seven Stars, the Eight Bagua, changing the course of fortune and opening the way to luck, opening the road to the disciple XXXX, that riches and prosperity are received.

By the command of Taishang Laojun.

Shen Bing Huoji Ru Lu Ling!

It is completed, CHI!!!!

The Master now lights the lamps.

6. With both hands make the Golden Ingot Mudra (Yuanbao Zhi). There now follows extensive invocations of the Wealth Gods.

ZHAOCAI ZHOU (Inviting Wealth Spell)

With respect I request Wu Caishen Xian Guan, Zhao Guangming Lishi Xian Guan, the handsome young noble, come and be present here. I bow and request Zhaocai Chen Jiu Guan to send the Child of Wealth, Cai Tongzi to assist the disciple XXXXXX who resides in XXXXXXX,

Zhaocai transports the treasures, profits and wealth.

I call the Five Directions Roads Caishen Lishi Xian Guan and Zhaocai Tianzun to bring riches.

Tianzun Zhaocai Shizhe to send the Child of Wealth to go to the … (the residence of the client), come to the incense that is offered by Divine Will.

Wealth continuously comes, treasures are bestowed, send great riches to the Disciple, transfer great wealth!

Shen Bing Huo Ji Ru Lu Ling!!

CAISHEN ZHOU
(Wealth God Spell)

Heavenly Spirit, Earthly Spirit, by command of Taishang Laojun, the Sun and Moon surround the Disciple XXXX with bright rays of light that bless and protect him. The work at hand is clear.

Every day, the Five Roads are open where great wealth shall travel. I request Jiu Tian Xuan Nu, the Nine Heaven Mysterious Girl to assist and send her heavenly warriors to the Disciple XXXXXX, our honoured guest, constantly inviting wealth from the ten directions.

I request Caishen Zhao Guangming Yuanshuai to come and command the Wealth Gods of the Five Roads to come.

From the East, the power of Wood, Caishen transports money.

From the South, the power of Fire, Caishen transports money.

From the West, the Power of Metal, Caishen transports money.

From the North, the power of Water, Caishen transports money.

From the Centre, the power of Soil, Caishen transports money.

The Five Directions, the Ten Paths of money and jewels come to the disciple named XXXX.

The Four Seasons and Eight Solar Periods, money continually comes.

Open the Four Seas and every year great wealth and riches come and those I have named descend to assist. The Gods immediately manifest their power and bestow on the disciple XXXX, day by day, constantly showering XXXX with blessings, health, wealth, longevity and riches.

Quickly come Liu Ding and Liu Jia, by command, immediately,

now! Assist the disciple XXXX at the place of XXXXXXXXX(name of home and or business), our honoured guest, and also his whole family who here offer incense.

Give prosperity day and night, transport money, DOU! Money comes constantly, DOU! Silver and gold money from the Five Directions and Ten Roads, move, arrive, transport wealth into the home of the disciple XXXXXX, money fills the hall, money fills the treasury, great fortune for all the family, vast and great prosperity, great richness, filling the bank, by command of the Mysterious Girl of the Ninth Heaven, Jiu Tian Xuan Nu.

Shen Bing Houji Ru Lu Ling!!!!!

7. The Master and the client again use personal heartfelt and sincere prayers to the Host God. Use the Moonblocks or I ching to determine if the operation has been successful. If not, repeat the invocations. If the divination marks a success, burn joss money and burn wealth talisman 1 and 2.
8. Place the safflowers in a bowl of water. You may also burn a Qingjing Fu. Let the client again pray for prosperity.
9. The client take home the clothes and the eggs. He or she wears this item of clothing without fail without washing it for 12 consecutive nights, sleeping in it.

The eggs, the client must walk exactly 49 steps from his home or place of business and throw and smash the eggs one by one saying:

Bad Luck Gone, Good Luck Come!!

Practical Chinese Magic ✷ 299

Doumu, Lady of the Chariot and Big Dipper Mother

33. Mysteries Of The Nine Stars

The ritual had reached its climax. He now had to perform the pace of the Big Dipper, drawing on the great celestial energies to catapult his consciousness into the occult planes of pure purple energy. His hands formed the necessary mudras, carefully he began to trod with crane-like steps, careful and gracefully. At each step, he drew unknown sigils calling the names of the holy stars of power. Each step seemed to become increasingly more difficult as a river of etheric force flowed in torrents around his feet. He made sudden and sharp veering turns, following the ancient pattern. Finally, the step was complete. The dimensions suddenly yawned before him as his soul went into freefall into the gaping darkness with its bands of twisting purple light.

The magician in the above description has used a special technique known as the Pace of Yu or the Big Dipper Step.

The Pace of Yu is an ancient technique deriving from the earliest shaman sorcerers of ancient China, The basic premise is to evoke supernatural presence and enter the kingdoms of the unseen by using consciously careful footwork to create an energy matrix on the earth, that reflects the heavens. The magician then literally traverses the universe. To understand this method one must understand the role of the Big Dipper in Chinese occult thought.

The Big Dipper consists of the well known seven stars that form part of Ursa Major. The Dipper seemed to the Chinese to be a huge ladle that constantly, and in cycles, made an annual pivot around the celestial axis. The Big Dipper was, therefore, for us on earth, a cosmic doorway to the realms of the Gods as well as a dispenser of the heavenly Qi.

Several threads of occult thought, some of which came from Indian tantra, by the way of Buddhism, found its way into the secret Taoist teachings of the Big Dipper.

Chief among these Tantric Indian influences was the goddess Doumu, the Great Big Dipper Mother. The Great Mother of Heaven is said to be the very same Goddess who revealed herself as Jiu Tian Xuan Nu, the Mysterious Girl of the Ninth Heaven, This is important because Jiu Tian is, of course, the Queen of Magic in the Maoshan tradition, Suddenly Jiu Tian and her attributes make sense. Part warrior, part sorceress and part teacher of the sexual mysteries under her guise as Su Nu, (The Plain Girl). In many ways, she is cast in the same mould as the Mesopotamian Ishtar or Astarte.

The image of Doumu is almost certainly from over the Himalayas in India, where she was called Marici. Marici and Doumu are depicted as beautiful women seated upon a lotus upon the back of a sow. Sometimes she is shown many armed and many faced, or with seven sows pulling her chariot. Various sutras in Tibet and China show her to be a very protective goddess. The Seven Dipper Stars are invoked to increase prosperity or protect the practitioner.

The nine stars of the Big Dipper, seven visible and two invisible or 'black stars' are said to be the sons of Doumu. We refer to them as the Beidou Jun, or the Big Dipper Kings. They are intimately linked with destiny, life and death of every living being on earth. In the novel The Three Kingdoms, Zhuge Liang observes the dimming of a star that is an ill omen. His death is forthcoming. Zhuge immediately sets about constructing a ritual that can extend his life by another twelve years. With a throng of strong men dressed in black and circling his great tent with black flags, he sets up seven lamps to represent the seven stars of the Big Dipper. They must remain lit through the whole night to extend his life. However, quite by accident a gentleman stumbles in and knocks over one of the lamps and Zhuge knows it is destined to die.

This ritual of the Seven Lamps still exists today as we will teach you in this book albeit in a simpler form than that performed by Zhuge Liang.

The pattern and shape of the Big Dipper is a fairly common sight on talismans and ritual implements such as the Seven Star Sword or Green Dragon Sword of the Taoist occult tradition.

The symbol of the much misunderstood Svastika is believed to be derived from the four positions of the Big Dipper around the celestial pole.

On occasion, such as in certain Maoshan meditations and rituals the practitioner must face the direction in which the Dipper is pointing. Why? That is the direction in which the Heavenly Qi is pouring into the realm of mortals.

The Big Dipper as mentioned before consists of seven visible and two invisible stars. These two black stars can only be seen by occultists of certain development and possessing the Tian Mu or Heaven's Eye.

The Seven Stars have the following names and attributes.

1. TAN LANG.

The name of this star in Taoism is the Greedy Wolf. In Western astronomy it is Dubhe. The Greedy Wolf is the Star that points directly at Polaris, which in Taoist theosophy is the central axis and location of the Heavenly Palace. You could be forgiven for thinking that the name Greedy Wolf is somehow negative in its connotation. This isn't so. This Wolf is 'greedy' for positive energy. Being close to the Heavenly Source, it is the vehicle of Pure Yang energy and is a direct representative of the Emperor of Heaven. Indeed Greedy Wolf is sometimes known as the Guardian of Yang, or the Guardian of Light. It has the quality of nourishing the Heavens. In divination and feng shui we call it Zheng Xing or the Star of Truth or Righteousness. Its associated direction is the North-west, the Gate of Heaven. The colour is white His Trigram in the Bagua is Kan, Water. The planet is Jupiter. In the Later Heaven sequence, the element is Wood.

2. JU MEN.

The name means Giant Gate. It represents the great feminine powers of Yin and is associated with the Empress of Heaven. Her colour is black and the direction is West. The element is the Earth, but in the Later Bagua sequence, it is Water. Her planet is also Jupiter. In a sense, Greedy Wolf is the cosmic phallus of creative Yang energy. Ju Men is the womb or vagina, the gate of life and death. Her trigram is naturally Kun, the Receptive. Ju Men is the giver and caretaker of the Dark Light of the Yin Essence. In divination and feng shui she is called the Fa Xing, the Star of Law or Justice. Giving shape and method to the pure energies of Tan Lang.

3. LIU CUN.

This name means Stored Wealth. It has a sense of retaining and storing energy, nurturing, capturing and retaining the Yin and Yang energies that come forth from the stars that precede it. It also represents the collective energies of all experience and so is associated with the energetic reservoir of knowledge of the Ancestors. For this reason, it is associated with the direction of the North East … the Gate of Ghosts. Its colour is light pale green like a milky jade stone. Its element is either Wood or in the later Heaven sequence, Earth. The planet is Saturn. The Trigram is Zhen, Thunder. In Feng Shui and divination it is named the Ming Xing, the Star of Destiny or Life. In this sense, destiny is linked to the ongoing chain of ancestral expression.

4. WEN QU.

Can be best translated as the Path of the Scholar. The energy of this star is about the expression of the energies in thoughts, words, ideas and names. The organisation of energy into thought. We can compare it to ancient Gnostic and Qabalistic ideas on the Logos. The Logos or Word-Reason giving shape to the raw energy of divine thought. In Taoist thought, the Yin and Yang combine in countless xing or forms. Its direction is the South and its colour is Dark Green…the condensing of the energies of light green Liu Cun. Its element is Wood but is Water in the Later Heaven. The planet is Mercury. The associated trigram is Xun, the Wind. The Wind being the carrier of ideas and inspiration.

5. LIAN ZHEN.

The name roughly translates as the Incorruptible Pure and True. It has no associated trigram and is associated with the Centre. The colour is yellow and the direction is the north. Its element is Earth, but Fire in the Later Heaven. Its planet is Mars. It rids one of impurities, refining the thought. In feng shui, it is the Sha Xing or Star of Death and Transformation.

6. WU QU.

Is the Path of the Warrior. The energy now is in action, expressing itself, coming into being. Its colour is white and is associated with the Southwest, the Gate of Man. In other words, energy now descends into a created being to experience existence. Its element is metal, the crystallisation of energy into form. The Trigram is Qian, Heaven. As above, so below The planet is Venus. Its other name is Wei Xing, the Star of Danger. The vulnerability felt on the path of action and manifestation.

7. PO JUN

The Broken Army. The form must face its dissolution and change. The colour is red and is associated with the East and the element of Metal and the planet Venus. Its alternative name is Ying Xing, the Star of Duty, Recognising the goal of existence and subject to the laws of the cosmos. Its associated trigram is Dui, the Lake or Marsh.

8. FU.

Is one of the invisible or dark stars that can only be seen by the Immortals. Its colour is white. It is the Left Assistant and is associated with the Earth element and the trigram the Mountain, Gen. The planets are Saturn and the Sun.

9. BI

Also an invisible or dark star. It is the Right Assistant and its colour is purple. Its trigram is Li, Fire. It is associated with Mercury and the Moon.

We can see from above that the Big Dipper represents a process of energy, a heavenly representation of the emergence and transformation of original Qi or spirit into manifestation. From point of origin to solid crystallisation in existence. On one level, therefore, when, say, pacing the Big Dipper, you are making that energetic journey either to or from that Origin of All.

The whole process can be altered for various magical and spiritual objectives so certain energies are traced or followed in certain ways. Thus there are numerous variations of the Big Dipper pace. The most basic being the Yin and Yang variations, which, I suppose we could call going to or going from. Going up or coming down.

The Big Dipper is strongly linked to the individual's fate or destiny. We may recall Zhuge Liang's fated death that he observed in the stars and his subsequent ritual to add twelve years to his life. The Sutras of the Big Dipper are largely concerned with the luck and fate of the individual, and therefore the aspirant conducts a ritual or sadhana to receive the blessings of Marichi and the associated Big Dipper Maidens.

The Sutra of the Big Dipper had such a massive influence that it found itself in Tantric Buddhism in China, Tibet and Mongolia as well as having a place in the massive Taoist Canon. The Mongolian version of this Sutra is the most complete and so therefore I will give a short precis of it here, enough to allow you to engage in the practice.

Practice Of The Big Dipper Sutra To The Seven Maidens

1. First you must know your star.

a. If you're born in the year of the Rat you come under the star, Greedy Wolf, and you should wear its Talisman. The correct offering is large grained millet

b. If you are born in the years of the Ox and Boar you come under the jurisdiction of Giant's Gate. Pearl millet is the offering.

c. If born in the years of the Tiger or the Dog then Lu Cun is your star. The offering is rice.

d. Those born in the year of the Rabbit or Rooster come under Wen Qu. The offering is wheat.

e. Those born under the years of the Dragon or Monkey come under Lian Zhen. The offering is hemp seed.

f. Those born in the years of the Sheep and Snake come under Wuqu. The offering is black beans.

g. Those born in the year of the Horse come under Po Jun and the offering is green beans.

2. The Mantra of the Eight Stars :

Om Sapta Jinaya Bhajami Jyasa Jambu
Dhama Svani Naksatram Bhavatu Svaha.

If it is recited 108 times daily you and your family are protected. If recited 500 times daily it brings greater protection from the Big Dipper

Ladies.

3. To invoke the Big Dipper Ladies to improve one's fortune and status.

The Altar is prepared and incense is lit. Around the incense pot, have seven bowls of grains as according to your star, and seven teas and seven fruits and wines.

4. Say the vow.

' I request with all my heart that the Seven Luminaries, the Venerable Stars, the Smashers, the Hungry Wolf, the Giant Gate, the Money Preserver, the Literary Song, the Pure and Upright, the Military Song and the Breaker of Armies, on the behalf of…….. (name) ……., that you free him/her from danger and lengthen his life so he will see one hundred autumns. I have set up the Altar! Show kindness and accept this offering. Protect ……….., free them from disasters and lengthen their life."

Say three times.

5. Make the Big Dipper Mudra. (see Chapter 26)

Fingers interlocked and thumbs on the nails of the middle fingers touch. Index fingers bent down and tucked and little fingers erect.

6. Recite the two mantras of Invoking the Big Dipper.

Nama samanta dara dara pacara hum.

Namah samanta darana ehyehi pax hai dai kai

rax murdara gharaham svaha.

7. Burn the offerings

8. Observe the natal star.

If it seems to change colour and scintillate with yellowish light it is good.

9. The text notes that one's good and bad deeds are said to be recorded

by the Controller of Fate every 57th Day of the 60 day cycle on the Keng Shen Day. Serious offences mean inevitable destruction and lesser offences are a sentence of twelve years.

The Big Dipper Ritual here is a combination of Taoist and Buddhist ideas and is a useful addition to the basic Daoist magician's arsenal, especially in terms of correcting fate and fortune.

We will now introduce some unique aspects of Daosit practice that in some way incorporate the mysteries of the Big Dipper.

The Big Dipper Talismans for the above ritual.

Read them from right to left.
Greedy Wolf. Year of the Rat.
Giant Gate. Years of the Ox and Pig (Boar).
Scholar's Store. Years of Tiger and Dog.
Scholar's Song. Years of Rabbit and Rooster.
Lian Zhen. Years of Dragon and Monkey.
Wu Qu. Years of Sheep and Snake.
Po Jun. Year of the Horse.

Pressing The Big Dipper Lamp

In the Great Dipper Ritual for a year of prosperity and fortune, longevity and freedom from calamity and illness this beautiful ritual calls upon the Great Mother Dipper Goddess, Dou Ma. She is said to rule the palace of destiny, (Changsheng Gong) fate and longevity of the hun or spirit of mankind.

She is in charge of the ever turning cycles of the years, seasons, months and days, and the processes of change that accompany them in the total human experience including suffering, aging, illness and so on.

Thus we often call this the
BEIDOU SOUL METHOD or BEIDOU HUN FA.

The ritual is centered around a ritual bucket or barrel, the Dou Tong. Note that the word for bucket, dou, in Chinese is also the word for the Dipper.

The bucket is filled with rice and then certain objects placed within it:

Cheng, the hanging scale.
Zhu Chi, a wooden ruler inscribed with the Big Dipper name.
Jiandao, metal scissors.
Jingzi, a round mirror.
Qixing Jian, a seven star sword.
Youdeng, an oil lamp.
Ri Yue Shan, the Sun and Moon fan

The whole thing is covered by a canopy or parasol with a golden peak and a fringe of tassels known as the liang san.

On an altar there are two red candles and an incense burner.
On a plate are three or five kinds of fruit.
Then there are three red bowls. Contained in two of the bowls is a

The Three Officials are shown in the front.
These deities rule the affairs of Earth, Water and Heaven

single steamed chinese sponge cake, in the third a Good Fortune Rice Cake. Some magicians in China may prefer the use of small balls made of taro called Qingyuan, as they represent the idea of eternity and Heaven.

There are three cups of chinese green tea and a further three cups of rice wine.

Right at the front is an unwashed item of the supplicant's clothes, usually a shirt. There are also bundles of money and the Big Dipper Fortune Talisman and a set of Kai Yun Fu, or Open the Luck talismans.

The magician will write a Shuwen (sparse text) that states the year, month, day and time as well as the purpose of the ritual and a personal prayer to the Gods and Immortals, especially of the Big Dipper. This is usually written on yellow paper that is easily burned.

This is a long and complicated ritual used when life is not what it should be. There may be illness, constant bad luck, a failure in business, a lawsuit, marital disharmony or even a total lack of love life, mental illness and depression, an important exam and so on. Thus when writing your shuwen or a shuwen on behalf of the client you should state your problems clearly and ask equally clearly for the blessing of them to be solved.

Now the Altar is set up both the magician and the supplicant take up sticks of incense and leave the ritual room to stand outside and request the Gods in a personal, heartfelt and improvised manner.

Now due to the length and complexity of this ritual let us take it step by step.

1. The mage lights the joss sticks and candles.

Tudi the Earth and soil God really represents the local spirit of a place

2. Recite the Qing Shen and Hushen spells given earlier in this book, ie Request the Gods, and Protect the Body.

3. Use a Jingshui Talisman as taught to purify the altar.

4. Recite the Incense Spell (XIANG ZHOU):

> The court of Pengying is bright,
> Sending gifts to the Heavens,
> The Sun is the King of Purity,
> Like a mirror, light dawning on this temple,
> The Qi is auspicious in the misty incense smoke,
> The heart declares the Secret Laws,
> Of entering the Path of the Dao and longing for immortality,
> Taishang commanded the Three Treasures Heavenly Worthy
> and the glittering gems vibrate,
> The midst of the kingdom is purified,
> The rivers and seas are calmed,
> The high mountains are swallowed by clouds,
> Ten thousand spirits salute,
> The request causes the Gods and the True to assemble,
> Heaven has no fear of terrors, even those concealed,
> The Earth dismisses the demonic aura,
> The empty cave is luminous and bright,
> Reaching the utmost High Jade Capital.
> Constant purity and constant calm, the Great Tianzun.
> The sincere heart is calm and pure, the Dao is our Master,
> Like unto the Middle Heaven Treasure,
> Emperor Tianbao, the Moon,
> Cleansing and sweeping away clouds of confusion and foolishness,
> One wheel emitting rays of light fills the Highest Great Void,

The Upper Medicine Body is in the centre,

Jing, Qi and Shen all people have them and are capable of not losing them and by doing so increasing their skill,

The ability to blend with and return to the Tao,

The Golden Tripod Cauldron, the yellow sprout daily generates one burning excellent fragrance that is the root of the Self-Nature,

The Yellow Court Incense Burner within emits an auspicious mist up into the empty sky, moving towards the floating clouds and sealing the Upper with blessings of longevity and life eternal,

The Dao acts, the Great are honoured, and so the door is opened to benefit humanity, Brilliance, clarity, and the fundamental laws and the scriptures thus exist.

5. Next in the ritual sequence follow the familiar Purifying Heart Spell, Cleansing Body Spell, Earth God Spell, the Spell of Heaven and Earth and the Spell of the Golden Light. See the section on the Eight Great Spells in this Book.

6. Two smaller Incense blessing spells follow the above:

Blessing With The Incense Spells (Zhu Xiang Zhou)

The Dao is the cause of heart-knowing,
The heart borrows sweetness passed on to it,
Sweetness burns in the Jade Furnace,
The heart accumulates the Supreme Being,
The True Spirit looks below,
The flag of the Immortals flies high,

The official order declares it's passage,
A direct path to the Ninth Heaven is attained.
The incense cloud rises,
Divine power spread over thousands of miles,
The incense cloud is thick,
The revealing excellence reaches to the Court of Heaven,
Above stands the Golden Tower,
Next to the Hall of the King,
The Golden Tower Royal Palace,
where the men of virtue with fragrance beseech the Tower,
Fragrance penetrates the Three Realms,
Penetrating the Three Realms with the Divine Talisman,
Sending forth the Worthy Talisman,
Listen to me for the incense-message is a mist
and is at one with the request of the virtuous person,
The incense cloud is thick and a mist on Earth and in Heaven,
A point rises and the incense-request passes through
the Gates of Dharma,
Southern Chen Big Dipper company descends,
A Five Colour brilliant cloud,
The Purple Palace opens in its midst,
the Peach Blossom Valley Cave Immortals receive the request,
O I courteously request the worthy Talisman Envoy,
I am also communing with the Earth Lord Tudi,
Taiyi Rescues from Hardship Celestial Worthy,
The Three Officials Great Lords descend to this Altar!!!

7. You may recall in an earlier chapter that magic cannot properly manifest in the material world without involving the Tudi, the Earth God. The Earth God in this context is more akin to the idea of a

local Earth Spirit or a Spiritus Loci. Thus we read the Earth Lord Spell.

The Root Direction Tudi,
God of the Spirit of the Earth,
Who communes with Heaven and yet reaches to Earth,
Who descends into the Underworld and on our behalf opens it for us without tarrying,
Rising into Heaven, descending to Earth,
The Ten Continents and Three Islands,
The talisman moves and the Seal moves,
Calling all together unceasingly we request,
Performing a great service on this day,
The Script Name of the Upper requests you to come,
Arrive at this Altar,
Come by my order,
It is so commanded by Taishang Laojun Chi!!
Ji Ji Ru Lu Ling!

8. Now follows the astrological power spells:

Big Dipper Spell
(BEIDOU ZHOU)

DOU! SHOU! QUAN! XING! BI! FU! PIAO!

Spell Of The Twenty-Eight Star Lodges
(ERSHIBA XIU ZHOU)

JIAO! KANG! DI! FANG! XIN! WEI! JI! DOU! NIU! NU! XU! WEI! SHI! BI! KUI! LOU! WEI! MAO! BI! ZI! SHEN! JING! GUI! LIU! XING! ZHANG! YI! ZHEN!

Spell Of The Heavenly Stems
(TIANGAN ZHOU)

JIA! YI! BING! DING! WU! JI! GONG! XIN! REN! GUI!

Spell Of The Earthly Branches
(DIZHI ZHOU)

ZI! CHOU! YIN! MAO! CHEN! SI! WU! WEI! SHEN! YOU! XU! HAI!

Spell Of The Five Elemental Phases
(WUXING ZHOU)

JIN! MU! SHUI! HUO! TU! (Metal, Wood, Water, Fire, Earth!)

9. The last preparation spell for this difficult ritual is asking the Divine Spirit of the Gods to assist you in the ritual.

Spirit Assisting Spell
(ZHU LING ZHOU)

By means of union,

By means of union with the Gods,

The essence of the Gods assists me

And I assist the spirit of the Gods

The true origin is one place,

And Ten Thousand Gods listen!

The mage now puts the name(s) of the client written on yellow paper on the lamp and holds the Jingshui or water purification talisman and recites:

Water and stone, send the spirit,

Sun and Moon send the spirit,

In the midst is concealed the Big Dipper,

Within the San Tai respond,

One cup of wine and Heaven and Earth change,

Two cups of wine and the Sun and Moon are bright,

Three cups of wine and here comes the Thunder Troops General!

Quickly as fire he comes and in his true form!

(sprinkles the water on the altar three times)

10. At this point he begins the ritual proper he prepares to light the lamp The name-paper will burn at this point. He chants the Dian Deng Zhou or lighting the lamp spell while holding the Golden Light Mudra as shown earlier in this volume:

The Spirit Mountain has the power of command,

Sending forth warriors,

The seven stars descend to tend to the true people,

Assisting on both the left and the right,

Manifesting magical power,

The Ferocious Great General commands the Celestial Troops,

The Five Thunder Envoy, the Six Jia and the Six Ding,

The Profound Lord of Heaven Supreme King,

Taichung Three Stars,

Quickly leave the Golden Pavilion,

Descend unto this mortal realm,

Rid of ill-fortune and rectify hardships,

Save life, prolong life and display your mighty power,

Emit strength,

Let the Evil Ones perish,

The three immortal souls shall protect the body,

The seven mortal souls defend us,

The Primordial Essence is radiant,

The body is a vessel of light,

Disobey the Dao and death follows,

The command presides over us and we follow life,
I command it by Taishang Laojun!
JI JI RU LU LING!!!

Before lighting the lamp, it is now up to the magician to infuse the rays of light with further magical force. In Daoist esoteric thought light is a carrier of 'magical information', both the will of the magus and of the deities he invokes. This concept goes quite far back to the earliest Maoshan and Lingbao texts. To this end he or she reads the Fa Hao Guang Zhou or Sending the Rays of Light Spell.

The Root Master of brilliance sends rays of light,
The Ancestral Master of brilliance sends rays of light,
The Seven Ancestral Immortal Master sends rays of Light,
Immortal Boy and Jade Girl send rays of light,
Launching rays of light, powerful and blazing light,
Launching rays of light that clearly illuminate,
Launching rays of light over a thousand miles
and the left eye is purified,
The right eye sees brightness,
In one burst all the rays of light come to the body and appear,
A second burst and the rays of the light in the body are visible,
A third burst and rays of light penetrate
and pass through and ascend to the Heavens,
By the command of Taishang Laojun.
Shen Bing Huoji Ru Lu Ling!

11. Using seven pieces of Longevity Money he lights the lamp and the name paper.

12. He then proceeds to consecrate the food so it is suitable for the Gods and Immortals:
    The spell used to do this is called Shi Shishi, Bestowing Food Spell:

    All you Gods, all you Gods listen carefully to the Spell,
    I declare the Taishang Spirit Order,
    This mortal food changes into Celestial Food,
    This Mortal water becomes Precious Jade Liquid,
    ZI! One transforms into ten!
    WU! Ten turns into one hundred!
    MAO! One hundred turns into a thousand!
    YOU! One thousand turns into ten thousand
    which changes into ten million and so the changes are endless!
    I offer the Celestial Immortals assembled here today, these offerings.
    Take this food in all the Ten Directions,
    All you Immortals and we hope for merit and virtue thereby,
    We give it to all,
    I offer to all those Immortals assembled a return to the Dao,
    OM FU MO LUO, MI SUO HE SAN DENG.

13. Both mage and client bow and burn the shuwen and some gold paper money.

14. The mage and client both approach the Lamp and cask with all the instruments within it. At this point the main meat of the ritual begins so to speak.
    The Seven Star Sword is associated with Fire and the South.
    The Ruler is associated with Wood and the East.
    The Scissors are associated with the element of Metal and the West.
    The Balance Weight Hook is associated with Water and the North.
    The Mirror is associated with Soil and the centre.

All these instruments are used to gather the soul or shou hun. In Daoist thought as we live life we lose fragments of our soul and in some way we are incomplete and not at our full potential. Due to soul loss we may experience more depression, ill fortune, relationship problems and so on. In this part of the ritual the magician calls back lost soul fragments.

> In the East, gather in the soul with the Iron Ruler,
> The General gathers in the soul in the head with the ruler,
> The disciple named xxxxxx's three souls path is unblocked and obstacles dispersed and he possesses the Jade Ruler that measures the soul to return,
> The Root Master assists us to gather the soul for its return,
> The Patriarch assists us to gather the soul for its return,
> The Immortals assist us to gather the soul for its return,
> The Jade Maiden assists us to gather the soul for its return,
> O gather the Soul Three Master Three Boys,
> O gather the soul Three Master Three Boys Officials,
> Quickly gather the soul, very quickly it shall arrive,
> Very quickly gather the soul,
> Very quickly let it return,
> Gather the soul back to the head, return!
> Gather the soul back to the feet, return!
> Gather the soul back to the Three Immortal Souls
> and Seven Mortal Souls, return!
> Return to the root of life and the place of the twelve meridians, spirit and mind, return to the root of life,
> The Three and Seven Souls of xxxxx return to the root of life!
> Shen bing huoji ru lu ling!
> QIAN YUAN HENG LI ZHEN!
> The Taiji directs us in the correct way to act!
> The Three Souls return.
> The Seven Souls are spirits.

The Three souls are at the root place.
The seven souls are at the root of life.
I request the Three Teachers Three Dao Sages Script Talisman Water
to gather the three and seven souls of xxxxxx to return!
Shen bing huoji ru lu ling!
The left hand in the Dao Seal and the ruler in the right hand present it to the East.
The mage continues:
In the South we harvest the soul with the Sword,
The Northern Pole bestows the power to cut the evil spirits,
The three souls path of the disciple is unblocked
and he also possesses the sword.
Slay! The soul returns
(Grasp the Treasure Sword right hand and left Dao Seal)
In the West we gather the soul with the Scissors,
Wang Mu bestows upon us the power to slice the evil spirits,
The Disciple's three souls road is unblocked
and he also possesses the Golden Scissors, the soul returns!
(Right hand grasps the scissors and left hand in Dao Seal)

In the North we gather the soul with the Precious Weighing Hook and hook and stop the wandering soul to return. The Disciple's three souls road is unblocked and they also now possess the Precious Weighing Scales Hook, the soul returns.

(Grasp the hook in right hand and make the Dao mudra with the left)

In the centre we gather the soul with the Bright Mirror,
Tai Wu Ying's Warrior Troops take the soul to return,
The Disciple's three soul road is unblocked and they also possess the Mirror of Clarity, soul return.

(Pick up the mirror with right, left Dao, but this time reflect light to the four directions)

Generally the magician will now perform a simple divination with moonblocks as they are called in the West. See Tools of the Trade chapter. If the result is favourable then proceed, if not repeat the invocation at step 14. Until you have a good throw.

15. Now push all the tools, the ruler, sword, hook, scissors and mirror firmly into the rice and do the Big Dipper Step, (see talisman chapter), but with these words at each of the seven steps and with the left hand in Dao Seal and the right hand in the Sword Seal:
    O the pure white Qi of the Primordial Chaos fills my form,
    The steps of Yu hasten the merging as I ascend to the brightness,
    Return to Heaven, Return to Earth, the Seven Star Steps!
    Shooting forth the paces of strength,
    the Steps of the Big Dipper Qi of the Nine Spirits,
    The lower points to the gathering of evil and the evil is shocked,
    The gathering of misfortune perishes,
    I have longevity! I have obtained longevity, longevity for longevity!

Yu the Great merges Heaven and Earth via the Dipper

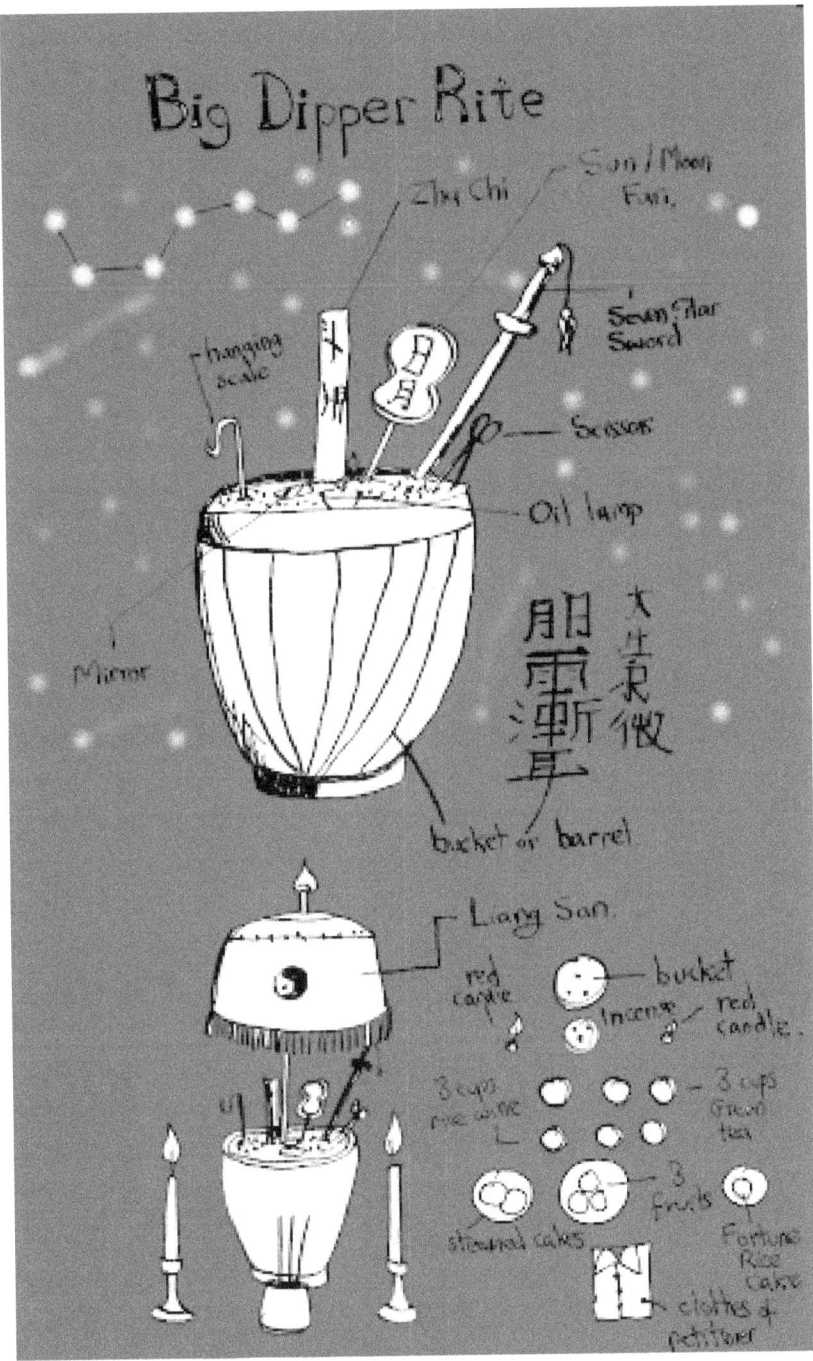

Ritual set up for the Northern Dipper Soul Technique
The Big Dipper Cultivation Methods

16. Finish by reciting the Golden Light Spell and the Calm Spell.

17. Burn some Gold Money.

18. Pressing the Lamp has many uses, but is especially good against illness, lawsuits, loss of mind, depression, exams, late marriage, runs of bad luck, curing disease, luck in legal matters.

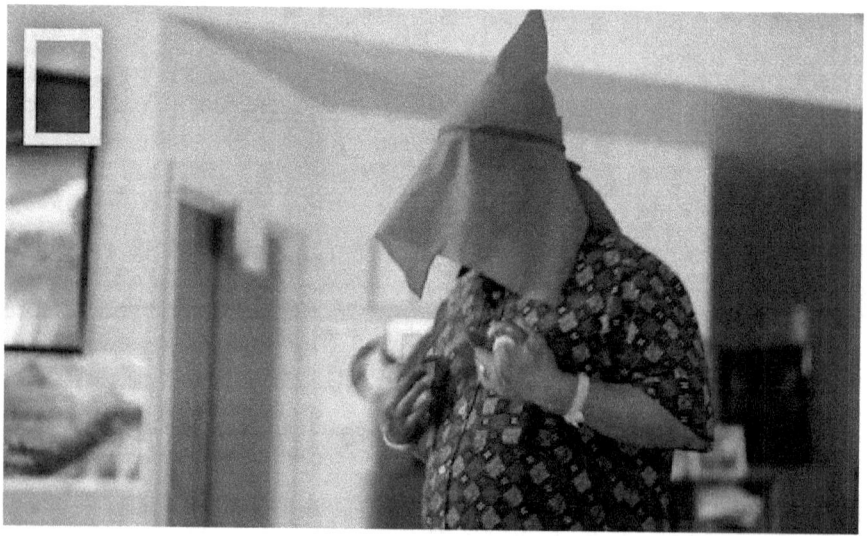

Hmong shaman with a veil similar to that used in veiled Dipper walking

Appendix
To Ritual Of Pressing The Lamp
The Big Dipper Sutra

This is a basic canonical text of a practical nature often employed in the rituals of Taoism. For example you will find it in Soul Retrieval, Fertility. Luck Changing, Healing and other rituals.

In the lore of the Dao the sutra was revealed by Taishang Laojun on the 8th day of the 1st lunar month in the Great Pure Realm (Tai Qing Jie) in the Taiji Palace. If not used within a ritual, it can be chanted alone with incense and offerings of green tea and fruit.

1. The Seven Origin Dipper Lords eliminate the Three Calamities.
   (San zai e) = the three lesser, War, Faminine, Plague.
   The three greater. Fire, Flood and Storm.

2. The Seven Origin Dipper Lords eliminate the Four Evils.
   (The four seasonal illnesses)

3. The Seven Origin Dipper Lords eliminate the Five Elements Evils.

4. The Seven Origin Dipper Lords eliminate the Six Evils.
   (Liu hai e. Evils arising from the Five senses plus mind.)
   Also six astrological illnesses arising from clashes (Chong) between the Earthly branches.

5. The Seven Origin Dipper Lords eliminate the seven injuries.
   (illness arising from excess in seven emotions)

6. The Seven Origin Dipper Lords eliminate the Eight Difficulties.
   (Eight kinds of disease and eight karma)

7. The Seven Origin Dipper Lords eliminate the Nine Star Evils.
   (Evil fate arising from the Dipper Stars)

8. The Seven Origin Dipper Lords eliminate the troubles between man and wife.

9. The Seven Origin Dipper Lords eliminate the troubles of boys and girls. (sons and daughters and courtship)

10. The Seven Origin Dipper Lords eliminates the troubles of childbirth.

11. The Seven Origin Dipper Lords eliminate the evil of unhappy departed ancestors.

Big Dipper Mudra

12. The Seven Origin Dipper Lords eliminate plague and disease.
13. The Seven Origin Dipper Lords eliminate illness.
14. The Seven Origin Dipper Lords eliminate evil spirits.
15. The Seven Origin Dipper Lords eliminates the dangers of wolves and tigers.
16. The Seven Origin Dipper Lords eliminate the danger of poisonous insects and snakes.
17. The Seven Origin Dipper Lords eliminates the danger of robbery and theft.
18. The Seven Origin Dipper Lords eliminates false accusation, imprisonment and punishment.
19. The Seven Origin Dipper Lords eliminate sudden and violent death.
20. The Seven Origin Dipper Lords eliminate witchcraft, evil spells and oaths.
21. The Seven Origin Dipper Lords eliminate the result of violating the Laws of Heaven.
22. The Seven Origin Dipper Lords eliminate the violations of the Laws of Earth.
23. The Seven Origin Dipper Lords eliminate the evils of swords and weapons.
24. The Seven Origin Dipper Lords eliminate the evils of fire and water. (euphemism for extremes of continual misfortune and misery)
25. The Seven Origin Dipper Lords are virtuous communicating by spirit and relieving the suffering of all living beings.

The Big Dipper Cultivation Methods

To really work with the Big Dipper in a fuller way, there are practices which 'tune' you into its energies. The Big Dipper Step is one way to do this. The practitioner can perform the Big Dipper step wearing a dark veil. Then, lying down, which can in western terms astrally project to the Dipper plane. In such a vision you may meet with any one of the Dipper Lords or Ladies.

This can be done by adopting a comfortable position wearing a veil. This should be a black, white or red cloth. Perform the Big Dipper Steps with the spell:

> Flying out of my body to visit the gods,
> My Qi turns to merit and guarding against spirits,
> Let the evil aura disappear.
> Ji Ji Ru Lu Ling!!

The disciple then sits or lies down, whatever is more comfortable, and forms a vivid image of the Big Dipper in the blackness or indigo of space directly above one's head. Continually repeat the spell and mentally visualise your light body emerging from the top of your head. You then mentally climb each of the stars as if they are rungs on a ladder to reach the immortal realms. To finish the exercise you simply reverse the procedure, climbing down each star in turn and re-entering via the bai hui point (fontanelle) and then remove the veil.

There are many such techniques for exiting and entering the spiritual realms.

Another version you hold the Seven Star Peach Sword to the chest and walk the Bugang. Then again repeat the procedure walking out from the top of your head and up the ladder of stars. This time however the aspirant visualises a ball of fire on the tip of the sword or sword finger in lieu of an actual sword and with each star traversed let it grow bigger and brighter until the flame seems to fill the cosmos. You would use this to burn away evil spirits before any ritual.

In other books in this series we will further investigate such methods of soul travel and sending the shadow as this book is of a fundamental basic level.

A more practical meditation method that doesn't involve the disciple exiting his body on an astral journey to the stars is as follows.

This method is called the Qixing Beidou Gui Yuan Nei Humo Zhen Fa, the Method of the Seven Star Northern Dipper Returning to the Origin and Guarding the Internal Reality Method.

1. Sit quietly in your standard meditation posture, let your thoughts slow down and settle with some light breathing.

2. When you feel ready, turn your vision in towards the Dan Tian area just below the navel and within the central axis of your body. Form there the image of a Golden Turtle, with its head facing towards your navel. Form it strongly until you feel its 'presence'.

3. Now turn your focus to the sky. The sky is dark and indigo and the Big Dipper is hanging there. Imagine that the Big Dipper is calling to the Tortoise at your Dan Tian and the tortoise responds.

4. Make the Big Dipper Mudra. The index and little fingers stand erect. The ring fingers touch at the tips. The middle fingers cross. The thumbs cross to touch the nails of the opposite middle fingers.

5. We then chant or rather vibrate the mantric spell to invoke the Big Dipper:

OM SABUDA JINAYA BANGJIA WEIJIA YA JIANG BUTA MA SI LU MI NA LA GE CHANG PA WA DOU SI WA HA.

As you chant the mantra one must visualise that the Seven Stars are sending rays of light, flying like bright meteors to your Dan Tian and there being absorbed by the shell of the tortoise. Feel and see the tortoise becoming brighter and brighter, hotter and hotter until it begins to illuminate the inside of your body and all the internal organs.

Once you are satisfied the meditation has reached a satisfactory point, we chant the following mantra to consolidate and absorb the Big Dipper Powers:

OM PAWA DOU SIWAHA

Recite 1080 times.

Using The Dipper To Know The Fate

In the esotericism of the Dao we are a combination of self and of fate or destiny. Fate is the sum total of how the self has interacted with the environment ... the fruit we have harvested, karma and action. As we now know our fate is tied to the cycles of the Big Dipper even if symbolically To know one's fate Maoshan sages devised this ritual.

Set up seven candles in the pattern of the Dipper. Tealight style candles are ideal for this.

Start walking from one point to the other beginning at the first star in the 'bowl' of the Dipper.

Count the number of candles you pass. The point where you forget the number or make a mistake is the significant star. You can if you wish, then sit next to that candle and meditate to gain further significant information. If lights seem to appear, their colour and shape will have meaning.

The self is defined as the true you, the true expression of who you are. You can discover this by the Southern Dipper of six stars. Setting up the candles as in the diagram. Follow the same process.

There is a large body of occult lore associated with the Big Dipper and we will certainly give more in future publications.

Other forms of magical stepping exist for all kinds of purposes

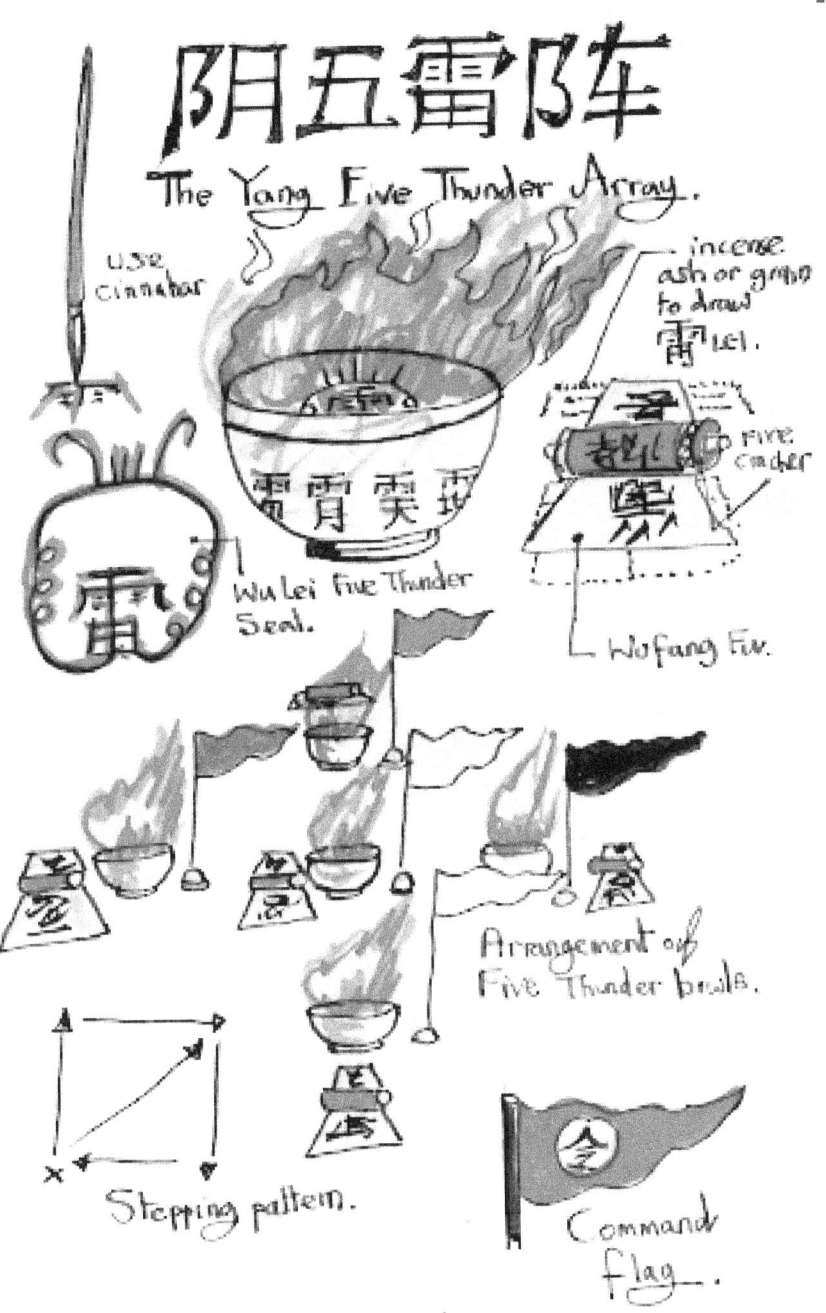

The Five Thunder Array Technique

and will be touched upon in those future publications, such as Ghost Steps used in necromancy, the Lo Shu Flying Star Steps and so on.

One powerful ritual that is a derivative of 'pace magic' is Yang Wu Lei Zhen or the Five Thunder Array Technique.

This a loud, powerful and very Yang ritual method used to drive away evil influences or even exorcise the possessed. I will only briefly describe it here and you will have to wait till a future volume of Intermediate Chinese Magic.

At the heart of the ritual are five bowls with talismans painted on them with cinnabar resting on a thunder sigil drawn on the ground with incense ash, rice or wheat flour. Each of the bowls is filled with chinese white wine or baijiu. Five sets of talismans, flags in the colours of the Five Elements and chinese firecrackers are all arranged in a specific pattern to be 'paced'.

At the climax of the ritual there is a crescendo of noise and colour as the bowls burst into flame and the firecrackers explode.

34. Of Ghosts And Ghouls

You cannot be a Taoist magician without a deep knowledge of, and interaction with ghosts and other beings of the dark world. They are a reality and in some ways the essence of many of the sorcerous arts of the Maoshan. Most western magicians would view a large number of Maoshan teachings and practices as unadulterated necromancy.

While generally speaking, the average westerner lives in a world free of ghosts, in the Far East, they are very much part of everyday life. They are constantly around. They live in your space, they are here. Right now as I write there are spirits surrounding me. They are near you.

Most of the time you won't be bothered by ghosts and you won't bother them, but now and again they become apparent, crashing into your reality when you least expect them.

The influence of ghosts is far more common than one would initially believe. So say the sorcerers in China. In fact, things happen and usually, you would not give them a second thought. However unbeknown to you, you have been influenced by a ghost. It could be as simple as a passing uncharacteristic mental thought, a strange dream, a run of bad or even good luck, a lack of energy, depression and so on. There are greater experiences that are far more traumatic too.

To understand the process of death according to Taoist beliefs, we must closely examine the idea of the soul and spirit in Chinese thought.

Man is considered to have two kinds of soul. The highest immortal and most beloved part is known as the Hun Soul. While the lower soul, which is said to be mortal in nature, is called the Po Soul.

In Taoist magic, the soul complex is referred to as the Sanhunqipo. That is the Three Hun and Seven Po. The three Hun represent increasingly 'higher' and more subtle forms of the highest spirit in man.

Will, true unconditional love and the divine consciousness all belong to the Hun. One of the dangers of the Hun, however, is its tendency to wander at night as we sleep and can on occasion get into serious trouble or even refuse to return. We will deal with this highly interesting matter in a future chapter.

The Po are seven in number and are our grossest spiritual attributes. They are the seat of the desires and passions. One traditional source relates them to the seven emotions of joy, anger, sorrow, fear, worry, and fright.

However, in discussing matters of practical magic we usually refer to the soul as a single entity, the Linghun Shen, or soul body.

So, man being but a vessel for the soul, there is at death a process of disengagement of the life force and soul from the body. Usually, under normal circumstances, this process takes around seven days. During which time the family takes special precautions to ease the transition from our yang world of the living to the yin world of the dead.

During these seven days, there are a number of traditional taboos and observations. For during this time it is believed that the soul of the dead is there, as close to familiar people and places as possible, revisiting the things they love and are worried about, before taking the final journey on the 'Yellow Spring Road' to the world of the Dead.

Death is considered not only a great loss to the family and sadness but a dangerous time in which the soul has to make a precarious transition into a new stage in the cycle of death and rebirth. The slightest thing can cause difficulties in this transition.

The corpse is firstly washed and kept clean to avoid impurities that attract darker forces at this vulnerable time. Family members must put aside their differences and trivial squabbles lest the spirit of the dead is so troubled that they cannot move on. The dead body is dressed in white or brown clothes, never red.

At the time of death, red is a taboo colour. Red is the colour of life and can cause the dead to return as a ghost.

There is a tradition that was practiced on occasion, usually by wronged women and has become a common motif in Chinese ghost stories. Typically a spurned lover or some other victim of the more brutal side of the affairs of the heart would don a red dress and adorn her face in makeup and red lipstick. At the stroke of midnight, she would kill herself by rope or knife. Then insisting to her co-conspirators that she be buried in that red dress she would return as a vengeful spirit to wreak havoc on the life of the man who spurned her.

At the moment of death, a lamp or white candles are lit to help the deceased find their path into the afterlife. A meal of rice and a boiled egg are placed at the foot of the bed. Family members will also burn special spirit money. All the women must let their hair down and remove makeup. The family altar with all the statues and images are covered with a white sheet. On the door is pasted a white paper with the Chinese character for death. Neighbours will often post a red paper on their doors. At the door is a bowl of water and a cloth so the soul can wash before hiking the great path leading from our world to the next.

A Soul Table is set up with a picture of the deceased. When family and friends enter the house they may speak to the deceased and offer apologies or praise and even tears. Gifts of flowers and fruits are placed on the Soul Table.

Meanwhile, an auspicious day and place are chosen for the actual burial of the corpse. A bad burial is after all the cause of the creation of many supernatural monstrosities. For this purpose, Feng Shui Master is usually consulted. The master will advise on a good time to bury the deceased according to data based on the Chinese Almanac, and the location will be based on the Pre-Heaven Bagua.

The final stage is wrapping the cadaver in coarse paper and putting a cloth over them. They are lowered into the casket. This is a time of very deep sadness as it will be the last time they are viewed. These observances will carry on for another seven to forty-nine days depending on region and family.

The Taoist view of the journey of the impure soul into the Underworld is indeed a grim one. The Underworld is known as Diyu. In many ways, it is similar to the idea of Hades in Greek mythology. It has its punishments and its guardians, its rulers, its great yawning gates and so forth.

On arrival in Diyu, the newly deceased soul is said to be greeted by the two psychopomps of the Underworld. They are a horse-faced deity known as Horse-Face and another with a minotaur like appearance simply known as the Bull-headed. These two imposing and armed Guardians of the Underworld lead the deceased to judgement.

In the First Hall, ruled over by King Qin Guangming, the ghost stands before a mirror which shows him his life and the good and bad deeds flash before him. Based on the true reflection in the mirror, the soul of the deceased must now pass through various halls to receive purification by various punishments.

The Second Hall belongs to Chu Jiang Ming. Crimes of theft and robbery as well as rape and allied misconduct cause the soul to be plunged in an icy pool of water and prodded with an iron fork.

The Third Hall of Di Song deals with frauds and liars, cheating in love and business, where they are said to feel crushed by stones.

In the Fourth Hall ruled over by Five Faced Mingwang, the soul of a murderer is thrown from the Nai River bridge to be washed away and cut by sharp knives.

In the Fifth Hall of King Yan Luo, destroyers of family harmony are further immersed in icy water.

In the Sixth Hall of Biancheng Ming Wang, those who abused their power had their tongues slashed.

In the Seventh Hall of Taishan Ming Wang, swindlers are further punished by cutting with sharp instruments.

In the Eighth Hall the unfilial, have their limbs amputated and their internal organs wrenched out and burned.

Finally, in the Tenth Hall, the men who refused aid and food to the weak and hungry have their tongues ripped out.

Most Taoists see this not so much as a 'real' experience but as partly symbolic of the purification of the soul after death. The various tortures represent the powerlessness, guilt and regret of the soul as it touches upon reality. We can compare it to, for example, the Bardo Thodol tradition of the Tibetan Buddhists.

However, things can go awry. Perhaps the spirit was a black magician in life and has the power to disengage from the common process of death. Or the ghost is unusually attached to the world, so much so that the spirit remains to engage in its desires, be it revenge, lust, love or even pure 'homesickness'. Or the soul was brought back into our mortal world by the magician. For example, the magician may have ghost servitors deliberately kept and even cultivated to provide certain capabilities and occult services.

Some ghosts as the cliche goes, do not realise they are dead and wander the earth oblivious to their condition. The saddest ones are the Lonely Ghosts who, having no family to remember them, wander as grey phantoms seeking the warmth and comfort of life and love.

Young mothers or babies and even aborted foetuses, brilliant young men and women, children and suicides are a great source of fear among the common population. Yet they are also considered a great source of magical power throughout Asia. The Sichuan plateau and much of South-East Asia specialised in this form of magic. In Thailand (and in Maoshan) the bones and spirits of such beings are cultivated as we shall see later in this work.

Another phenomena that may seem unique to the western ear is the Ghost Bride. Among some Chinese communities, there is a great fear of the ill-fortune and unhealthy psychic influences that can be brought about by the unhappy ghost of a young and unmarried girl or boy who has died. Every home, for example, has a family ancestral altar with the spirit tablets of dead family members carefully placed on it and tended with love. However, dying unmarried, one cannot display such a tablet. This is said to wreak further havoc and sadness. Hence the solution was the so-called Ghost Marriage. Sometimes this was another dead person. However, sometimes the ghost girl was married to some hapless passerby. The most common means was to leave a wallet or even a hong bao (red packet) containing money. The ignorant man would pick up the money and find himself the unwilling bridegroom to the dead girl. In richer families, a full marriage ceremony was conducted including effigies of the girl and bridegroom if dead. There are also tales of ghostly girls requesting certain men and even consummating their passions.

In fact love, sex and desire is the leading cause of ghostly visitation and haunting, such is the power of the erotic impulse. With my Master, I had visited several of these cases and it is hard to deny the evidence.

My master told me that as a young man it had happened to him and that is the very reason he had gotten into the path of magic in the first place. The experience had truly opened his eyes. If it sounds like an erotic dream come true, it is not. Due to the Yin nature of the ghost, no matter how beautiful or handsome, the yang life force of the individual is drained away. I have seen with my own eyes such a case.

I visited a small house in Changsha with my teacher. The woman was in her mid-twenties and living at home with her parents. I saw her photos in the family pictures scattered around the apartment. She was a typical, rosy and robust Chinese girl. Then I saw her and frankly, it was startling. Despite voraciously eating, she was near skeletal. Eyes were sunken into deep grey hollows. This girl was emaciated and sickly with a bluish-grey tinge to her skin. The room felt depressing. She talked to the Master. She explained she had a boyfriend who visited her in the night and made love to her. She divulged that it left her underwear soaked and was so embarrassed that she would throw them away or secretly wash them. The ghostly lover at first had merely felt like a gentle breeze but over time the phenomena became stronger. She could make out the figure of, but not the details of her nocturnal visitor. The Master was very concerned. Eventually after a kind of seance a deal was struck between the family and the ghost. Unlike in the movies, Taoists do not go rushing in with guns blazing banishing spirits. The first step is talking with them to find out what is going on and how the situation can be resolved. This is a kinder and less dangerous path. The ghost had told the teacher that he was in love with the girl. The Teacher, in turn, explained to the ghost that he was harming her by his actions. The ghost relented. The family instead were to offer the ghost fruit, foods, and spirit money on a regular basis instead. Happy with the arrangement the girl soon recovered and the house had a benign protector.

What is notable is that in the Chinese practice, ghosts and spirits are not automatically exorcised, the magician bursting in guns blazing like in popular movies and novels, rather the magician approaches the spirit in a spirit of dialogue and compromise between the mortal and spirit worlds.

Ghosts can, in a sense, become friends of the magician, and indeed it is common in Chinese magic for ghosts to be what western magicians would call familiar spirits, serving and performing certain tasks on behalf of the sorcerer.

It should be understood that the ghost used in such necromantic work is usually the shell, the etheric corpse left behind when the higher spirit or consciousness of the deceased has passed on to other, higher spheres of existence. This part, as we have seen, is called the Po, as opposed to the higher part called the Hun. The Po or astral shell is fed with food, incense, and the magician's own mind. The astral shell grows in intelligence and objective presence.

There are a number of famous stories in China where the ghost can be developed to such a high degree it can become visible to all spectators. The most famous is the tale of a Taoist magician who would reveal a beautiful dancing girl before his audience. Sometimes the ghost's silhouette was visible behind a paper screen and the rapt audience would watch the slender figure of the graceful and lithe ghost dance before disappearing.

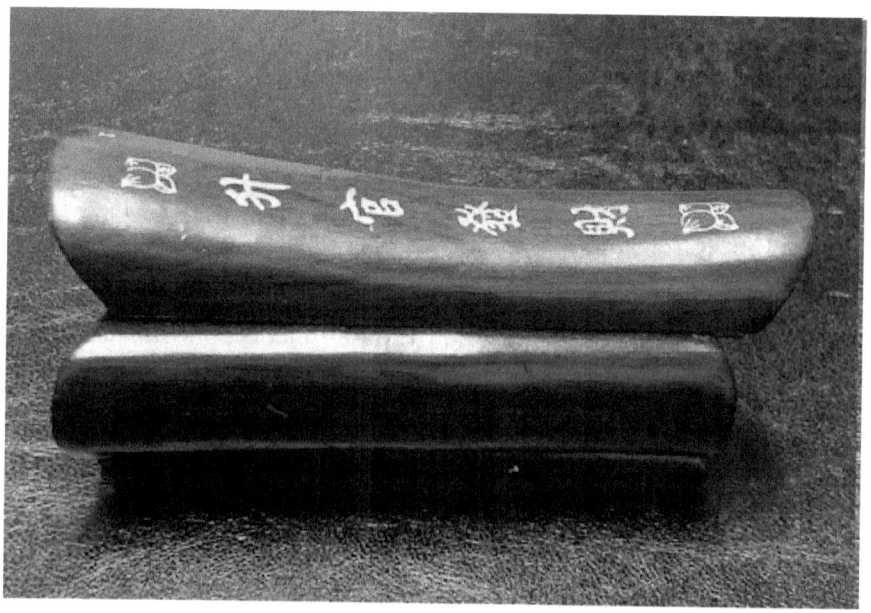

Chinese Lucky Coffins used in Feng Shui can be used for this ritual.

Daoist Ghost Magic

A whole branch of Maoshan magic is devoted to the use of ghosts in magic and is so extensive that we have a whole volume devoted to that topic. The most famous practice being that of the Five Ghosts or Wu Gui.

The Five Ghosts are frequently used in Chinese magic for a myriad of purposes. Originally they seemed to have been plague gods but over time were seen as lesser ghosts representing the Yin Gui Qi (ghost Qi) of the five directions.

One common use of the Five Ghosts is in wealth magic. As this is an introductory volume we will not go too deeply into the topic as there is a book devoted to that topic alone in this series.

However, magicians are a practical lot and we shall here give an example of Five Ghost Magic used to increase prosperity. This will be a good place to start the practice of ghost magic, for this art is one of the more powerful methods of Maoshan magic. The Gods are often the most tardy to act on behalf, they are high cosmic deities or immortals who though they do respond, take longer. Ghost magic is far more quick to act and bring results to fruition, simply because they are closer to the mortal realm.

However, the pay off is that the ghost art is far more dangerous and should only be practiced once you have a minimum of a year or even two under your belt. One needs to know how to safely communicate with and cultivate the 'Po' spirit of the ghost, and eventually to release it back into the afterlife with special spells. A failure to do this properly can have serious consequences, among which is the ghosts you have cultivated will not allow you an easy death, a sign of which is the magician's corpse bleeding from the eyes, nose, ears, mouth and anus.

Fortunately, this spell of the Five Ghosts will be fairly safe for the beginner.

Five Ghosts Fortune Spell

This method called the WuGui Tai Guan Shu, the Five Ghosts Riches Method is said to have come from the Longshan Mountain region and passed into the Luban tradition.

The sorcerer is instructed to make a miniature Chinese style coffin from the wood of the Scholar Tree, that should be 2 inches long and about a half inch wide. For practical reasons, western readers can buy a small wooden coffin from a Feng Shui shop or online.

In Chinese magical thought, the word for coffin sounds like the word for fortune.

Have a small piece of red paper and write the words Guan Cai, meaning Wealth Official 9 (see illustration). Put it inside the coffin with some powdered gold. The less affluent can put inside three chinese coins.

Also have a small plinth made of either willow or the wood of a poplar tree. Place the coffin on top of this.

On a Yin Day, that is a day when the Earthly Branch is one of the Yin Branches, and in a Yin Month, place the coffin and plinth in a secret part of your home in a Southeast corner but facing Northwest.

Obtain some yellow paper or card, and cut out the shapes of five human figures. These are zhiren, or paper dolls and they are frequently used in Chinese magic.

With the consecrated brush, ink, water and inkstone write the following on the ghosts.

1. 東木鬼 East Wood Ghost
2. 南火鬼 South Fire Ghost
3. 西金鬼 West Metal Ghost

4. **北水鬼** North Water Ghost

5. **中土鬼** Centre Soil Ghost

Place the paper ghosts in the correct direction around the coffin on the plinth, but the centre ghost of soil is placed underneath the coffin.

Put five sticks of agarwood incense in the burner (never sandalwood or any of the Yang incenses as this is a Yin Class spell). On either side of the set place two red candles. Light them all with a yellow paper.

The ghost master now chants the spell:

I ask you, the Five Directions of Metal, Wood, Water, Fire and Soil, O you the Five Element Ghosts, come to this altar and transport to me a great fortune.
I shall aspire to give due reverence and heartfelt desire for this to practice, help my store of fortune and may it bring merit to us all, and great fortune to me!
By command of the Ancestral Master!
Ji Ji Ru Lu Ling.

When you are in need of a financial boost, on a yin day and month set up on the floor near the coffin and ghosts a censer with five sticks of incense and five small bowls of rice, and say this simple spell:

In the Southeast and Northwest,
Metal, Wood, Water, Fire and Earth,
the Five Ghosts hear my command,
the coffin of the Wealth Official is esteemed.
We invite you Wealth and Treasure to channel to us a great fortune, bringing us good luck and banishing ill luck.
By command of the Ancestral Master!
Ji Ji Ru Lu Ling.

35. Tools Of The Taoist Magician

The tools of Daoist magic are every bit as wide and as varied as any magical culture, and some spells will call for more than is listed here. This is a recommended list of essential basics that will, in essence, be a starter kit that will be built up over time. On top of this the Daoist magician will collect herbs, stones and so forth but in an introductory volume such as this we will not venture there.

1. Altar.
A small to medium table is ample for the beginner. Oblong or square is a good shape and made of natural wood.

2. Censer.
Initially a bowl filled with rice but later you may want to invest in a larger chinese style tripod or urn.

3. Talismanic paper.
This is made of xuan paper and can be bought online in large rolls from specialist Taoist stores. Yellow will be the most common colour that you will use, but red is also common.

4. Command block.
The command block is tapped or struck against the altar's surface in certain rituals. It is usually a piece of peach or mahogany wood carved with names of deities, an ancestral master of the lineage etc. I recommend the Five Thunder Block for most operations.

5. Bowls and cups.
Buy the chinese style porcelain rice bowls and tea cups. You will need a minimum of 12 of each.

Command Block

6. Incense sticks.
Sandalwood for yang operations and agarwood for yin operations.

7. Cloth.
You should buy in five colours, red, yellow, blue, black and white. Buy 2 metre squares, in cotton or silk. They will be used for making command flags, pouches, altar cloths, headscarves and bowl covers.

8. Tea.
A good quality chinese green tea, for example the Guanyin brand.

9. Rice wine.
Can be bought from Chinese supermarkets where it is called Bai Jiu.

10. Coloured thread and string in the five colours.

11. Rice.
you will get through alot!

12. Beans in the five colours.

13. Seal or chop.
We recommend the Bagua Chop for stamping talismans.

14. Robes.
One black and one yellow.

15. Spirit money.
The minimum types needed are gold and silver money, Shoujin and Jiama.

16. The Four Treasures of the Scholar, brushes, ink and inkstone.

17. Bell.
A Buddhist bell is fine or a real Taoist one with three prong termination.

18. Moon blocks for inter-ritual divination.

19. Peach wood sword
Some of these tools will need some explanation.

The Command Block

The Command block is a ritual tool that could be very loosely compared to a combination of the pentacle and the wand in Western Magic. It is usually ascribed to the Five Thunder Powers, the Heavenly Five Elements. It gives power to an order when used. Typically the magician when reciting the spell or command will slam it on the table to send out the order. The wooden Five Thunder Command Block has characters and sigils graven on it that represent the magical authority borrowed by the magician. In the above example you can see the Ziwei or mark of the 28 Stars (Purple Palace) and the order, literally, The Five Thunder Command. 五雷號令 .

Traditionally and ideally it is made from wood taken from a peach tree struck by lightning. However this is unlikely except in rare circumstances, so we can rest assured that less exotic ones will work very well. You can find Command blocks on Chinese e-markets such as Taobao.com.

Spirit Money

Throughout the rituals given in this text you will have seen references to burning gold money. Do not worry, you are not literally burning gold!

In Chinese magic, nothing is free. There is a reciprocal relationship between you and the Gods and Spirits, and even more so, the Universe itself. If you take, you must give. This is an unbendable law of Chinese magic.

The tradition of Spirit Money comes from this idea. It is a distillation of several ideas found in ancient spiritual and shamanic culture.

1. PROVIDE FOR THE ANCESTORS

I recall a story about a shaman who once asked a western anthropologist, "Do the white men bury their dead?" The anthropologist answered of course we do, but further enquired why did the old shaman think we do not. The shaman replied that whenever he looked at foreigners in the spirit vision they were usually accompanied by hoards of their dead relatives, hence his assumption. In many cultures the dead are not simply buried and forgotten, but remain part of the family. They are not forgotten but respected and remembered, given gifts and their passage to the spirit world eased.

Furthermore, the prosperity of a family is thus strongly linked with the ancestors. A poorly retained link and even disrespect for our dead ancestors leads to poverty and ill fate for many generations. This is part of the logic of having as part of our altar dedicated to our ancestors who have passed on, and it was also the main purpose of the original feng shui.

The infamous terracotta soldiers of Emperor Qin in Xian are an extreme example of offerings to the dead to ease their passage in the afterlife. The same is true of most cultures. The ancient Egyptians had special tomb chapels where one could regularly honour the dead and even write them letters. The Romans respected their ancestors as the Lares and Penates who would return the favour by giving tranquility and fortune to a household and allowing the family name to survive.

Indeed, it is only in modern times and in our striving to insulate society from death that the practice of ancestral respect has driven a wedge between us and the spirit world.

Spirit money, sweet incense, food, water and wine are all considered excellent offerings to our ancestors. As well as yearly visits to maintain their graves and tombs.

To the Chinese, talking about spiritual cultivation, magic, and communicating with spirits is just talk unless you first have a viable connection with the spirits of your own bloodline and your immediate masters. The author can confirm that a large percentage of a student's personal problems and lack of currency in the spiritual realm is due to a fracture in the ancestral continuity.

For the ancestors silver money was considered the standard offering. More recently the infamous bank of hell money has become popular, though in fact it is less traditional.

2. SHOWING RESPECT

Paper money is given to show a conscious acknowledgement by yourself of the Gods and Spirits from gratitude.

3. PAYMENT

Spirit money is burned in gratitude for an effect or result having come to pass. Nothing is free.

The money symbolises energy you have given back in lieu of energy spent on your behalf.

Types Of Spirit Money

Many centuries ago, spirit money would have been actual gold and silver foil, but obviously this is very expensive.

Also Spirit Money has evolved many kinds that are used for either specific classes of spirits or gods, or for specific purposes. The following kinds of spirit money are the most commonly used in Maoshan and thus in this book.

1. Kanjin or Cut Gold Money

Which usually consists of yellow paper with a gold foil rectangle. This is used for purification and offerings to Celestial Deities and Immortals. For cleansing, usually seven pieces are held together,

sometimes sandwiching a talisman. It is then lit with a yellow paper and the resulting 'gold fire' is used to cleanse the person, altar or object.

2. Xiaoyin or Little Silver
is used for ancestors and ghost working.

3. Shoujin.

Longevity money is used for many rituals. It is intended to bring blessings and enhanced life, health and fortune to the practitioner and the spirits.

4. Jia Ma.

This is used for Celestial Troops and sometimes the Five Ghosts. It is money used for sending spirits to perform a task.

36. Hand Seals Used In Daoist Magic

Chinese magic has a rich tradition of using various hand seals in its magical art. Some were passed to Daoism via Indian Tantra, but others were developed in China long before the Tang Dynasty connection with India via the Buddhist stream.

There are many hundreds of specialised hand seals or Shouyin used in Daoist magic. I give some of the more popular ones here.

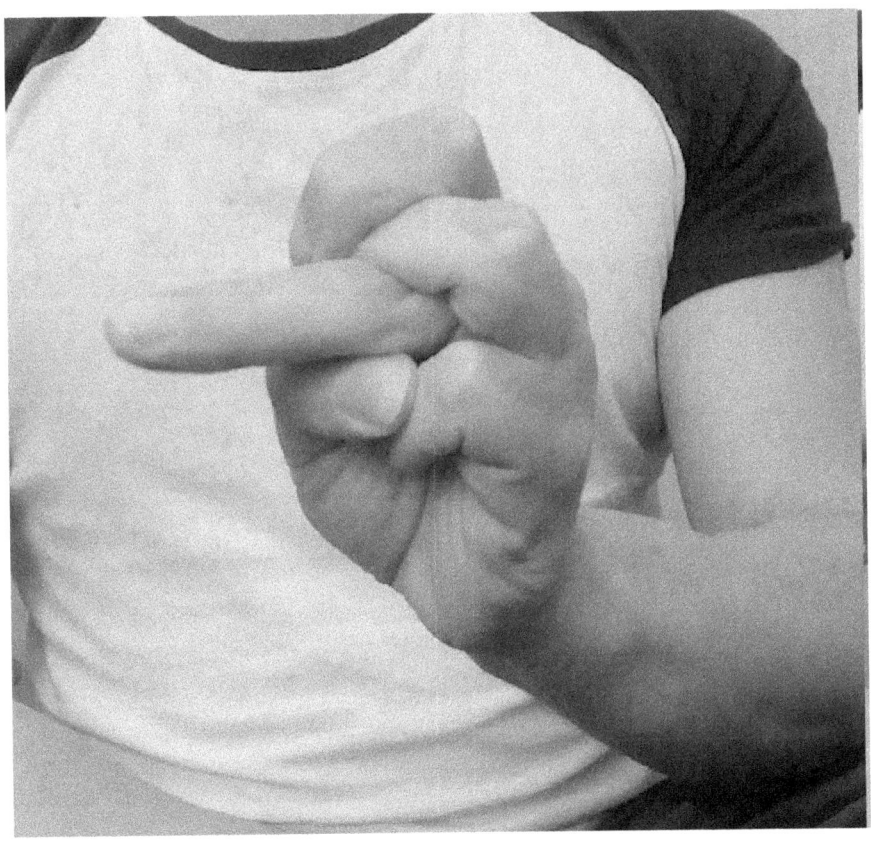

1. The Vajra Seal also called Heaven King or Open Heaven

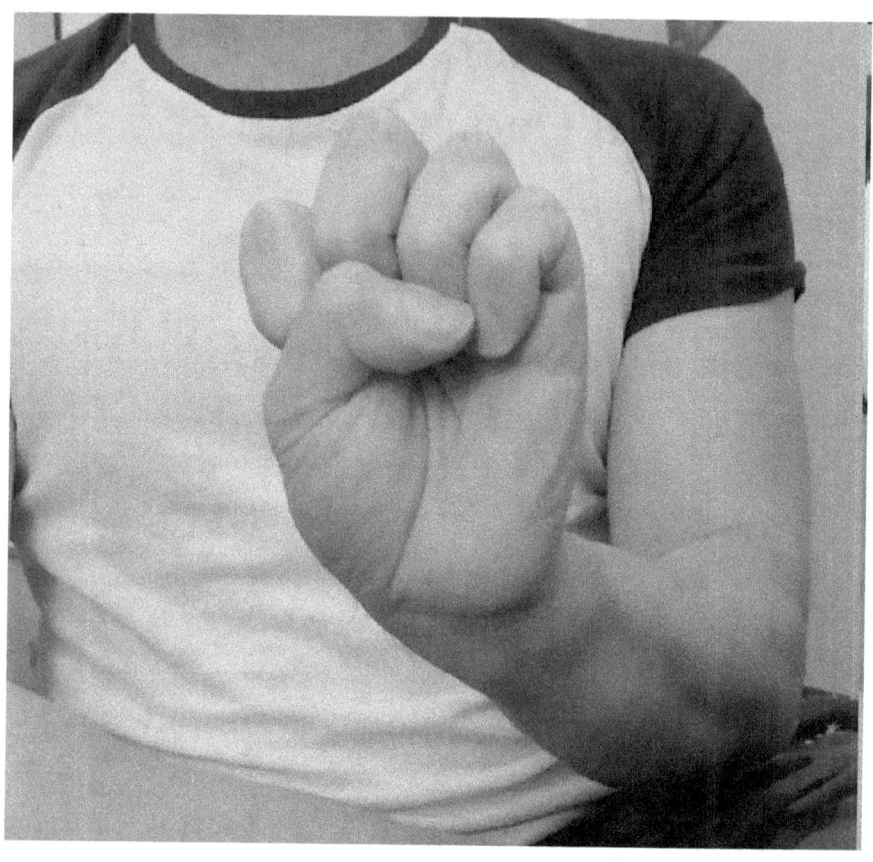

2. Wu Lei. Five Thunder Seal

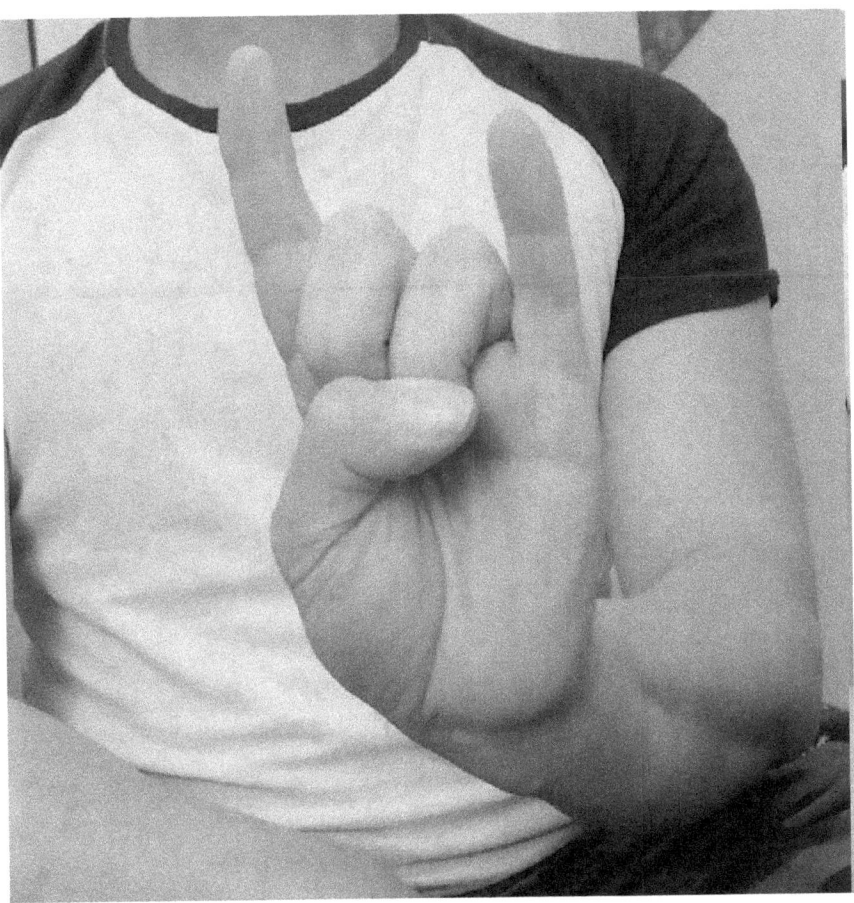

3. Dao Seal

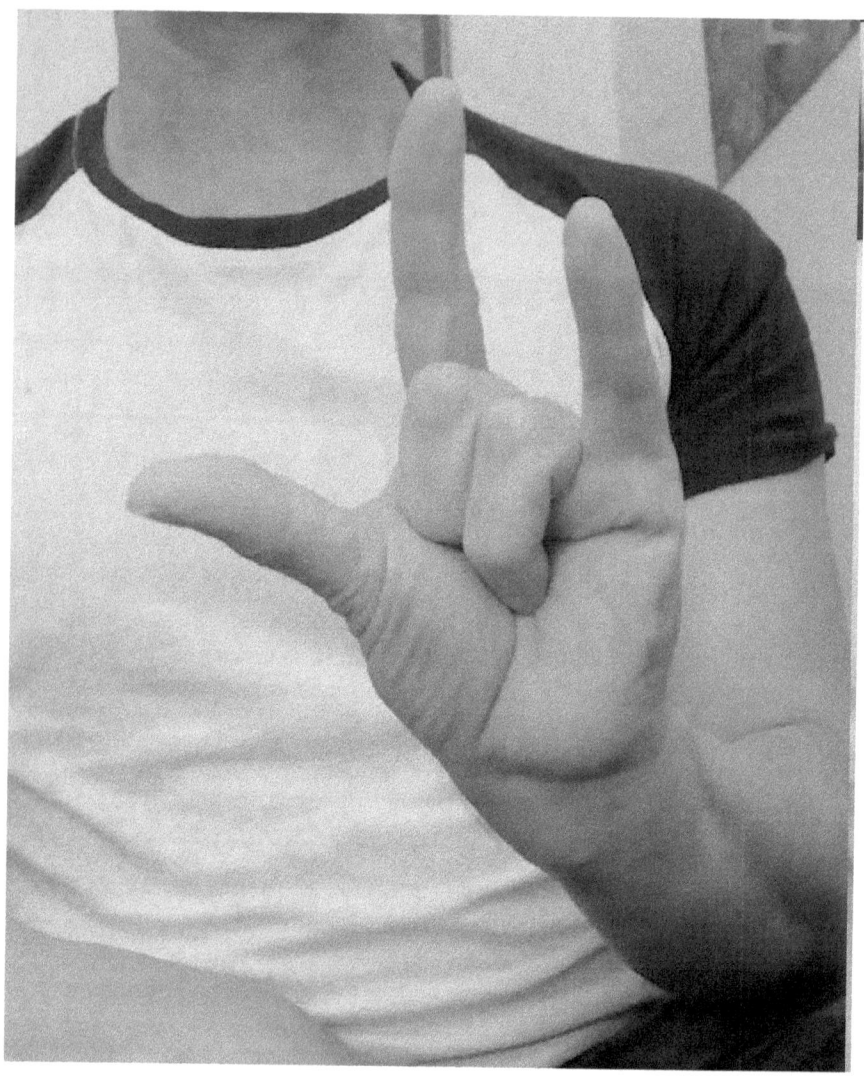

4. Sanshan Yin. Three Mountains Seal.
This one is usually used for holding a bowl or cup

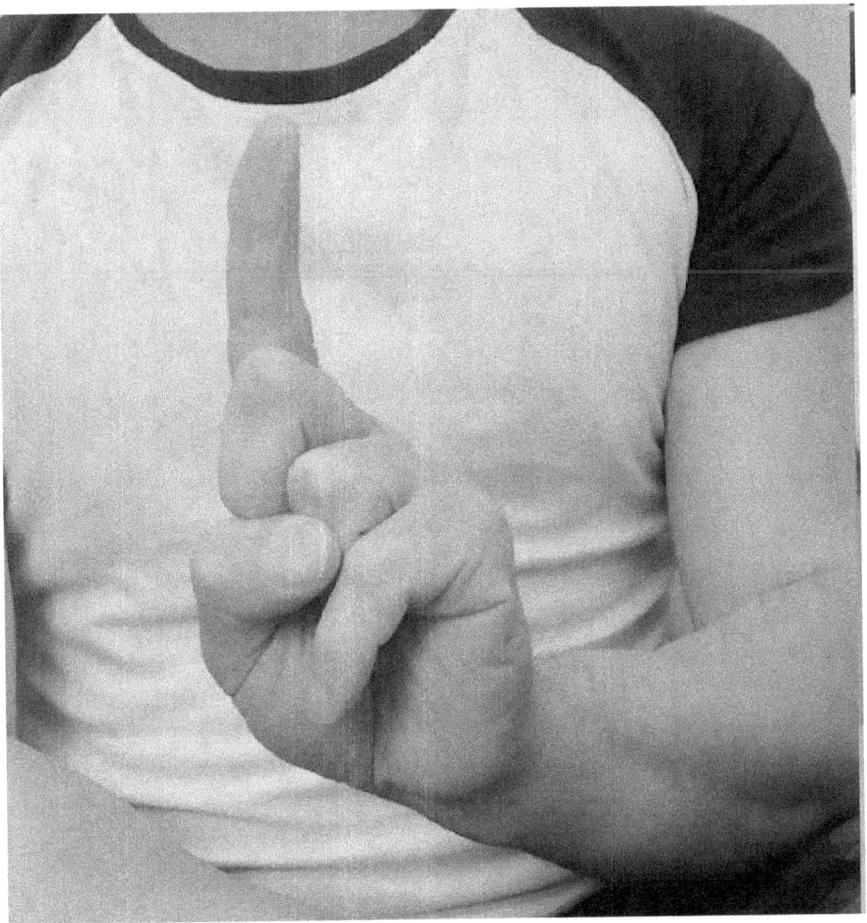

5. Mysterious Heaven or Purple Palace Seal

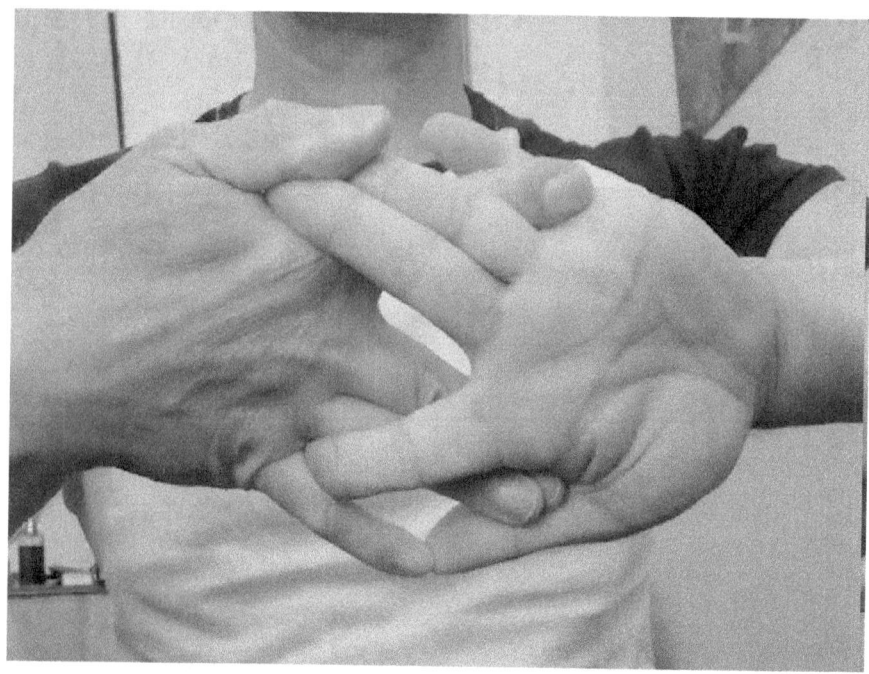

6. Pre Heaven Bagua Seal. Right palm is up

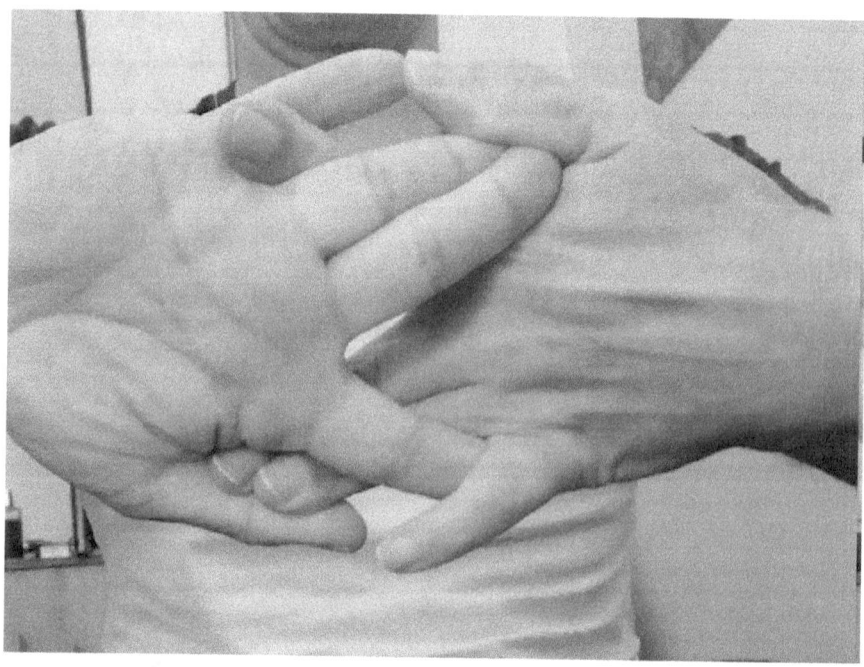

7. Post Heaven Seal. Right palm is down

8. Zushi Yin. Ancestral Teacher Seal

9. Request the Gods or Guan Yin Seal

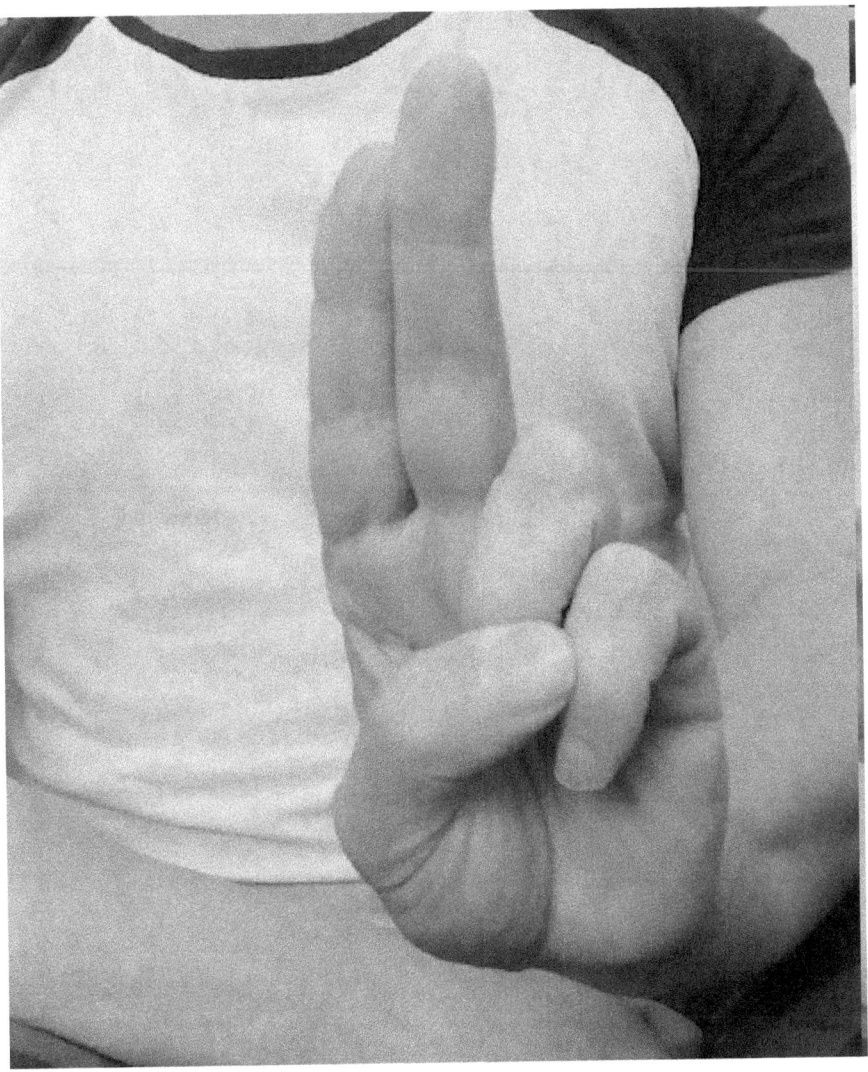

10. Sword Seal

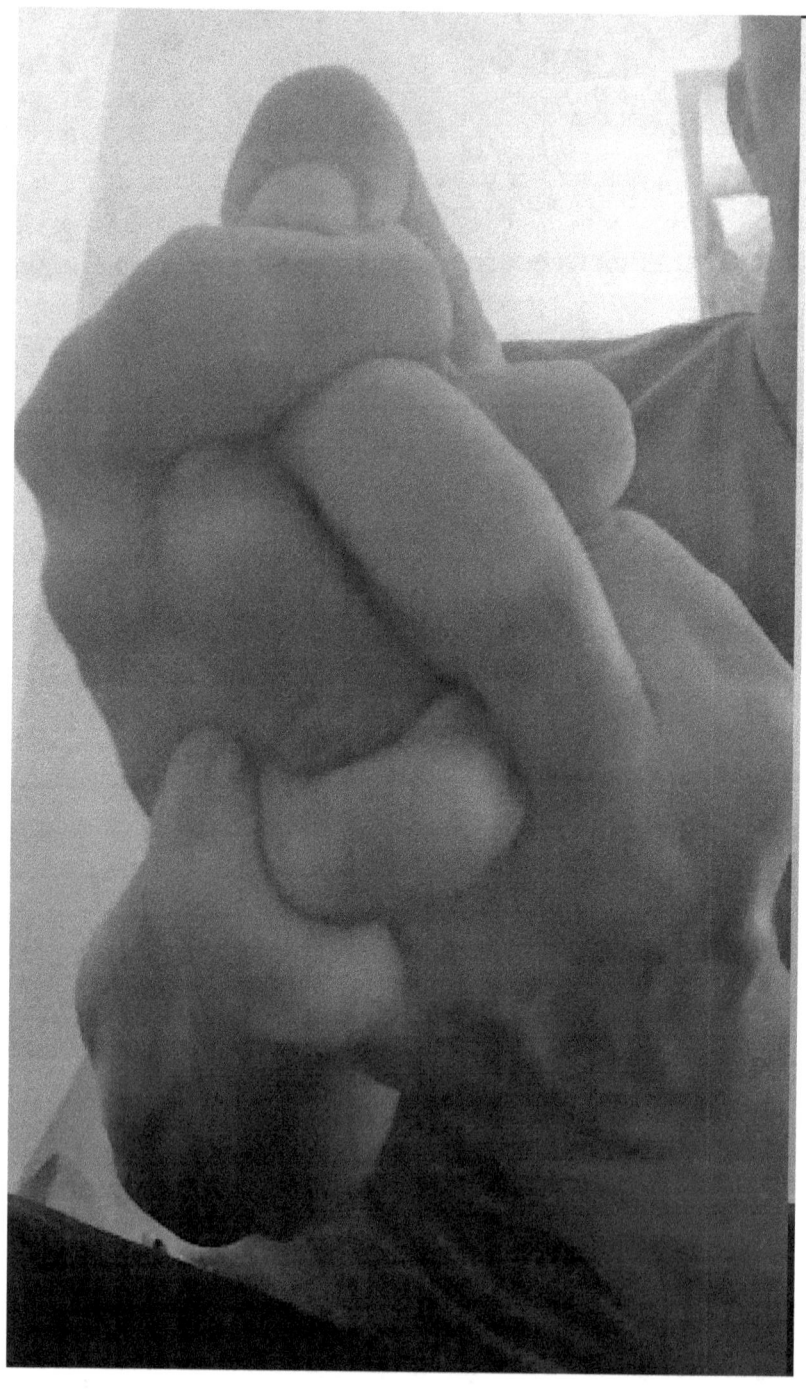

11. Taishang Laojun Seal

The Nine Character Seals

The most famous mudra sequence is called the Nine Character Seals or Jiuzi. They were first mentioned in public print by Ge Hong in the Baopuzi Classic, but most people know them from their manifestation in Japanese culture.

Here we will look at them from a Chinese magical point of view as there are many books and articles describing their Japanese Buddhist application but very few that talk about them from a Chinese point of view despite their origin being Chinese!

Ge Hong uses them as a kind of protection magic before entering a mountain wilderness, to defend from spirits and wild animals. He suggests the Daoist hang up silk banners in the five elemental colours and perform the nine mudras and chant the spell. The spell in fact calls the Six Jia spirits. The Six Jia spirits are six celestial troop generals or warriors that can protect the sorcerer.

The magic of the Nine Character Seals is strongly linked to the Goddess Jiu Tian Xuan Nu who is said to have taught them to Huangdi, the Yellow Emperor in his war against the demon king. They are also linked with the stars of the Big Dipper, and in some cases the seals and spell can be made while walking the Big Dipper Pace.

To properly do the Jiuzi you could set up the five colour flags as recommended in the Baopuzi, but it isn't essential.

Wash yourself thoroughly, ideally pouring water downwards over your head from a bowl, and it should be cold water.

Face the North and exhale, visualising all the dark impurities leaving your system. Then turn to face the East and inhale new pure Qi.

Tap the teeth 3 times. Repeat the Eastern Breath and the teeth tapping thirty-six times.

Finally lead fresh invigorating qi to the dantian.

Form the hands into a prayer like position. Bow three times and do the seals in as flowing manner as possible. The incantation in Chinese is

LIN BING DOU ZHE JIE ZHEN LIE!

It can be translated as Be present, warriors, fight, them, all, in the battle array, line, at the front, act!

As you chant this visualise six beautiful but warlike girls lining up one by one before you or the Six Jia Generals

Practical Chinese Magic ☙ 367

The Six Ding Maidens of Jiu Tian Xuan Nu

The Six Jia Generals

The mudras are as follows:

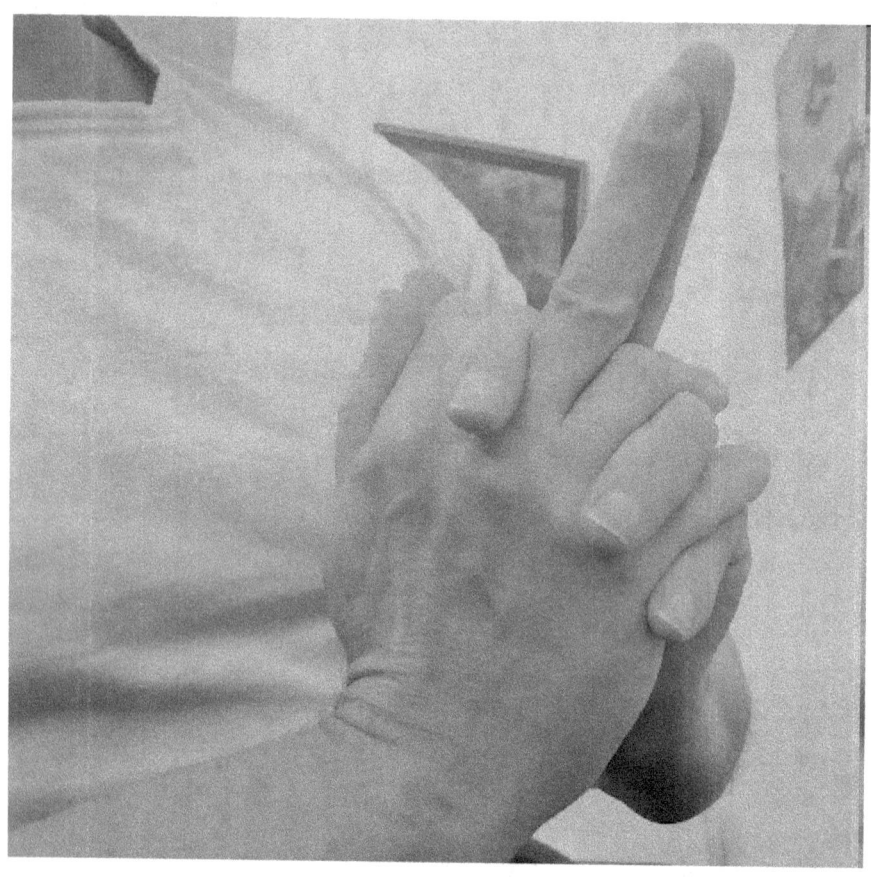

I.LIN!

Practical Chinese Magic ∞ 369

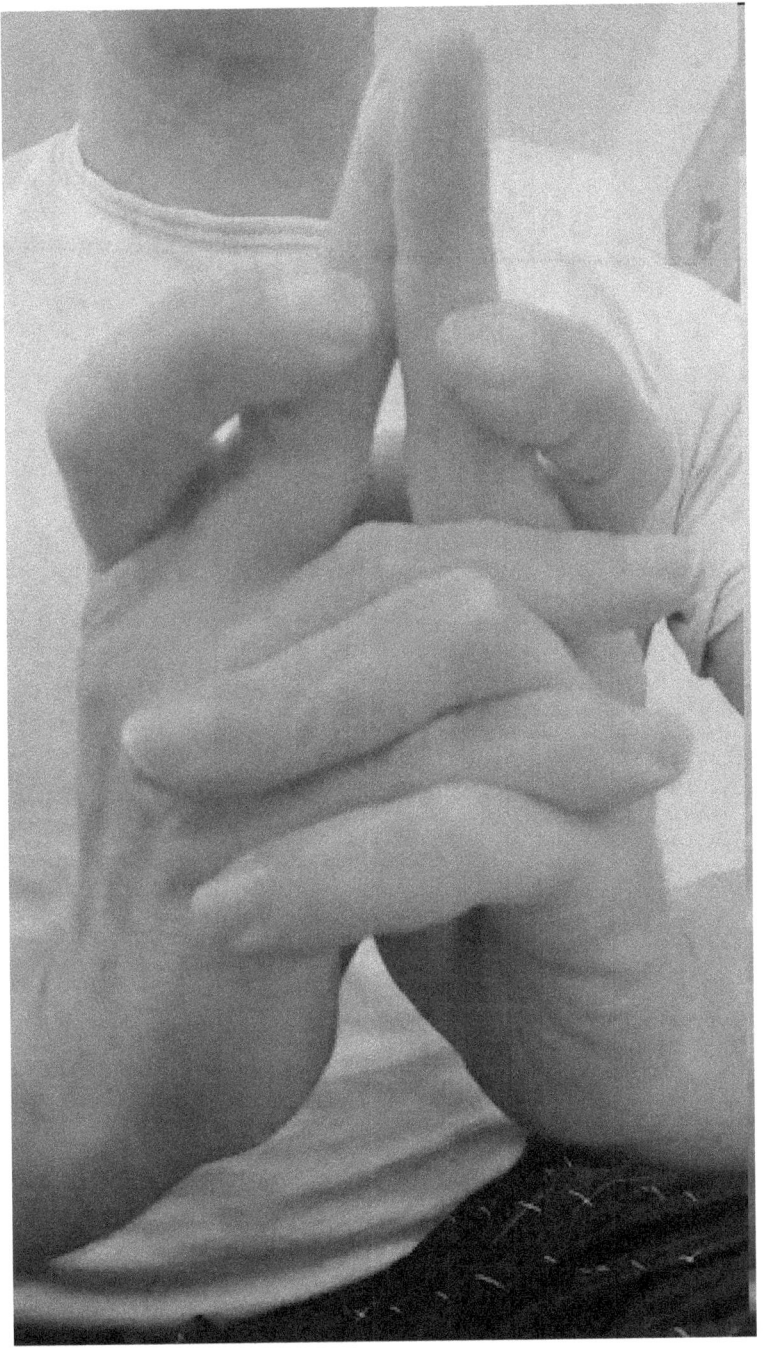

2. BING!

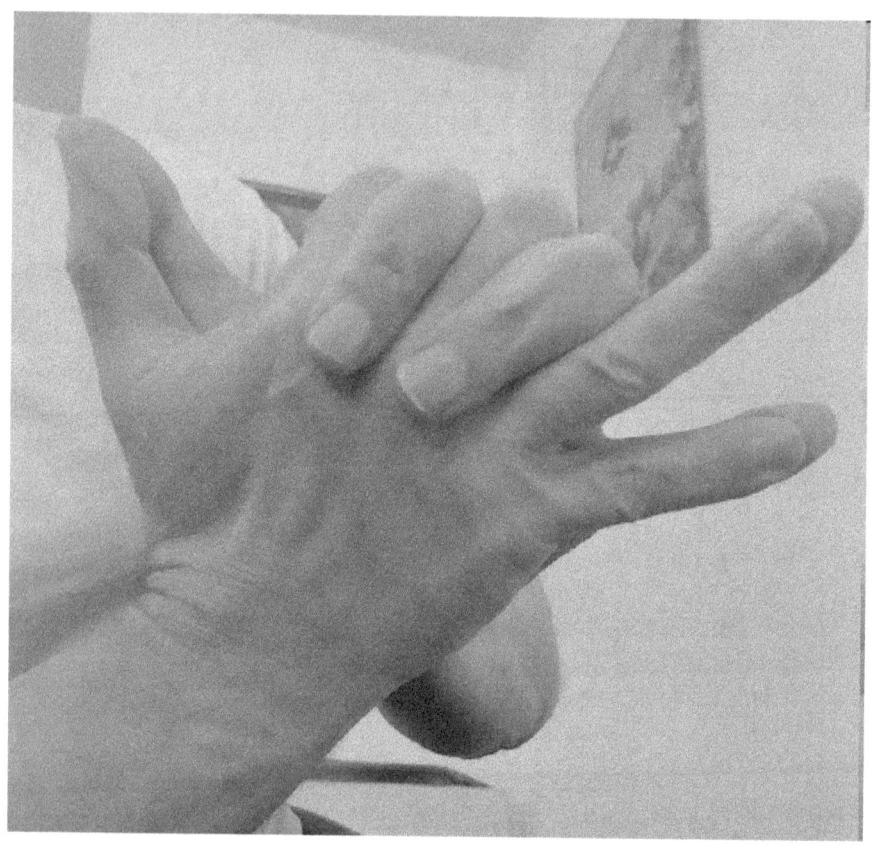

3.DOU!

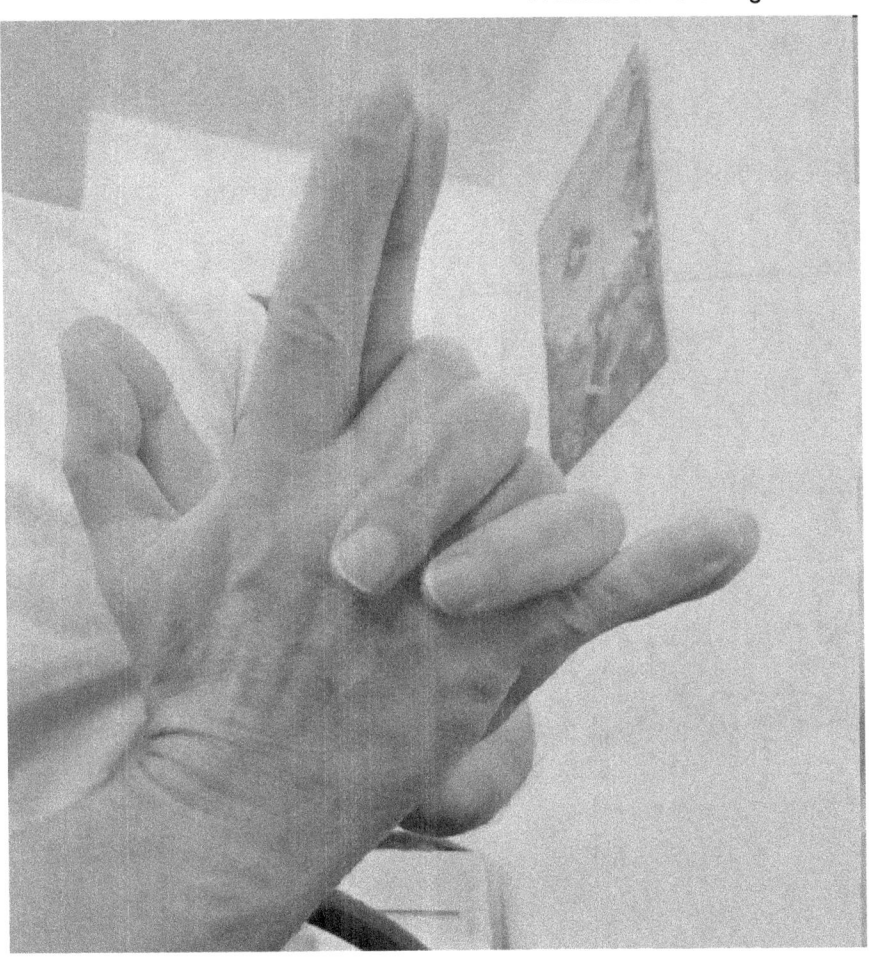

4.ZHE!

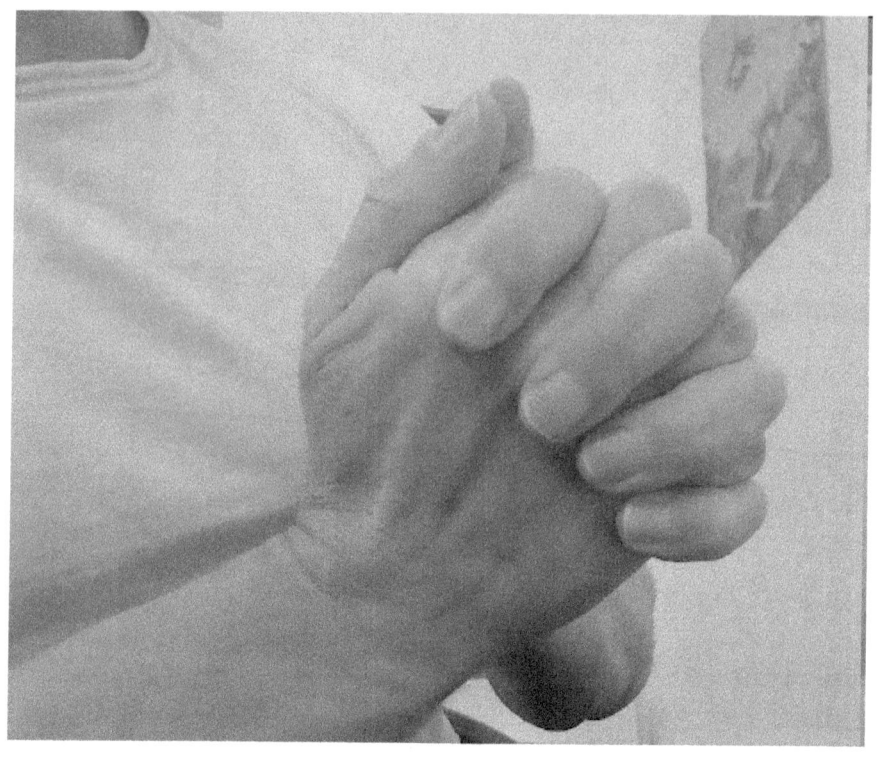

5. JIE!

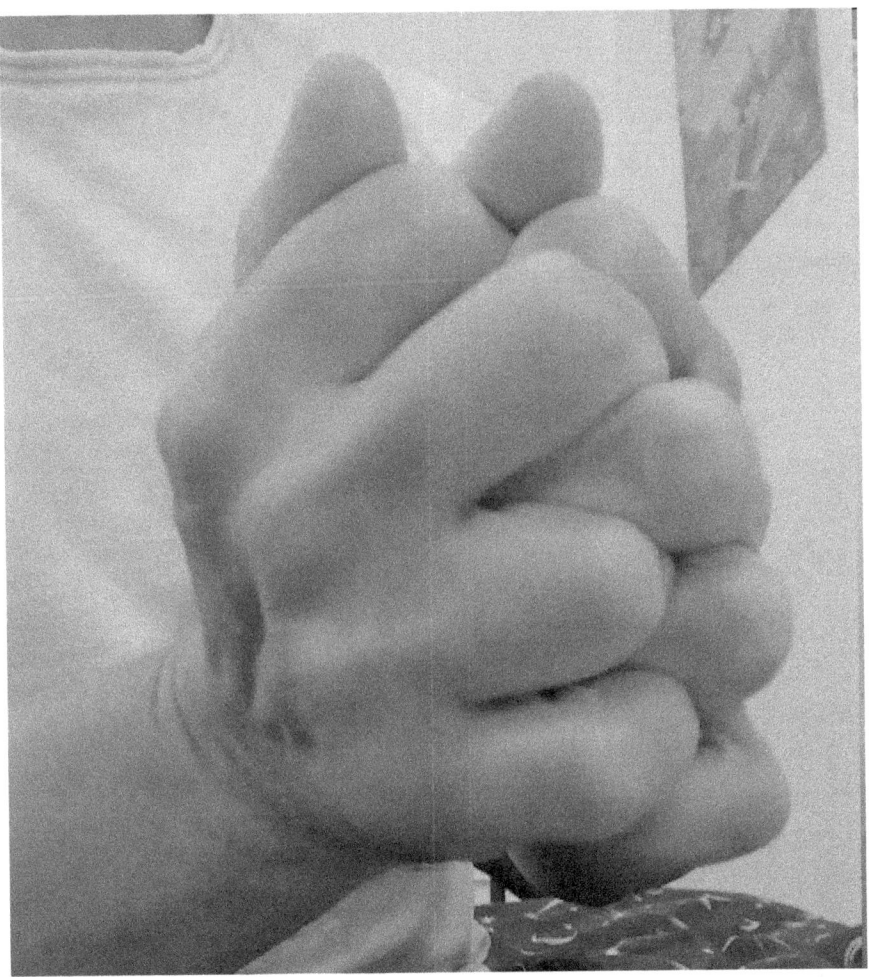

6. ZHEN!

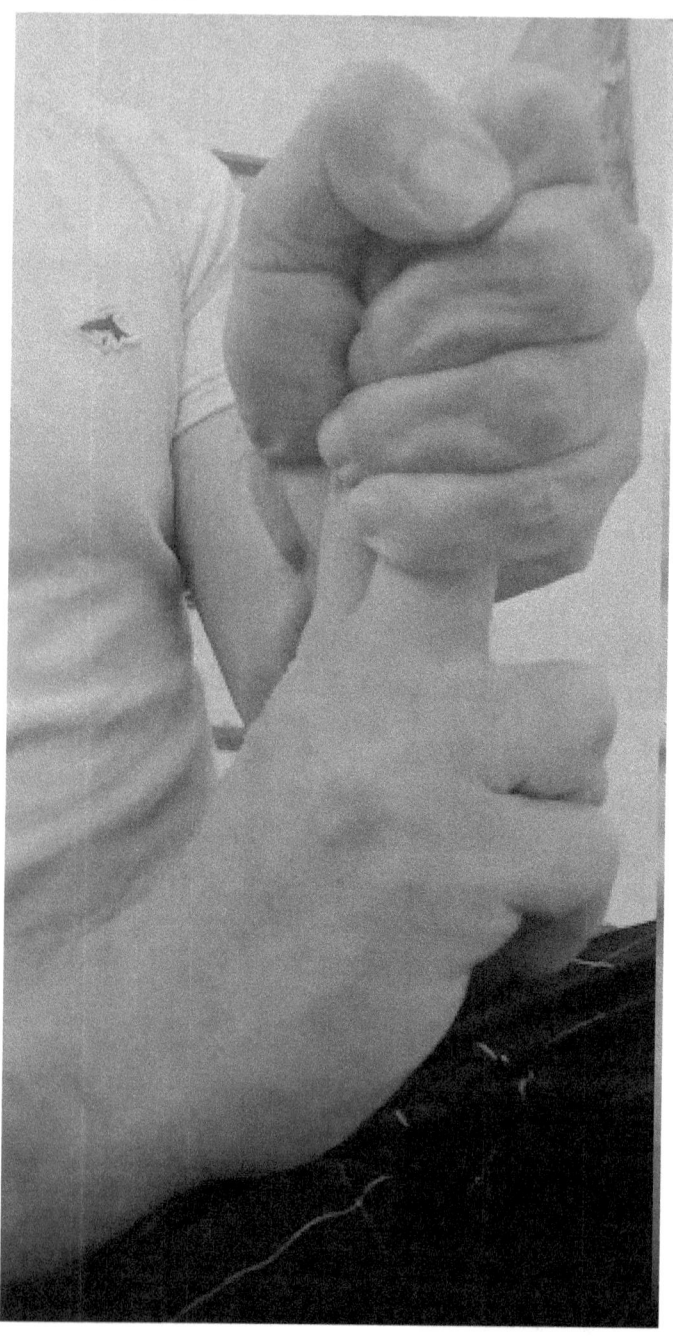

7. LIE!

Practical Chinese Magic ∽ 375

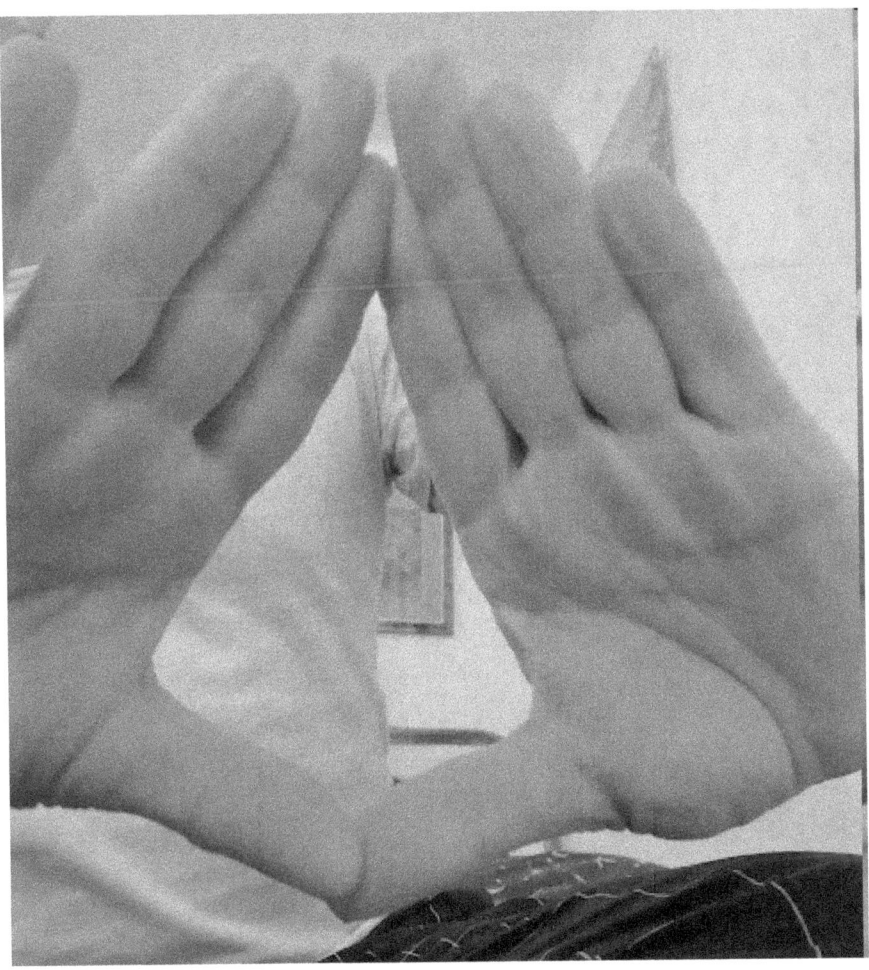

8. QIAN

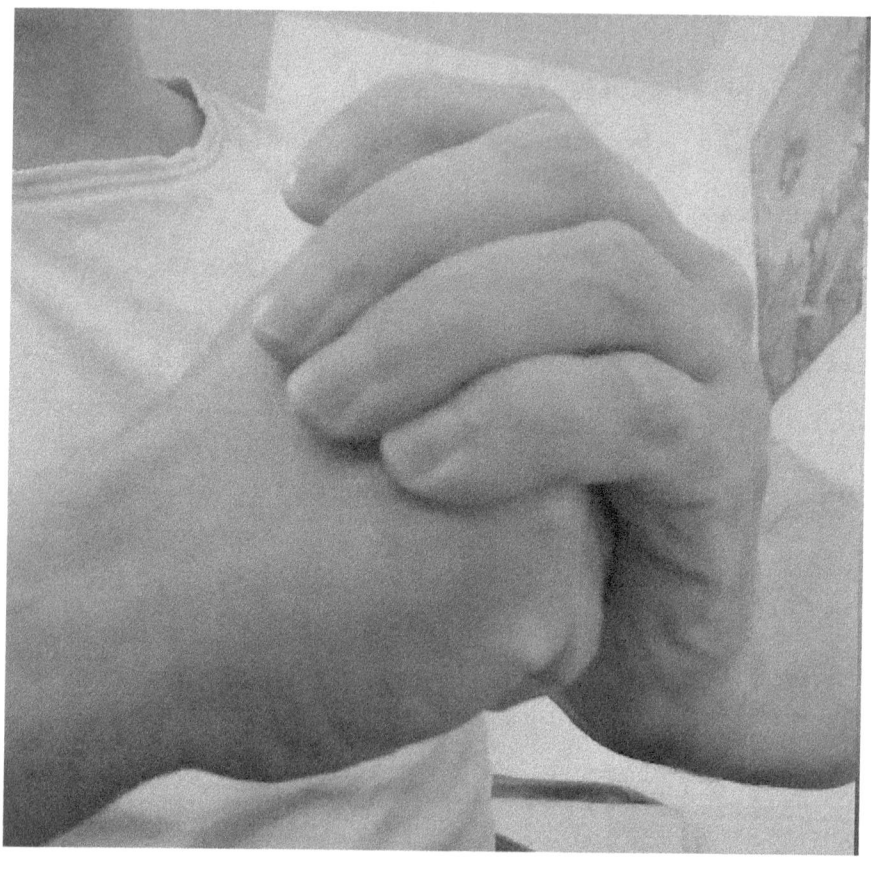

9. XING!

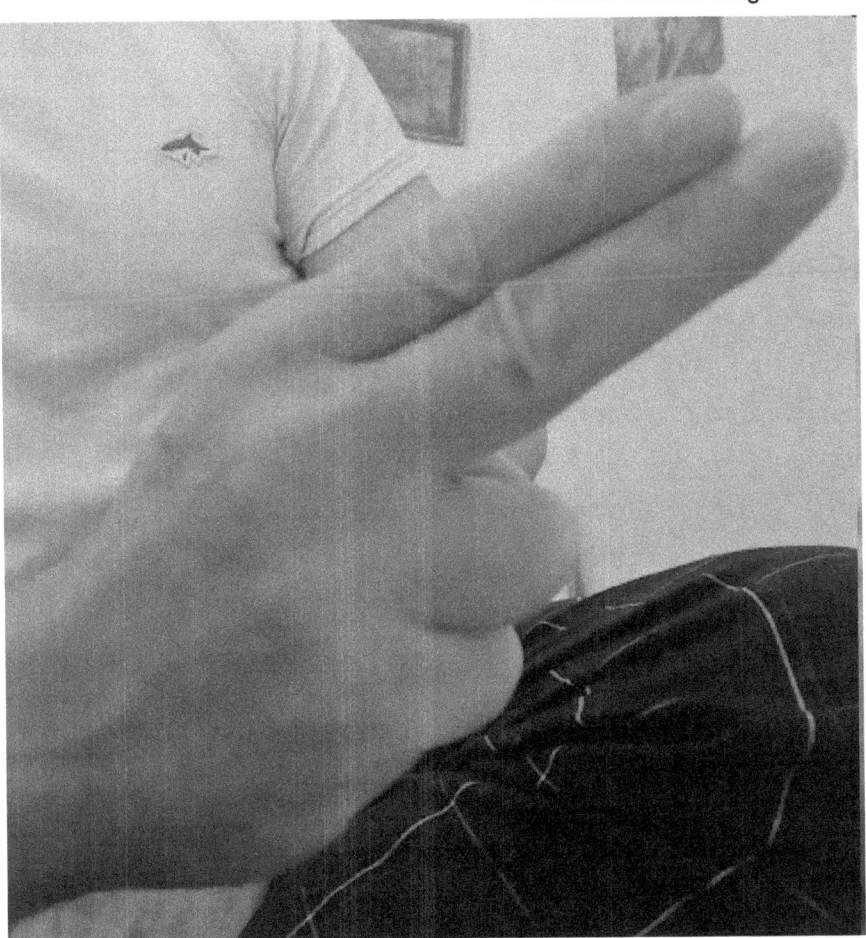

10. PO
We can use these mudras at any time we feel endangered or when cleansing the self and the immediate environment. The final Po is not one of the Nine Characters but a final stabbing exorcism towards the target, for example an unclean force. Po means break or destroy.

37. Divining With The Ling Gua

Divination in China is highly developed and the practitioner of Daoist magic has many arts at his disposal.

The Yi Jing is well known though to Westerners they are more familiar with the Confucian form as popularised by authors such as Richard Wilhelm. In fact the Daoist rarely uses the 'book method' preferring more intricate and accurate systems such as Plum Flower Yi Jing or Six Lines Yi Jing which go well beyond the rather vague readings of the book method.

More complex arts are Chinese astrology, the most popular being Bazi, literally Eight Characters, which uses the year, months, days and hours of the client's birth or an important moment to build up a complex chart of associations. Purple Star astrology could be described as Bazi on steroids and takes the art even further in interpreting future trends that may affect the client.

QimenDunjia means 'Wonderful Door Escaping Art', and is said to have been given by no less than the Mysterious Girl of the Ninth Heaven to the Yellow Emperor. In essence Qimen analyses the flow of qi on three levels using three 'plates'. The plate of the Earth analyses the flow of Qi in the earthly environment, the plate of Humanity looks at the status of Qi in the life of men and women, in the mortal world. Finally the plate of Heaven looks at the workings of Qi on the heavenly and spiritual levels. The diviner then combines the three plates to get a total picture of the interaction of forces. It is an uncannily accurate depiction of a situation, and I can attest to its accuracy.

Another method is called Da Liu Ren. This is considered the creme de la creme of the divination arts. It takes into account astrology, hexagrams of the I Ching, movements of the Big Dipper, the 28 Lunar Mansions and other factors to create one of the most powerful divination systems in the world.

Of course there are simpler arts such as analysing how incense sticks burn and others which we will leave to specialist texts that are forthcoming from yours truly.

Now when you are doing a ritual and you want to know if the result is good, bad or indifferent we need a simpler method. For obvious reasons, we cannot suddenly, within a ritual, break our concentration with long and lengthy calculations to construct a qimen or bazi chart. That is when the Ling Gua method is used.

First off the term moonblocks is awful and a remnant of colonial misunderstanding.

The proper term is Jiaobei among conventional folk and Ling gua with the esoteric masters.

There are two ways to use Ling Gua. They can be thrown for simple yes and no answers to spiritual questions directed at the Gods and Spirits especially during rituals so you can ascertain if the ritual goal has been successful or not.

Ling Gua (Spirit Symbols) are just that and not a plaything or for fun with friends.

They are a consecrated and holy tool for communicating with the Gods. They generally remain on the Altar.

If you mess with the Gods or Spirits, play with them like a parlour game you will never receive truthful answers.

In rituals, we use the simple form of yes, no, or laughing to know if our rites have worked or our offerings accepted, NOT whether your date is a nice girl/guy!!

Now as you know the Lingua are two horn shaped pieces of wood,

Jade, etc with one flat side (ping mian or Yang) and a curved side (huxing/yin).

In the second method in the more esoteric forms of lingua we throw three tosses to find combinations or GUACI.

The three possible throws are:

1. Sheng Gua. One Yin and one Yang.

2. Yin gua. Both are Yin.

3. Yang gua. Both are yang.

In three throws you might get the combination of Sheng Gua, Yin Gua, Yin Gua for example and this has a specific meaning more than just yes or no.

The order matters too. Yin Gua, Sheng Gua and Yin Gua are different from Yin Gua, Yin Gua, Sheng Gua.

There are traditional verses given by the Goddess Jiu Tian Xia Nu for each Gua combination.

For example for the combination of Sheng, Sheng, Yin:

此卦占的有些凶，
飞蛾入火难脱身，
点灯照亮遇狂风，
进山又遇凶猛虎……

"The gua is somewhat inauspicious, the moth enters the flame but it is difficult to get away when the lamp is lit and there is a strong wind, ascending to the mountain the inauspicious meeting with the wild tiger…"

This is only part of the Jiu Tian texts, but does show you the difference from a mere yes, no, maybe and we will give the full version in Advanced Chinese Magic.

However within a ritual it is the simple answer that is needed.

A set of Ling Gua

So for example, let's say you have just finished the money spell and you wish to know if it has worked.

You pick up the ling gua holding them together at the ends. Ask your question mentally or verbally out loud and circle them through the incense smoke three times. Lightly toss them onto the altar.

You will have one of four answers:

1. Sheng Jiao.

Literally means Holy Cup. It will have one yang side and one yin side up. This is a positive response.

2. Nu Jiao.

The Angry Cup. This has both Yin sides facing up. It is a resounding negative response.

3. Xiao Jiao.

The Laughing Cup. Has both yang sides up. It means the answer is obvious or the question cannot be answered as it is too vague or not understood. Redefine the question and repeat.

4. Li Jiao

Standing Cup means the ling gua fall on their sides and are therefore neither flat or curved. The divination is void and must be repeated.

So in our ritual if we get a Nu Jiao we must repeat the ritual until we do get a sheng jiao. It is very simple.

APPENDIX

Shen pei or god tablets that are useful for altars.

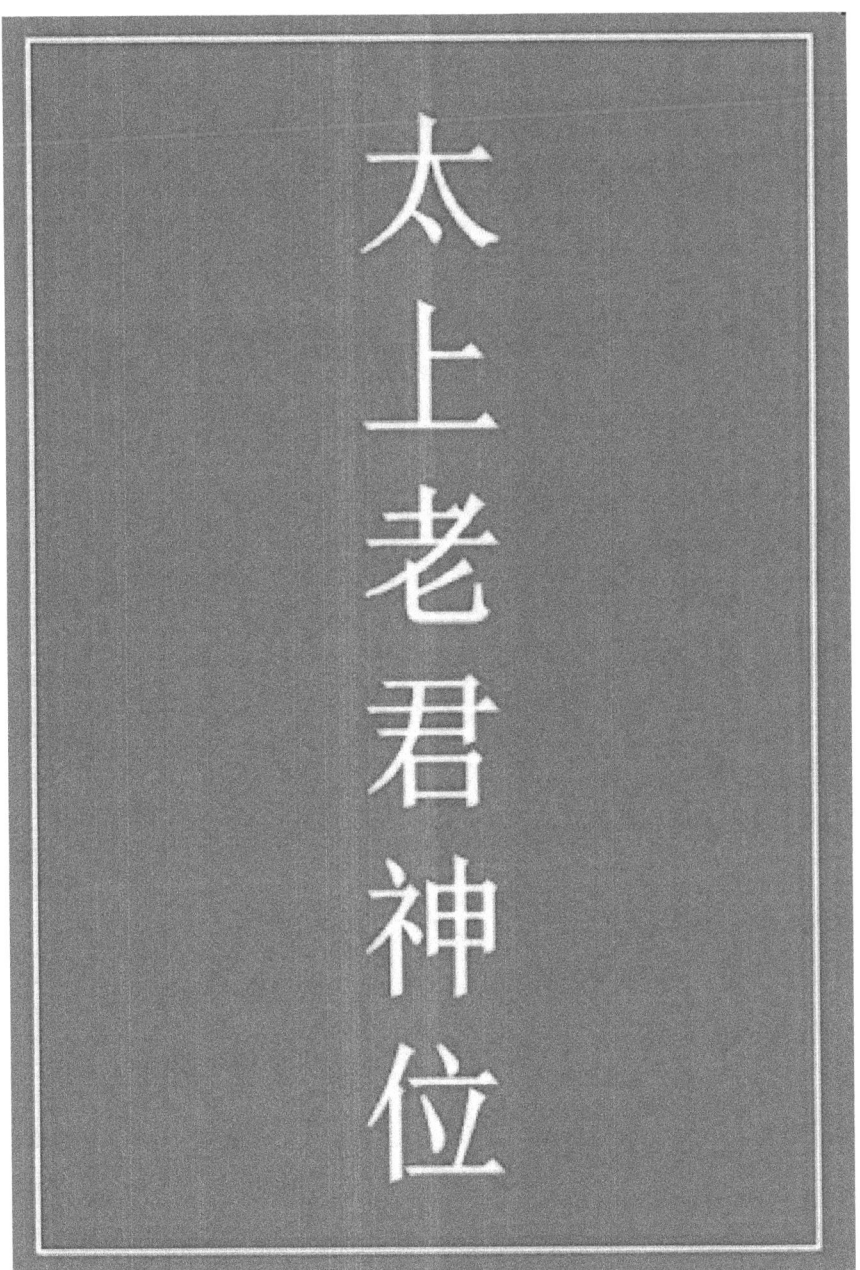

Shen Pei for Taishang Laojun.

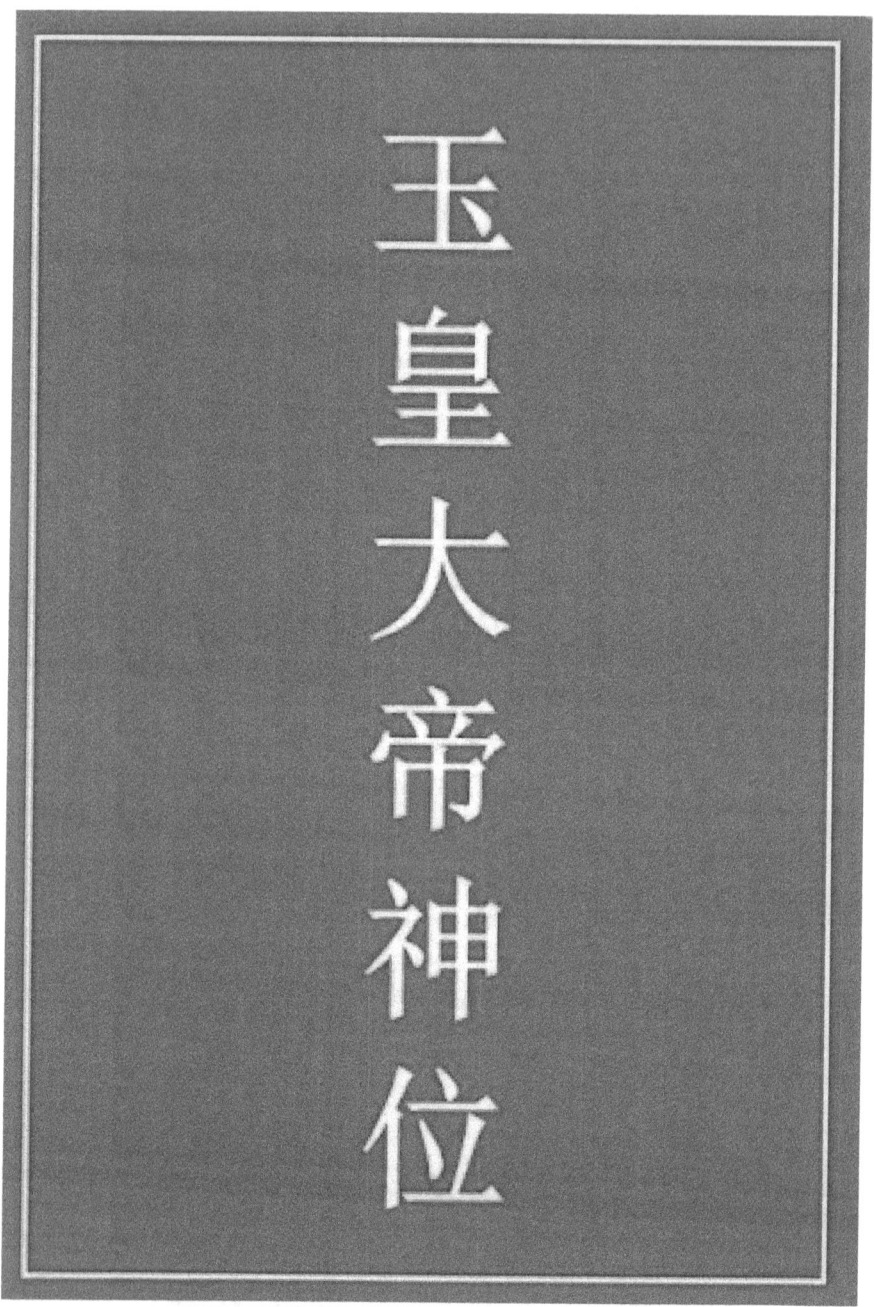

Shen Pei for the Jade Emperor

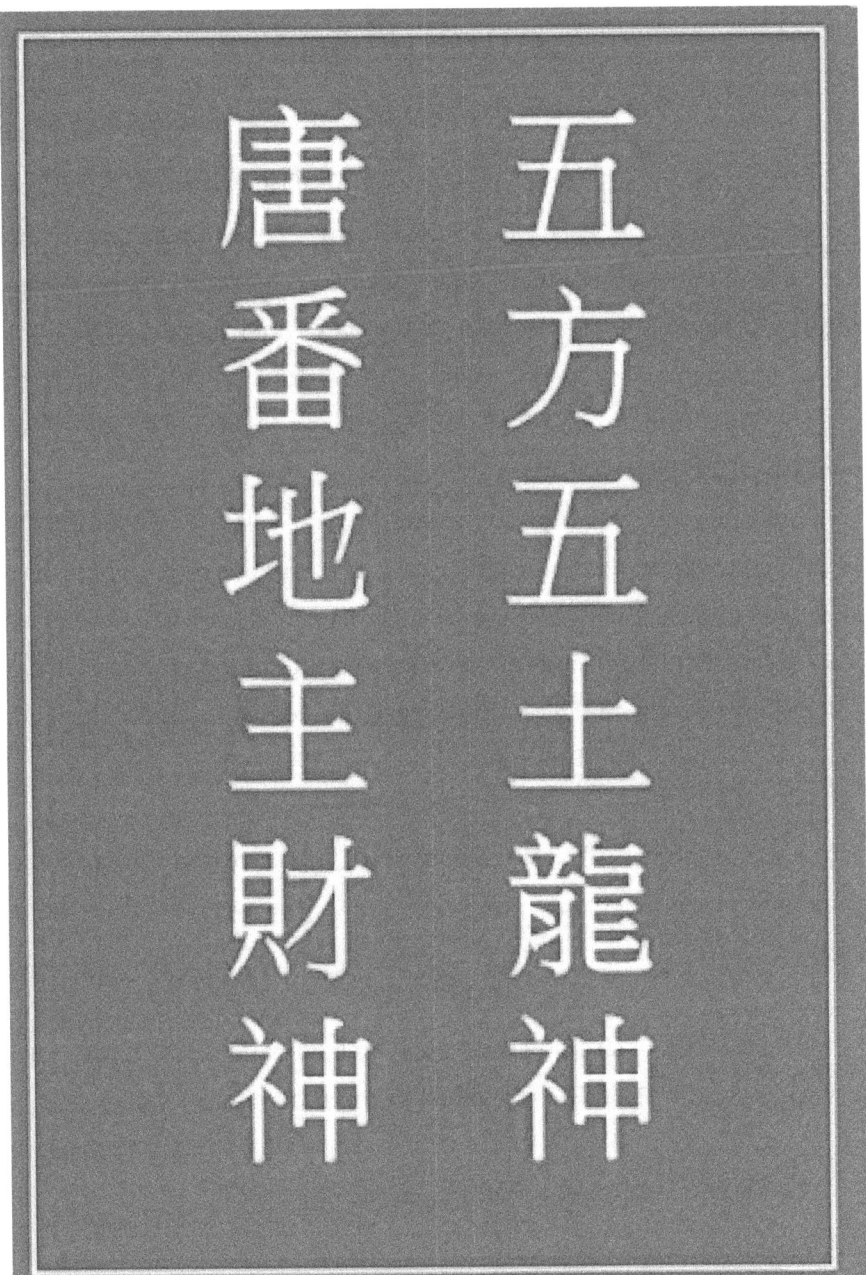

Shen Pei for Tudi

Conclusions

I truly hope you have enjoyed this brief introduction to Taoist magic. In this book we have covered many of the fundamentals but have had to cut short at points which could have been the starting point for many chapters or even volumes. However in your hand you hold the basic fundamentals for practice. Those who are more inclined to western magic or 'mixing it up' may find some unique points you can add to your own practices.

Maoshan is a folk tradition in the hands of the people and not a sacerdotal tradition telling you that you cannot do this or that. Maoshan as we have seen is quite organic and changes and adapts to time and place. Maoshan has picked up tricks so to speak in the countries it has entered into due to the diaspora of the Chinese peoples into Thailand, Malaysia, Vietnam and Indonesia.

I would however exhort the reader to keep it fairly pure at the beginning of his practice, as the saying goes, "Chase two rabbits, catch none".

The fundamentals in this book will prepare you for more advanced and specialised work to be published in the near future.

I wish you luck on your journey in the Dao.
J.R 2022.

Glossary

Amitabho
The Great Buddha of the Western Paradise, The Buddha of Immeasurable Light and Life. In Chinese he is known as the Great Buddha of the West or more simply as Emítuófó. In Maoshan and other forms of Chinese folk magic he is especially associated with healing, driving away evil, longevity and ensuring an easy passage at death and a favourable reincarnation. To this end the Rebirth Mantra was often used.

Bagua
Bagua literally means the Eight Holy Symbols. The chief holy symbol of Daoism and magic though it perhaps predates Daoism by possibly millenia. The Bagua was said to have been discovered and revealed by Fu Xi. The Bagua reveals the essence of the manifest and unmanifest cosmos. The Bagua must be thoroughly understood in all its implications in philosophy, cosmology, medicine, magic, divination and so on.

Baijiu
Chinese white wine, a powerful spirit distilled from rice.

Baopuzi
Important text that is a compilation of many Daoist beliefs and practices mainly evolved from the Lingbao tradition. Written in the Jin Dynasty around 260 CE. The general theme is how mortals can use inner and outer techniques of alchemy to attain immortality.

Baoying
A concept of folk Daoism that refers to cosmic retribution. In many ways similar to the Buddhist idea of karma yet also quite different from it. Daoist thought states that we live in a cosmos which is essentially good in nature and is harmonious. We are not separate from this cosmos

but have a reciprocal relationship with it. Our acts decide our fate or mingyun and our chance encounters and meetings with good and bad events and people, yuanfen.

Bazi

Literally Eight Characters.

Refers to the 8 characters of the Stems and Branches that are calculated from a person's year, month, day and hour of birth. This represents the energetic signature of the person and can be used in magic to link with a person, for example written on a paper doll, or for divination.

Bazi is also a term for the simplest form of Chinese Astrology that has the Bazi as its starting point.

Benshi

Root Teacher in a school of DAO or folk magic. An ancestral master in the tradition similar to the Tantric idea of the Root Guru.

Bugang

A term used in both Orthodox and folk Daoism for special stepping patterns that serve several functions. They can invoke energies by using motion to carve an energetic pattern on the ground, be used to induce trance, or serve as a ritual dance as is more common in modern Orthodox Dao. The most famous are the Seven Star Dipper Steps, but there are hundreds of other specific patterns.

Caishen

The Chinese God of wealth and fortune.

Chi ling

A command or imperial edict. This can represent the will of the magician or a God in talisman making and spoken spells.

Confucius (Kong Fu Zi)
Revered philosopher of the Spring and Autumn Period. Confucius is revered in Daoism as an esteemed ancestor for his wisdom. His philosophy is concerned with human virtue and social equilibrium.

Dantian
The literal translation is the Cinnabar Field. Cinnabar in ancient alchemy being the basis of transformation. There are three major dantian in the energetic body of the human organism, The lower just below the umbilicus, the central at the heart and the higher in the head.

Dayue
Great Moon. A month with more than 29 days.

Di
Chinese for Earth, one of the Three Principles. See Tian and Ren.

Dizhi
The Twelve Earthly Branches most popularly known as the Twelve Animals.

Dizi
A disciple in Daoism.

Doumu
The Big Dipper Mother, an important Celestial Deity of Daoism. She is in charge of time and by default, fate and fortune.

Ershibaxiua/Su
The Twenty Eight Stars or Lunar Mansions. Divided into four sections ruled over by one of the four auspicious animals.

Fali
Literally 'law power', magical power or mana developed in meditation and ritual.

Fangshi

A term for a Chinese magician, a master of magic or a sorcerer.

Feng

A chinese character found on the talisman head requesting the service of a deity or Immortal Master.

Feng Shui

An ancient art of understanding the Qi of the earth through direction and shape.

Firestar

A circle or loop usually found on the edge of a talisman representing further power, like small 'batteries' for qi.

Flying serpent

A form of magical attack that manifests as lesions, spots or rashes on the skin.

Four Auspicious Beasts

The four beasts are similar in function to the Kerubim or Four Archangels of Western Magic. They represent the elements and four directions. They also mark the head of the four quadrants of the celestial sphere in Chinese astrology. They are the Green Dragon, the White Tiger, the Dark Warrior and the Vermillion Bird.

Fu

Chinese term for a paper, wooden or cloth talisman.

Fudan

A special seal at the base of most talismans that seals in the power so they do not leak power or allow unwanted and intrusive forces within it. It translates as Gallbladder of the Talisman.

Fuxi

A major demigod and immortal in Chinese magic and myth. The founder of the Bagua. Sometimes he is referred to as the Bagua Master.

Ge Hong

Author of the Baaopuzi, a major influence on Daoist magic and alchemy and an inheritor of the ancient Ling Bao system.

Golden Boy

A figure important in Daoist magic. An eternal youth or tongzi who is associated with wealth and prosperity.

Gold money

A kind of spirit money burned for the higher gods and immortals or used in some spells such as for purifying the altar or treating sickness.

Gu

A kind of poisonous magic using insects, spiders, toads, lizards and scorpions. Gu or Ku was believed to have developed among Hmong girls and was mainly used to control a lover, and occasionally kill. Though Gu powder could be hidden in the victim's food , far more dangerous was the creation of a Gu Spirit.

Guanyin

The Buddha of Mercy and Compassion who sheds tears for the world. Guanyin is also frequent in Daoist magic and worship as a saviour and merciful healer.

Guizu

The soul of a non cultivated person after death as opposed to one who is cultivated in spiritual disciplines.

Hetu
The River Map, an important cosmological and magical diagram expressing the relationship of numbers in relation to Yin and Yang. In legend, Hetu was used to help control the rivers and their flooding.

Huangdi
The legendary Yellow Emperor and ancestor of all Han Chinese, the Peoples of the Dragon. Many early teachings are attributed to him in Daoism such as treatises on alchemy and medicine.

Huang Di Neijing
Important foundational text on Chinese medicine attributed to the Yellow Emperor.

Huazi
Literally, Flower Words. Characters or seals that are usually superimposed on the fudan or base of the talisman to increase and consolidate its power.

Hu shen
The Fox Spirit Goddess. Usually depicted as a slender and strikingly beautiful lady. She has a deep knowledge of alchemy and can be either vampiric or helpful in nature.

Immortal rope
A twisting, curving line often with loops and/or hooks that channel qi or fali in specific patterns on a talisman.

Jade girl
A Chinese spirit depicted as a beautiful young girl. An immortal with exceptional powers in fortune, beauty and wealth. Her companion is the Golden Boy.

Jade wine
Alchemical and magical term for saliva that has been magically transformed by meditation. It is then swallowed to absorb its powers.

Jiaguwen
One of the earliest forms of Chinese script written on bones or turtle plastrons. It is worthy of study to ascertain the origins of modern Chinese characters. It literally translates as Bone Writing.

Jian jue
Commonly used seal or mudra representing the Seven Star Immortal Sword.

Jiaobei
Crescent shaped pieces of wood, ivory or shell used in divination.

Ji Ji Ru Lu Ling
A common ending to many spells that means Quickly Quickly realise the command! The Chinese version of the western So Mote It Be. It has considerable mantric force.

Jing
Sexual essence, the foundational substance of Chinese alchemy that is preserved, stored and transformed into higher energies including magical power, spirit or shen and even an immortal magical body.

Jiu Tian Xuan Nu
Major and important goddess in Daoism and especially Maoshan. She was the magical tutor of the Yellow Emperor and revealed major teachings in war magic, divination, alchemy and in sexual alchemy.

Kaiguang
The ritual act of consecrating a statue, image or painting to allow divine consciousness to enter into it.

Kunlun
Holy mountain and axis of the cosmos in Chinese symbolism.

Laozu
The earthly manifestation of Taishang Laojun whose role is to administer the teachings of the Dao. He was the author of the Dao De Jing.

Leigong
The God of Thunder, with beak and claws and a magical drum.

Lingbao
Important school of Daoism developed in 400 CE by Ge Chaofu. Its major text is the Book of Five Talismans.

Ling gua
See JiaobeI

Liu ding liu jia
A family of spirits and deities of a martial nature representing time and space and its powers.

Luban
Legendary carpenter and craftsman who had a secret knowledge of feng shui and magic. The Book of Luban was a treasured secret with a reputation as a powerful grimoire.

Luoshu
The Luo River Map. A grid of nine chambers with nine places and numbers representing the elements, big dipper stars and bagua.

Lushan
Major magical Daoist school often sharing teachings and methods with Maoshan.

Maoshan

A school of magic that branched off from Shanqing some centuries ago. It absorbed many shamanic and witchcraft teachings in Hunan, Sichuan and Fujian.

Neigong
Any number of spiritual alchemy systems whose goal is spiritual immortality, as opposed to qigong whose goal is chiefly health and healing.

Ninja
Incorrect term for shinobi, a warrior class of spies and assassins whose training included elements of Taoist derived magic.

Nongli
The Chinese lunar calendar.

Nuwa
Ancient primordial Dragon Mother Goddess who created human beings and taught the arts of civilisation.

Oracle bone
A sheep scapular or tortoise shell plastron that was heated until cracked. The diviner would then read the cracks to divine the will of the spirits and the Cosmic God, Shangdi. Such cracks might well be the origin of the I Ching hexagrams and thus its relationship to the Vision of the Turtle.

Paces of Yu
A term for the Big Dipper Steps or Bugang used in Daoist magic. Yu the Great was a legendary figure who could change to and from a bear, thus indicating a shamanic origin. He was said to have a limp and to this day some forms of Bugang have a dragging step in honour of Yu.

Pai
A school or branch.

Pangu

Primal giant god and first living being in this manifested cosmos who emerged from the cosmic egg. By default he is the Ancestor of all living beings. He is often depicted holding the Yin Yang symbol or the Sun and Moon. He is also shown as hirsute and horned. Certain spells and factions revere Pan Gu.

Peach blossoms

A branch of Chinese magic skilled in love and marriage magic.

Peach Blossom Grove

An afterlife abode of Taoist magicians.

Penglai

A mysterious island that is home to the immortals.

Post-heaven

The state of life after birth into the mortal realm.

Pre-heaven

The state of life as it exists before birth.

Pressing the lamp

A ritual using the powers of the big dipper to heal or unblock the road of fortune of any unseen obstacles.

Qi

The universal force of life, the Cosmic Breath.

Qigong

An exercise using mind, breath and posture to gather Qi for health or martial arts benefits.

Qimen Dun Jia

An ancient art of divination taught to the Yellow Emperor by the Mysterious Girl of the Ninth Heaven. Originally it was used by military advisors to plan strategies by analysing the Qi of Earth, Heaven and Man and their interaction.

Ren

Mankind, humanity. One of the Three Powers or San Cai.

Sanbao

The Three Treasures. Three forces or energies manifest in man, Jing or sexual innocence which is also tied to ancestral essence. Qi, the refined cosmic breath, and Shen or the divine spirit.

Sancai

The Three Powers of Heaven, Earth and Man.

Sanguan

The Three Officials, three Gods who are the immediate executives of the Jade Emperor who act through Heaven, Earth and Water.

Sanhunqipo

The Three Immortal Souls and Seven Mortal Souls.

San Mao Jenzhun

The three brothers who popularised Shanqing Maoshan and were later immortalised.

Sanqing

The Three Pure Ones, the highest and most abstract deities in Taoist theology.

Shangdi

Chinese term for the supreme and highest God, a term going back to at least the Shang Dynasty.

Shen

A term meaning God, spirit and divine depending on context. In man it is the divine energy and one of the three treasures.

Shendao
The Way of the Gods and origin of the term Shinto in Japan.

Spirit Money
Sometimes called Joss paper. Various kinds of paper money burned as offerings to the Gods, Immortals and Ancestors.

Sunu
The Dark Girl, the teacher of the sexual mysteries in Chinese mysticism.

Taiji
The Supreme Ultimate, the origin of all and symbolised by the Yin and Yang in perfect equilibrium.

Taishang Laojun
A mysterious being whose role is to guide and lead man to spiritual progress. Both Fu Xi and Lao Zu are his avatars on Earth.

Tan
Chinese term for the altar.

Tian
Heaven or Sky, the realm of spirit and the first of the Sancai.

Tiangan
Heavenly Stem. Essentially combinations of the Elements in Yin and Yang polarities.

Trigram
A gua or holy symbol of three lines that form the Bagua.

Tudi
The Earth God, or rather the spirit of the local environment.

Willowboy
A wooden puppet imbued with life.

Wudi

The Five Emperors of the Five Directions and Elements.

Wufujing

The Book of Five Talismans, an influential book of the Lingbao Sect.

Wuji

The state beyond polarity.

Wushu

Chinese term for witchcraft or the shamanic art.

Wuxing

The Five elements in Chinese thought.

Wuyue

The Five Holy Mountains

Xian

Immortal or fairy. A being who by cultivation has transcended the accidents of manifested reality and become an immortal being who is an executive force in Nature.

Xiwangmu

The Great Mother of the West. A goddess who holds the keys of immortality in the form of magical peaches.

Yanluo Wang

The Lord of the Underworld.

Yinshan

A magical school that specialises in working with ghosts

Yin Yang Water

A blend of cold and hot boiled water.

Zaojun

The Kitchen God, rules the heart of a home, the hearth.

Zhang Daoling

The ancestral master of all Daoist magical schools and the first Celestial Master

Zhenren

A true man or woman.

Zi wei ling

The Purple palace seal which represents the entire essence of all the stars in the cosmos.

Index

Symbols

28 asterisms 176

A

Agrippa, Heinrich Cornelius 59
Alchemico 184
Alchemy 23, 34
Altar 347
    Prosperity and Wealth 292
Amitabho, The Great Buddha 141, 387
Ancestor 253
Answers 382
Astrology 378
Auspicious Beasts 390

B

Ba Gua or Eight Diagrams
    15, 16, 222, 387
    Spell 254, 272
    Talismans 274
Baijiu 387
Banish Evil Spirits 244
BAO YING balance 51
Baopuzi 387
Baopuzi (Book of the Masterr) 34
Baoying 387
Bazi 378, 388
Beans 349
Bell 349
Benshi 388
Bestowing Food Spell 320
Big Dipper
    18, 53, 219, 287, 300, 324, 379
    Cultivation 325, 330
    Lamp 309
    Mother 299, 301
    Mudra 328
    Pattern 199
    Soul Technique 325
    Step 300
    Sutra 306
    Talisman 308
    To Know The Fate 332
    Veiled walking 326
BING 369
Black 124
    Pen of Art 250
Blessed Land 106
Blue 124
Bowls 334
    And cups 347
Boxer Rebellion 46
Branches 84
Breath 138
    Six Healing 138, 143, 148
Brushes 349
Bugang 388
Burial 337

C

Caishen 388
    Wealth Children 288
Calendar 18, 84, 91, 100
Celestial Masters 29
Censer 347
Chaos 12
Chi ling 388
Chinese Occult 44
Chu 22
Cinnabar
    Field or Dan Tian 138
    Ink 235
    268
Cloth 349
Coffins
    Lucky 342
Colour 191
Command
    Block 347, 348, 350
    Character 214, 214–216
Communism 35
Condensing 181

Constellations 93
   Black Turtle Of The North 95
   The Azure Dragon (East) 94
   Vermillion Bird Of The South 97
   White Tiger Of The West 96
Cosmic Axis 108
Creation 70
Cultivation (Lian) 50, 52
   Jade Wine 184
Cursed Girl 130

D

Damage 190
Dantian 389
Dao 26, 76
Dao De
   Jing 30
   Tianzun 111
Daoism
   Qi Absorption Circle 197
Dark Lady 19
   Dark/Occult Girl of the Ninth Heaven 116
Days
   Law Of 100
Dayue 389
Dead 336
Defence 264
Deluge 36
Demons 14
Destruction 70
Di 389
Directions 290
Disposing 245
Divination 378
Dizhi 389
Dizi 49, 128, 250, 389
DOU 370
Doumu 299, 301, 389
   Lady of the Chariot and Big Dipper Mother 299
Dragon 13, 51
   King 18
Duck 208

E

Earth 54, 67, 79, 310
Earthly
   Branches 86–91, 90
      Twelve 87
   Pillars 220
Ecliptic 98
Ecstasy 22
Eel 208
Egg 12
Egypt 56
Eight
   Characters 378
   Great Spells 150
   Holy Symbols 76–83
Elements 137
Elixirs 36
Emperors
   Five 122, 123
Equinoxes 98
Ershibaxiua/Su 389
Ershisi, The Solar Terms 98–99
Eye 235
   Evil 64

F

Fairy Ropes 218
Fali Meditation 178, 389
Falungong 46
Fang Shi 23, 390
Feng Character 216, 390
Feng Shui 337, 342, 390
Fire 80, 142, 305
   Stars Or Coins 218
Firecrackers 334
Firestar 390
Flood 14
Flower 286
   Word or Hua Zi 233–245
   Word or Hua Zi. 211
Flying serpent 390
Fortune 264
Four
   Auspicious Beasts 13
   Treasures 204

Frog 208
Fu 390
Fudan 227, 390
Fuxi, Emperor 14, 15, 16, 76, 391

G

Gallbladder (FU DAN) 223
Gang symbol 221, 223
Garlic 208
Gate 132
Ge Hong 391
Geography 102
Ghost 52, 224, 253
   Eye 254
   Magic 343
Ghouls 335–346
Giant 13
God 128
   Of The Dao 102, 107
   Tablets 383
Golden Boy 391
Golden Light 148
   Mantra 40
   Mudra 147
   Spell 165
Grades 51
Grant, Kenneth 47
Green 124
Gu 391
Guanyin, the Great Goddess of Mercy and Love 118, 119, 391
Guizu 391
Gunas 61
Gurdjieff, G 136
Guru 26, 128

H

Han people 11
Heaven 54, 77, 310
Heavenly Stems 84–88, 85, 89
HENGSHAN 105
Hermetic 59
Hetu 392
Horse-faced deity 338
Hour 207
House Protection Bagua Talisman 264

Hu shen 392
Huang Di Neijing 392
Huang Di, the Yellow Emperor. 17, 116
Huangdi 392
HUASHAN 104
Huazi 392
Hun 335, 342

I

I-Jing 15, 24
Immortal 127, 128, 146
Incense 349
Ink 204, 349
   Stone 205, 349

J

Jade
   Emperor 112, 113
   Girl 22, 392
   Girl and Gold Boy 120
   Wine 184, 187, 393
Ji Ji Ru Lu Ling 393
Jia Ma. 354
Jiaguwen 393
Jian jue 393
Jiaobei 393
Jing 393
Jinying school 44
Jiu Ge (The Nine Songs) 22
Jiu Tian Xuan Nu 19, 116, 117
Jupiter 303

K

Kaiguang 393
Kanjin or Cut Gold Money 352
Khechari mudra 184
Kunlun 394

L

Lake 81
Lamps 289
Lao Tzu 26, 27
Lao Wei (foreigner) 49
Lao Zi 57
Laoshan Taizun 113
Laozu 394

Lei Gong 122, 394
Lie 374
Lin 368
Ling Gua 52, 378, 381, 394
Lingam 77
Lingbao Tianzun 108, 110
   Wizards Of The Divine Treasure 36
Liu ding liu jia 394
Lord 257
Luban 24, 394
Lunar 91
   Blocks 24, 349
   Mansions 93
   Months 92
Luo Shu Square 17
Luoshu 394
Lushan 107, 394
   Lu Mountain Faction 43

M

Magic 45, 53, 127
   Chain 169
   Square 270
Man 128
Mandarin 12
Mantra 306
Mao 45
Maoshan 21, 24, 49, 118, 130, 394
   School 41
   Zushi, the Maoshan Patriarch 10
Mars 304
Martial artist 61
Master 23, 169
Medicine 18, 70
   (Neidan), Inner 35
Mercury 304
Metal (Jin) 68, 142
Ming Dynasty 40
Mishu (Secret Book) 49, 132
Money
   Gold 391
Monkey 116
Mothers 127
Mount Heming 31
Mount Kunlun 14, 102, 103
Mount Meru 103

Mountain 79
   Immortal Fairy Girl 22
   Wuyue: The Five Sacred 104
Mouth
   Roof of the 185
Mudra 203, 368
   Ancestor 172
   Teacher 173
   Sword 172
Music 22
Mysterious Heaven or Purple Palace Seal 359

N

Neigong 395
Neophyte, KAI WU 52
Neoplatonic 59
Nine
   Hand Seals 35
   Heaven Mysterious Girl 297
   Palaces 222, 224
Ninja 395
Nirvana 56
Nongli 395
North 176
Nuwa, Queen 14, 395

O

Occult 45
Oracle bone 395

P

Pai 395
Pangu 13, 396
Paper 208, 347
Peach
   Blossoms 396
   Grove Flowers 178
   Wood sword 349
Pen 204
Penglai 23, 105, 106, 396
   Abode Of The Immortals 106
Phoenix 13
Po 51, 336, 377
Poets 103
Poison

Of Gu 130
Post-Heaven 82, 270, 396
Power 52
Pre-Heaven 81, 82, 268, 396
  Bagua 338
Pressing the lamp 396
Projection 181
Prosperity 286
Protection 181
  Bag 252
Purple Palace 175
  Seal 359

Q

Qabalistic 76
Qi 19, 55, 56, 63–
  65, 143, 179, 181, 344, 396
  Gathering 189
Qigong 28, 35, 62, 137, 154, 196, 396
Qimen Dun Jia 396
Qin, Emperor 106
Qing Jing Fu 285
Quanzhen 8
Queen Mother of the West 115

R

Rain 253
  Ghost 253
Red 124, 208, 287
Ren 55, 397
Rice 349
Rice wine 349
Ritual Of Money And Prosperity 286
Ritual Of Pressing The Lamp 327
Robes 349
Rope
  Immortal 218, 392
Ropes
  Law 218

S

Safflower 286
Saliva 184
San Cai or Three Potencies 53
San Mao Zhejun, the Three Mao Brother 42

Sanbao 397
Sancai 397
Sanguan 397
Sanhunqipo 335, 397
Sanqing 397
Sanshan Jiu Hou 127
Seal 349
  Ancestral Teacher 361
  Ba Gua Hand 254
  Character
    Nine 365
  Dao 357
  Five Thunder 356
  Golden 233
  Hand 152, 355–375
  Post-Heaven 360
  Request the Gods or Guan Yin Seal 362
  Sword 363
  Taishang Laojun 364
  Three Mountains 358
Secret Character 175
Seven
  Star Lamps 287
  Stars 302
Shaman 18, 21, 326
Shandi, Emperor 108, 397
Shanqing
  Masters 37
  School 39
Shen 107, 397
Shen Pei 383
  Jade Emperor 384
  Taishang Laojun 383
  Tudi 385
Shendao, Way of the Gods 50, 398
Shiva and Shakti 23
Shoujin 354
Sigil
  Of Maoshan Master 171
Silk 18
Six Jia Generals 367
Soil 142
Solstices 98
Soma 184

SONGSHAN 105
Sorcerer 40, 41
   Wars 44
Soul 335
South 97
Spell
   Books 233
   Eight Great 149
   Five Elemental Phases 317
   Five Ghosts Fortune 345
   Incense 314
   Inviting Wealth 296
   Of Purifying The Body 154
   Of Purifying The Heart 150
   Of Purifying The Mouth/Voice 152
   Of The Earthly Branches 317
   Of The Golden Light 160
   Of The Heavenly Stems 316
   Of The Mysterious Gathering 163
   Of The Offering Of Incense 161
   Of The Twenty-Eight Star Lodges 316
   Replenishing The Essence 187
   Requesting Gods 242
   Sending the Rays of Light 319
   Spirit Assisting Spell 317
   To Purify The Heavens And The Earth 158
   To Purify The Spirit Of The Earth 156
   Work 202
Spirit
   Money 287, 349, 350, 352–360, 398
   Of a place 312
   Water 174
Stars
   Nine 300
Stems 84
Stopping Strike Spell. 255
Storytellers 75
Su Nu, (The Plain Girl) 301, 398
Sun 156
Sword Finger 40, 198

T

Tai Chi 28, 60, 137
Taiji 58, 398
Taishan 104

Taishang Laojun, Lord 47, 48, 398
Talisman 36, 202, 207–209
   Bringing Peace, Calm And Purity 283
   Bu Gang 240
   Disposing 245
   Five 260
   Protection 250
   Qingjing 284
   Step By Step 235
   Structure 210
   Fu Shen or body 218
   Zhaocai 295
Tan 398
Tantric 26, 184
Tao 60
Taoism 22, 26, 335
Tea 349
Ten
   Heavenly Stems 135
Terracotta soldiers 351
Three
   Officials 310, 316
Thunder 80
   Array Technique 333
   Gods 122
Tian 398
Tiangan 398
Tiger 13, 32
Times 100
Tools 347, 347–354
Tortoise 13
Tourist 47
Training 130
Transmission 169
Treasures of the Scholar 349
Trial 137
Trigram 398
Tudi 287, 398
   Earth and soil God 312
Turtle 76
Twelve
   Earthly Branches 135

U

Underworld 124, 338

V

Vajra Seal 355
Venus 118, 304
Vermillion 236
Visualisation 192

W

Wang Mu Niang niang. Queen Mother of the West 115
War 51
Washing The Marrow 187
Water 78, 142, 310
Water Margin, The (Novel) 19
Wealth
   Gods 290, 296
   Spell 296
Wei Huacun 38
West 96
White 124
Willowboy 398
Wind 78
Wolf 302
Wood (Mu) 66, 140
Wu Shamans 20, 114
Wudi 399
Wufujing 399
Wuji 12, 60, 399
Wushu 399
Wuxing 137, 399
Wuyue: The Five Sacred Mountains 104, 399

X

Xi Wang Mu 103, 114, 115
Xian 47, 399
Xiaoyin or Little Silver 353
Xing 376
Xing cheng shen ling 50
Xiwangmu 399

Y

Yan Luo. Lord of the Underworld 124, 125
Yang 13
Yanluo Wang 399
Yarrow stalks 24
Year 207
Yellow 124, 209
Yellow Emperor 18
   Internal Classic 19
Yellow River (Huang He) 11, 17
Yellow Spring Road 336
Yi Jing 54, 76
Yin 13
   And Yang 57
Yin Yang Water 399
Yinshan 399
Yoga 34, 154
Yu the Great 15, 18, 324
   Paces of 300, 395
Yuanshi Tianzun 108, 109

Z

Zaojun, The Kitchen God 124, 126, 399
Zhang Daoling 400
Zhaocai talisman 293
ZHEN 373
Zheng Daoling 29, 32
Zhou Dynasty 25
Zi wei ling 400
Zishi 207

The Chinese Magick Series

The mysteries of Chinese occultism have long been hidden from the West, largely due to the cultural and language barriers between us. Also because of the reluctance of the Chinese Masters to part with their knowledge.

For this reason we are producing this series of books to fill that gap in the knowledge of most western magicians. This knowledge comes from both oral and written sources that can only be found in Chinese communities. The author has travelled extensively in China and Malaysia and personally learned under several teachers from a school of practical magic known as Maoshan.

Maoshan is a school of magic dealing with the interaction of the seen and unseen worlds, with a knowledge base dating back thousands of years to the time of the ancient shaman kings who ruled that area of China known as the Sichuan Plateau. Over many generations the Maoshan school developed hundreds if not thousands of unique techniques to alleviate the challenges of life as well as to explore our spiritual nature and that of the cosmos.

Maoshan, the school devoted to practical magic is unveiled in these books for the first time in the English language. We hope this opens a door to the mysterious world of the ancient chinese sorcerers. Forthcoming volumes include:

Thunder Magic.
Secrets of Chinese necromancy.
Chinese love and sex magic and alchemy

Mysteries of Chinese Star magick.

Chinese talismanic Magick.

The Book of the Nine Tailed Fox. (this volume)

Chinese Magickal Healing and Rejuvenation.

Chinese Magick of Fortune and Gambling.

The Training of a Chinese Sorcerer.

Chinese Magical Defence and Attack.

www.ingramcontent.com/pod-product-compliance
Lightning Source LLC
Chambersburg PA
CBHW071356300426
44114CB00016B/2088